More Hand-Manipulated Stitches
for Machine Knitters

Susan Guagliumi

More Hand-Manipulated Stitches for Machine Knitters

Susan Guagliumi

Second Edition ISBN 978-1-7333121-2-7
First Edition ISBN 1449987710

Library of Congress 2010901420

© 2010 Susan Guagliumi

All rights reserved

www.guagliumi.com

Other books by Susan Guagliumi
Hand-Manipulated Stitches for Machine Knitters
Hand Knits by Machine
Twelve Sweaters One Way: Knitting Cuff-to-Cuff
Twelve Sweaters One Way: Knitting Saddle Style
Handmade for the Garden

GUAGLIUMIDOTCOM

For my grandfather, Robert Fleischer, who gave me Chinatown, Fenway Park, Boston Common and unconditional love.

Contents

Introduction

Acknowledgements

**Part One:
Bridging Methods**

Chapter 1
Bridging Defined

  3 The Mechanics of Bridging

  5 Needle Positions

Chapter 2
Bridging to Increase Stitch Size

  9 Ideal Stitch Dial Setting

  9 Cable Exercises

13 Combination Cables

14 Woven Stitches

Chapter 3
Bridging Manually

19 Hand-Knitting Large Stitches

20 Knitting with Beads

23 Wrapping Stitches

23 Making Chinese Knots

28 Open Effects

Chapter 4
Bridging to Add Rows

33 Raising Cables

34 Combination Cables

37 Popcorns and Nops

45 Ruching

47 Short-Rowed Textures

50 Bridged Fills

52 Oversized Cables

57 Triple-Crossed Horizontal Cables

Chapter 5
Bridging with the Free Yarn

61 Wrapped Stitches

66 Fence Knitting

68 Midrow Cast-On and Bind-Off

Chapter 6
Combining Methods

73 Lazy Daisy Stitch

75 Knotted Ties

76 Twisted Eyelets

77 5-Stitch Popcorns

80 3-D Flowers

82 Petal Clusters

Part Two: Knitting the Patterns

- 84 About Your Machine
- 84 The All-Important Schematic
- 86 Swatching
- 87 Keeping it all Straight
- 87 Scrap Knitting
- 88 Short Rows
- 88 Finishing

Appendices and Resources

- 143 Appendix 1: Metric Schematics
- 154 Appendix 2: Make-do Garter Bar
- 156 Glossary of Symbols and Abbreviations
- 159 Bind off Methods
- 163 Finishing Stitches
- 165 Sources of Supply
- 166 Index

The Patterns

- 90   Tied Up in Style Cardigan
- 96   Loopity Lou Hat
- 100 Faux Crochet Cardigan
- 106 Puppet Scarf
- 112 Ruched Cardigan
- 118 Wrapped in Ruffles Scarf
- 122 Horizontal-Cable Pullover
- 130 Purple Posies Tote
- 136 Hugs and Kisses Shawl

Acknowledgements

I have been fortunate over the years to cultivate an interesting and exciting group of friends — many of whom are knitters or have experience in the publishing process.

Jeanne Criscola, who owns Criscola Design here in Connecticut, produced all of the charts for *Hand Manipulated Stitches for Machine Knitters* when she worked at the Taunton Press back in the 1980's. She also did all of the graphic work for *Studio Design Magazine*, which I edited when I worked for Studio — so many of you are familiar with her work already. Over the years, she has been my coach as I struggled to gain a grip on Illustrator software to produce my own charts and (with the patience of a saint!) she is responsible for whatever graphic ability I have honed over the years. Jeanne created the 'grid' for this new book and has acted as general design consultant.

Deborah Cannarella has been "my editor" for many years, going back to the years when she, too, worked at the Taunton Press. A stickler for detail and clarity, Deb is the one who makes sure that I make sense on the printed page. She edited the two hand knitting books I did for Creative Publishing International two years ago and has always encouraged my efforts.

Gini Woodward is a well known machine knitter and one of the few people I know who could spend hours pouring over manuscripts and schematics checking for accuracy. Without her review, I would have much less confidence in all the computations it takes to write a pattern in five sizes!

Samantha Frank is a talented, recent graduate of Southern Connecticut State University, where my husband teaches. Samantha photographed all of the projects for the second half of the book. I wish I could have had her next to me at the machine during the months that I spent knitting samples and photographing my own process shots. I am sure you will be able to detect a difference between the process/swatch shots that I took and Samantha's beautiful, crisp project photos!

Erica Udoff is a graphic designer and a good enough friend to offer her services editing and adjusting the photos that I produced. Photographing work on a knitting machine is challenging business and although black and white photographs would have been easier to manage, I think that, with Erica's help, the color photos convey much more information.

Special thanks to Terri Burns, Lynne (McClune) Garwood, Anne Morrison, Mary Anne Oger, Nancy Roberts, Toni Salerno and Shannon Strain for proofing patterns and doing the final read-throughs so I could be sure when I referenced a chart "at left", that it really was at the left and not on the next page. There are never enough trained eyes when it comes to a project like this.

I always enjoy working with the very best yarns I can find and want to thank Cascade for all of the "220" I used for the swatches. Thanks also to Berroco, Brown Sheep, Cascade Yarns, Knit Picks, Knitting Fever (Noro), Trensdetter Yarns, Westminster Fibers/Nashua Yarns for the gorgeous yarns I was able to use for the projects in Part Three.

The "make-do" garter bar on page 154 is the brainchild of Colleen Smitherman. Many thanks for allowing me to share this great idea with my readers!

Susan Guagliumi
Northford, Connecticut
January, 2010

Introduction

Nearly 20 years ago, the Taunton Press published the first edition of *Hand-Manipulated Stitches for Machine Knitters*. Soon after the book was released, I found myself wishing I had included (among other things) a chapter dedicated to bridging. Bridging is the method of managing individual needles or groups of needles in order to alter stitch size midrow or to work extra rows in specific locations. Sometimes bridging enables the needle bed of the machine to behave more like a pair of hand-knitting needles, in terms of flexibility and midrow variation; other times it simply facilitates certain actions, like crossing an entire row of cables without undue strain. There are dozens of ways to use bridging, and I find it the single most liberating method for producing hand-manipulated stitches on a knitting machine.

I wrote this book to provide greater detail on the subject of bridging. *Hand-Manipulated Stitches for Machine Knitters* contains lots of bridged techniques, shown as examples in each of the major chapters in which bridging was simply a silent partner—sometimes making stitches easier to manage and other times creating more pronounced textures. In this book, I have reorganized some of those bridging methods and also added new ones in chapters of their own. I have also included expanded explanations that should make bridging a fluent part of your knitting vocabulary. .

After the publication of the first book, knitters told me that it would be easier for them to understand individual techniques if I also provided practical applications. So, this book contains, in Part Three, patterns for garments and projects that feature expanded directions, highlighting and clarifying the way a particular stitch is executed and offering little tricks I used when I knitted them.

To make best use of this information, you should be an experienced machine knitter, familiar with your machine and its various functions. Because there are so many different machines in use and because each one has its own specific terminology, I have tried to write all of the directions in this book as generically as possible, keeping abbreviations to a minimum. The first chapter of *Hand-Manipulated Stitches for Machine Knitters* covers the essentials of how knitting machines work. I recommend reviewing that chapter if you have difficulty with any of the bridging directions in this book. With few exceptions, I knitted the samples for this book on a midgauge machine with Cascade 220 (100% wool) worsted, with stitch size 7-8.

There simply isn't enough space (or need) to show you every possible variation for any of these methods, but keep this in mind: When there is a repetition or regularity in what you do with your hands and tools, you will create a pattern in the resulting fabric. When you begin to vary your motions and methods—by altering the number of stitches or rows, changing the frequency with which you do something or the direction, lifting, crossing, or otherwise manipulating stitches—you will be on your way to creating new patterns. For example, in my earliest experiments with hand-manipulated stitches, I found that I could produce nice little popcorns by knitting extra rows over certain needles with a separate strand of yarn and then lifting the base stitches onto the needles above it. The technique worked quite well, but I soon tired of finishing off all those extra strands—and so bridging was born! There is no telling what you, too, might invent when you begin to play with the many variables in machine knitting.

I suspect that this book will no sooner be completed than I will find myself demonstrating at a seminar or teaching a class somewhere and yet another bridging variation will come to mind—most likely because of a question or suggestion from a student. You have always been my best teachers!

PART ONE
Bridging Methods

The actual mechanics of bridging should not seem like a totally new concept even to novice machine knitters because most machine knitters are aware that their machines have the capability to hold needles in certain positions. Bridging, however, exploits the variety of ways you can apply the holding capabilities of your machines to explore a wide range of exciting new stitches.

CHAPTER 1

Bridging Defined

Bridges are the groups of needles between "special effect" needles. Like a highway bridge, these needles get you from one place to another—or, in this case, from one group of special-effect needles to the next. Simply stated, the technique of bridging allows you to use the holding position (HP), which is available on most knitting machines, to knit a single row in several steps for three special purposes. When bridging, you can work individual needles/stitches or groups of needles/stitches to increase stitch size, to add rows, or to access the "free yarn" between the carriage and the last stitch knitted.

The Mechanics of Bridging

Before you begin, it is important that you understand how your machine holds needles. All of the Japanese machines, the Superba/White, and most plastic hobby machines handle needle holding in pretty much the same way. In the Passap system, pushers control the holding position and some other functions of the machine. Because this system differs so much from most other machines, I encourage Passap knitters to rely closely on the holding instructions in their machine manuals.

All knitting machine carriages include some type of triangular pathway amid the cams on the underside. This pathway channels the needle butts forward so that old stitches slide behind the latches. Then the carriage feeds new yarn into the open hooks of the needles before they are pulled back into working position (WP), ready for the next row. The number on the stitch dial determines just how far back the carriage pulls the needles, how much new yarn they take on, and, ultimately, how large a stitch they form. (The first chapter of *Hand-Manipulated Stitches for Machine Knitters* explains how some carriages work, so you may want to refer to that book for a more detailed description.)

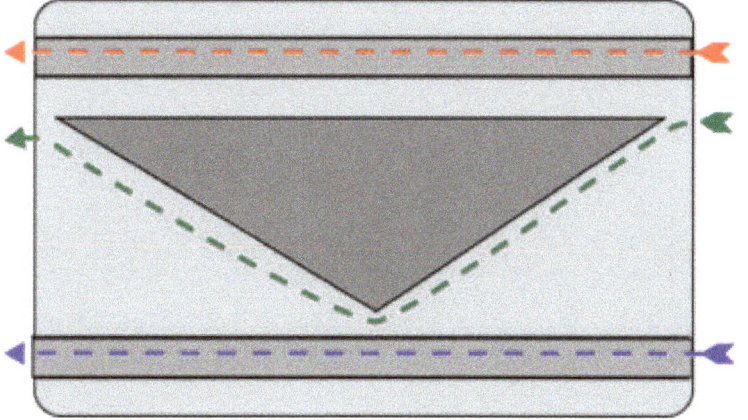

Rear channel for needles in nonworking position (NWP)

Triangular pathway where working needles will knit (WP)

Forward channel for needles, which can usually be set to hold needles (HP) or return them to working position (WP)

Most carriages provide these three pathways for the needle butts to travel through—noted by the three different-colored dotted lines in the drawing. Some machines also provide levers or controls to open and close the forward channel (holding position, or HP). More-sophisticated carriages also include a variety of cams in the triangular pathway, which are responsible for specific patterning features. All but the simplest machines include a stitch dial to alter the length of the triangular pathway to change stitch size.

In addition to the triangular pathway, there are usually two more channels on a knitting machine carriage. At the very back of the carriage, there is an open pathway that allows needles in nonworking position (NWP) to pass through. This pathway is too far back for the needle butts to enter the triangular pathway.

The second channel is at the very front of the carriage and, when open, allows needle butts in HP to pass straight through. HP is as far forward as the needle butts can be on the bed. Most carriages provide buttons or levers to open or close off this front channel from either side of the carriage.

Silver Reed machines call the levers Russel Levers, and Brother refers to Holding Buttons. Check your manual to see what your machine manufacturer calls them. (Incidentally, I have never been able to find out why Russel Levers are called Russel Levers and haven't a clue as to who Russel might be!)

The important thing to know about these levers/buttons is that they control the needle butts on *the leading side of the carriage*—in other words, the side where the butts enter the carriage with each pass.

If the upper channel is open on the leading side of the carriage, the needle butts will pass straight through and simply exit at the other end while still in HP, regardless of how the trailing lever/button is set.

If the pathway is closed off on the leading side of the carriage, the needle butts will be pushed slightly back on the needle bed so that they are in line with the entrance to the triangular pathway, and the needles will begin knitting.

Early on, most knitters find that if they are careless about putting empty needles into NWP when decreasing (for example), the needles get bumped into WP as the carriage moves across the bed. With bridging, it is imperative that the needles are fully and securely in NWP.

On most machines (with the exception of some plastic hobby machines), the needles are tensioned in the bed by means of a sponge bar or brake spring. This tension prevents the needles from slopping around in the bed, keeps them in specific needle positions, and—because the needles are fairly stable—makes it easier for you to use transfer tools. If the sponge bar is worn and flattened, however, the needles may tend to slip back from HP to WP when you least expect—or want—them to. For this reason, I make a point of replacing my sponge bars about once a year. I also shift the bars around whenever I change a needle to equalize the wear on them. There are about 4" at each end of a metal bed where there are no needles, so you have some leeway to shift the positioning of the sponge bars.

Bridging Tips

Rule 1: When bridging to modify stitch size, bridges knit with the same stitch size as the background fabric.

Rule 2: When bridging to add extra rows or to access the free yarn, bridges only knit once.

Rule 3: Turn off the row counter at the beginning of a bridged row and turn it back on at the end, advancing the count by only 1 row.

Needle Positions

Not all machines manufacturers describe needle positions in the same way, so check your manual—but there are usually four primary positions:

Nonworking Position (NWP) The needle butts rest against the back of the needle slots and are too far back to enter the triangular pathway on the carriage. These needles do not knit. Most knitters think of holding position (HP) as the most forward needle position on the bed, but you can also use NWP for holding.

Working Position (WP) The needle butts are roughly one-third of the way forward in the bed so that they are in line with the entrance to the triangular pathway. They knit, often according to cam lever instructions.

Holding Position (HP) Needles are all the way forward in the needle slots so that their butts are above and do not enter the triangular pathway. Depending on how you set the levers that control the pathway, the needles will either remain in HP or be pushed back to knit again.

Upper Working Position (UWP) Needles in UWP are halfway between WP and HP and will enter the triangular pathway to knit. You'll use this needle position when you need to leave *some* needles in HP and want to return others to WP, because you cannot use the automatic levers/buttons without returning all the needles to WP. UWP is also the position for most intarsia knitting.

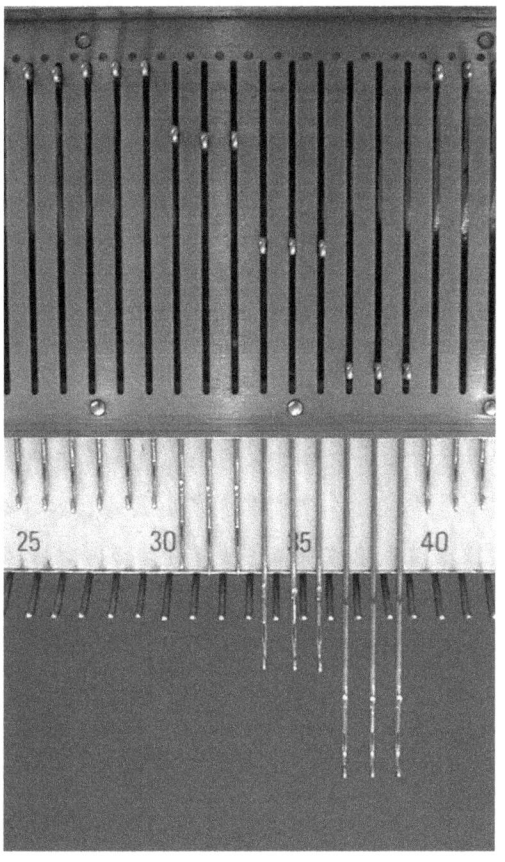

(NWP)
Nonworking position

(WP)
Working position

(UWP)
Upper working position

(HP)
Holding position

The name may differ from one manufacturer to another, but there are four standard needle positions on all knitting machines.

Half-Working Position (HWP)

There is also an unofficial fifth position that I call half-working position (HWP). Needle butts are lined up halfway between WP and NWP so you can manually hand-knit the needles to produce stitches larger than the stitch dial but not quite as large as knitting them all the way back to NWP. The needles *cannot*, however, remain in this position because they do not line up with any of the carriage pathways, and the carriage would bump into them. Rather, the needles are placed in HP before knitting the next row. I usually lay a thin dowel or piece of wood lathing across the back of the bed, in front of the NWP needles, to act as a guide so that all of the stitches I hand-knit to HWP are the same size. Then I remove this guide because the carriage will be unable to pass and I carefully move the needles to HP.

Some Helpful Notes

Please keep the following information in mind as you work through the various samples and methods in this book:

1. All of the charts represent the way the stitches will look on the back of the fabric when you are seated at the machine. You'll find all the stitch symbols on the charts defined in the glossary at the back of the book.

2. The serpentine arrows on most of the charts indicate the direction in which the carriage is traveling and also note each time that the carriage is interrupted.

3. When bridging for stitch size or to access the free yarn, the extra passes of the carriage simply indicate the backing-up motion of the carriage as it knits each section. When bridging to add extra rows, the arrows indicate exactly how many extra rows to work in each section.

4. The bridged row is always worked prior to crossing the cables or otherwise manipulating the stitches. When the bridged rows vary within a pattern, I have included additional arrows on the chart. The arrows appear only in the first repeat of a bridged sequence—not for every bridged row, as the additional arrows would make the charts difficult to read.

5. In some charts, the needles are numbered from right to left to cross-reference with specific text instructions. These numbers do not correspond to the needle numbers on your bed. When working a sample of any new technique, however, it will be easier to follow the directions if you work to the left of center zero on your bed so that the numbers do correspond.

6. After you've completed some manipulations, it will be easier to knit the next row if you set the carriage to knit all needles back from HP. Make sure that you reset the needles to HP before the next bridging sequence.

7. Sometimes, after bridging a preparatory row, most of the needles are in HP. For clarity in the photographs, I have returned some of the HP needles to WP before working the specific pattern stitches—it is usually not necessary to do. (Throughout the book, I have noted in the text when I have made that adjustment in the photos.)

8. On any manipulated row, bridge stitches only knit once, and they always knit at the same stitch size as the background fabric.

CHAPTER 2

Bridging to Increase Stitch Size

Stitch size can be a very limiting factor when executing hand-manipulated stitches. You might find, for example, that—even though the stockinette swatch you started with was perfect—when knitting a sweater with several columns of 3x3 cables, the carriage resists or jams after crossing the cables. Chances are that the cables will look better and cross more easily if they are knitted a little looser than the surrounding stockinette or rib stitches. Bridging makes it possible to knit just the cable stitches with a larger stitch size by changing the stitch dial midrow or by hand-knitting needles back to NWP.

Usually, you only need to increase the stitch size by one or two numbers, so don't get too carried away once you realize how much freedom you have with these methods. Most cables require some cross-tension in the stitches to give them shape and make them stand up crisply from the surface of the sweater. If you increase the stitch size too much, cables tend to be flat and lifeless. As a general rule, only increase the stitch size enough for the carriage to pass without undue strain, in order to avoid damage to needles, carriage, or yarn.

Not all rows require bridging. For example, you'll only have to bridge the row prior to crossing cables (unless the pattern specifies otherwise). My directions for bridging generally start with the carriage on the right end of the bed so that I can offer directions in a standard format throughout, but you could just as easily begin with the carriage on the left.

No matter which machine I am using, I try to use yarns that work right in the middle of the stitch dial. The middle of the dial is where every machine is the happiest. At that setting, which is the manufacturer's average calibration for the machine, you need to make the fewest concessions to knit special stitches or accommodate yarn.

Heavy and fine yarns are likely to require special maneuvers as you work higher or lower on the stitch dial: for example, extra weights, a slower knitting pace, and needles placed in HP. Of course, you should feel free to make full use of the range of stitch sizes (and the respective yarns) available on your machine. I just want to caution you that some techniques will be more successful at the middle setting. It will be easier, for example, to cross lots of cables at stitch size 5–7 on a midgauge or chunky machine (sizes 6–8 on most standard-gauge machines) than it will at stitch size 10. At the middle setting, you won't have to fret with as many little details. This is one of the reasons that many machine knitters own more than one machine.

Increasing Stitch Size with Stitch Dial

Step 1. Begin with the carriage on the right and set to hold needles in HP.

Step 2. Turn off the row counter. Set the stitch size as for the background fabric. Bring all needles to HP except the first bridge on the carriage side.

Step 3. *Knit one row, bring the needles just knitted to HP and return the carriage to the right end of the bed.

Step 4. Change the stitch size. Place the next group of needles into UWP.**

Step 5. Repeat * to ** across the entire row.

Step 6. Cross all cables (for example), turn on the row counter, and advance it by one row. Work to the next bridged row.

Cable Exercises

The following directions offer step-by-step instructions for making the preparatory row for three columns of 4x4 cables with 5-stitch bridges between them. The first example enlarges the stitch size of all eight cable stitches; the next two sets of examples enlarge only half of the cable stitches.

Enlarging all of the Cable Stitches

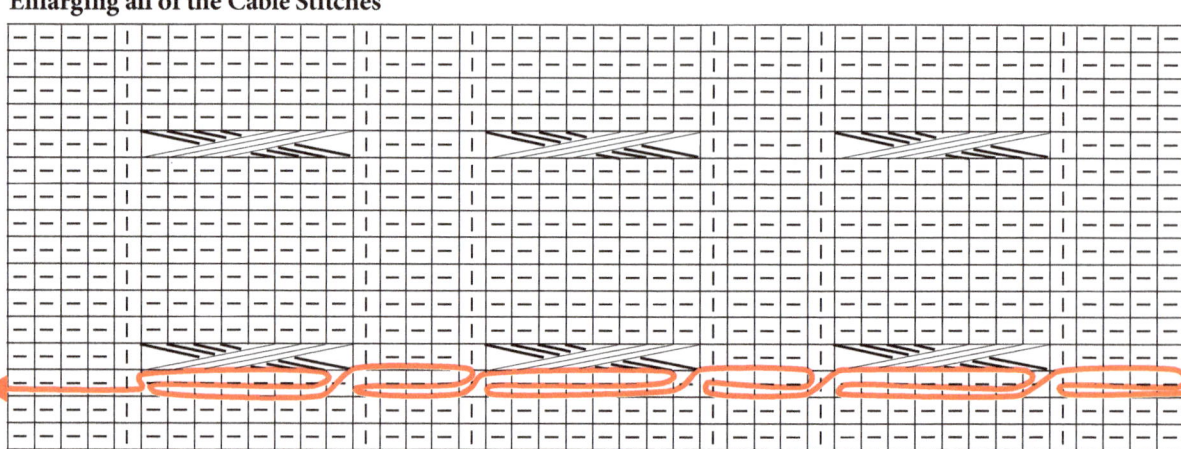

This chart shows 4x4 cables crossing on rows 4 and 12, with rows 3 and 11 bridged in preparation. The carriage follows the serpentine path indicated by the arrow overlaying the chart, changing stitch size with each section. Only the first pass of the carriage over any section actually knits; the other passes back up the carriage and move it to the next section. The cables are crossed at the end of the bridged row. When all of the cables are crossed, bring their needles to HP and set the carriage to knit them back before knitting the next row. The chart also shows a single reformed stitch on each side of the cables, which helps them stand away from the background fabric. If you don't have a pair of 4-prong transfer tools, hold two 2-prong tools in each hand.

Crossing 4x4 Cables

This is the method I use when I need to increase the stitch size by several numbers for sufficient crossing ease.

Begin with COR, set to hold needles in HP. RC 2. Stitch size for background fabric and RC off.

Hold all needles except the first five bridge needles (1–5) on the carriage side.

Knit one row and then hold the bridge needles just knitted. Return COR.

Raise stitch size by one number. Place the next group of eight needles (6–13) into UWP. Knit one row, hold the needles just knitted, and return COR.

Drop stitch size by one number. Place next group of five bridge needles (14–18) into UWP. Knit one row, hold the needles just knitted, and return COR.

Raise the stitch size by one number. Place next group of eight cable needles (19–26) into UWP. Knit one row, hold the needles just knitted, and return COR.

Drop stitch size by one number. Place the next group of five bridge needles (27–31) into UWP. Knit one row, hold the needles just knitted, and return COR.

Raise stitch size by one number. Place next group of eight cable needles (32–39) into UWP. Knit one row, hold the needles just knitted, and return COR.

Drop stitch size by one number. Place the next group of five bridge needles (40–44) into UWP. Knit to the end of the row. COL.

Cross all cables. The chart shows right-cross cables so first the four stitches on the right are replaced on the needles at left. Then the left group of stitches are moved to the right. Turn on RC and advance by one. RC 3.

Set carriage to knit needles back from HP and knit cable-crossed row. RC 4.

All of the cable stitches in Swatch #1 (page 12) were enlarged and are barely detectable. Stitches at left were also enlarged, but not crossed.

Enlarging half of the Cable Stitches

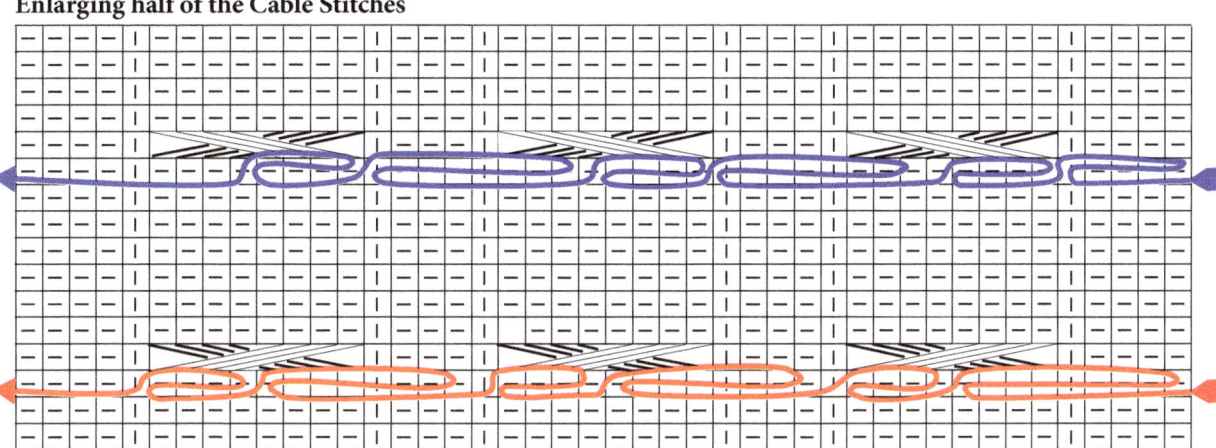

The serpentine arrow describing carriage motion is different for left- and right-cable crosses, but, in each case, half of every cable group knits at the same time as an adjacent bridge. As a result, one-half of the cable stitches knit at normal stitch size, and the other half are enlarged. The cables shown in blue are left-cross cables. The stitches on the right half of each cable group will be enlarged and will lie on the back of each cable cross. The cables shown in red are right-cross cables. The stitches on the left half of each group will be enlarged and will cross on the back of the cable. The single reformed stitch at each side of the cables helps them stand away from the background fabric for emphasis.

By the time you've knitted one bridged row like this, it should be pretty clear why you need to turn off the row counter at the start of a bridged row. In this example, the carriage moved back and forth a total of 13 times, but actually knitted only one complete row. Although the serpentine arrow on the chart indicating the carriage movement snakes back over itself, when bridging to change stitch size with the stitch dial, all of the needles knit only once by the time the carriage ends up on the left end of the bed. Some of the carriage motion can best be described as "dead passes"—the carriage only knits when traveling from right to left over needles that have not yet knitted in that row. This result is not true for all bridging methods, but it is the rule when bridging for stitch size. Also, each group of bridge needles (in other words, the needles with non-cabling stitches) knit at the same stitch size as the rest of the garment, which underscores one of the basic bridging rules: *Bridges always knit with the same stitch size as the background fabric.*

Enlarging Half of a Right-Cross Cable

It is seldom advisable or necessary to enlarge all of the stitches that will be used to cross a cable. The stitches may not need that much extra ease, and the cables would then lose their depth. In the previous example, I would probably only increase the stitch size for needles 10–13, 23–26, and 36–39, because these are right-cross cables and the larger stitches can be hidden on the back of the fabric. When I want to enlarge only some of the cable stitches, the procedure changes somewhat, as follows:

Begin with COR, set to hold needles in HP. Stitch size for background fabric and RC off.

Hold all needles except the first five bridge needles (1–5) and the right half of the first cable (6–9). Knit one row and then hold all the needles just knitted. Return COR.

Raise stitch size by one number. Place the next group of four cable needles (10–13) into UWP. Knit one row, hold the needles just knitted, and return COR.

Drop stitch size by one number. Place next nine needles (14–22) into UWP (includes the next bridge and half of the next cable's needles). Knit one row, hold the needles just knitted, and return COR.

Raise the stitch size by one number. Place next group of four cable needles (23–26) into UWP. Knit one row, hold the needles just knitted, and return COR.

Drop stitch size by one number. Place the next nine needles (27–35) into UWP. Knit one row, hold the needles just knitted, and return COR.

Raise stitch size by one number. Place next group of four cable needles (36–39) into UWP. Knit one row, hold the needles just knitted, and return COR.

Drop stitch size by one number. Place the remaining needles (40–44) into UWP. Knit to the end of the row. COL.

Cross all cables, first returning the right group of stitches in each group to the needles and then returning the left group, so that the enlarged stitches are hidden on the purl side of the fabric.
Turn on RC and advance by one. Knit cable-crossed row.

Enlarging Half of a Left-Cross Cable

If, on the other hand, I were crossing left-cross cables, the other half of the cable needles would be enlarged as follows:

Begin with COR, set to hold needles in HP. Stitch size for background fabric and RC off.

Hold all needles except the first five bridge needles (1–5). Knit one row and then hold the needles just knitted. Return COR.

Raise stitch size by one number. Place the next group of four cable needles (6–9) into UWP. Knit one row, hold the needles just knitted, and return COR.

Drop stitch size by one number. Place next nine needles (10–18) into UWP. Knit one row, hold the needles just knitted, and return COR.

Raise the stitch size by one number. Place next group of four cable needles (19–22) into UWP. Knit one row, hold the needles just knitted, and return COR.

Drop stitch size by one number. Place the next nine needles (23–31) into UWP. Knit one row, hold the needles just knitted, and return COR.

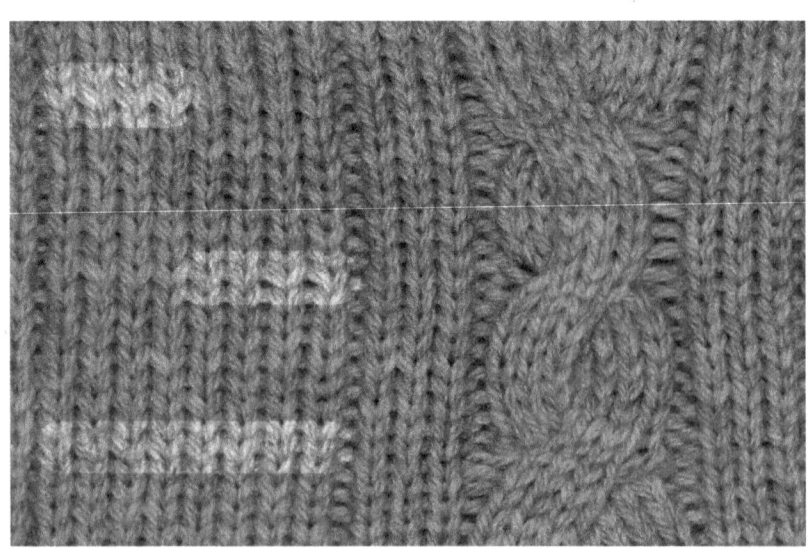

Swatch 1: The background stitches in this sample were knitted at stitch size 7, and the cable stitches were enlarged to stitch size 8. You can just barely see that the stitches inside the highlighted areas (at left) are slightly larger than the surrounding stitches; the difference does not show at all in the second and third cables. The edge stitches in the first cable do look a little looser, but the difference is barely noticeable, and the knitting ease the bridging provides more than makes up for it.

Raise stitch size by one number. Place next group of four cable needles (32–35) into UWP. Knit one row, hold the needles just knitted, and return COR.

Drop stitch size by one number. Place the remaining needles (36–44) into UWP. Knit to the end of the row. COL.

Cross all cables, first returning the left group of stitches in each group to the needles and then returning the right group, so that the enlarged stitches are hidden on the purl side of the fabric.

Turn on RC and advance by one. Knit cable-crossed row.

Combination Cables

The preceding examples involve entire rows of right- or left-cross cables, but there will be times when you will have combination cables in the same row. For example, wishbone cables and X and O cables (also called Hugs and Kisses cables) are formed by pairs of opposing cables.

For these types of combination cables, you need to combine the techniques described above so that some cable groups have enlarged stitches on the right and others have enlarged stitches on the left. Before I begin knitting, I always make a chart with a serpentine arrow to clearly illustrate the bridged rows, as shown below. After you've worked through a couple of samples, you'll find that this process isn't as complicated as it seems.

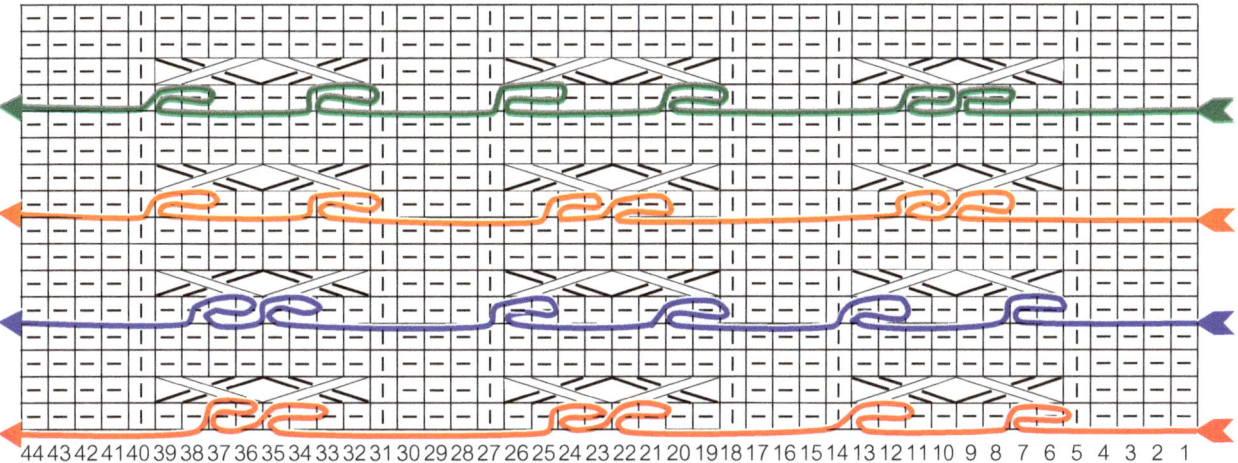

Combination Cables

All of the 2x2 cables in this chart are crossed every four rows, and all are paired so that they cross toward or away from each other, forming various combinations of X and O (Hugs and Kisses) cables. The row prior to the cable crossings is bridged according to the serpentine path described for each combination of cables, shown in different colors. In every case, the enlarged stitches lie on the back of the fabric where they do not show, providing ease for crossing. The single reformed stitch on each side of the cables helps them stand away from the background fabric for emphasis.

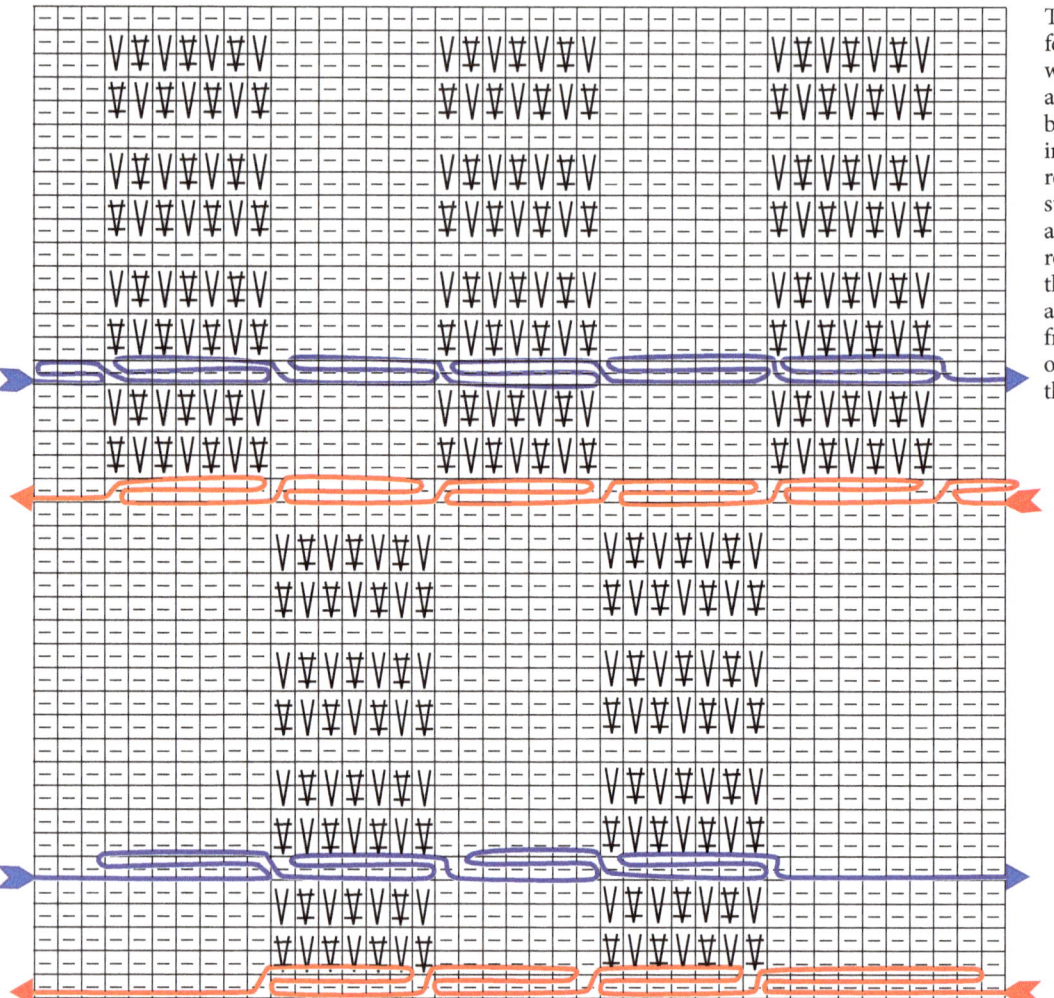

The serpentine path differs for each block of the woven slip stitch pattern, as shown by the red and blue serpentine arrows in this chart. The pattern requires enlarging the stitches shown by the arrows before each four-row sequence. Notice that the slip stitches alternate from back to front and that the blocks of pattern also alternate throughout the fabric.

Woven Stitches

Having been a weaver in a "previous lifetime," I am especially drawn to knitted woven-stitch designs (Swatch 2). Most of these designs require some lengthened stitches. Keep in mind that woven stitches usually combine stockinette and slip stitches. The slip stitch portions of the fabric will be shorter than the rest and may produce irregular fabric edges. Usually this creates a pleasant scalloped effect, which can be exploited as a design element of the garment. The difference in take-up or row gauge will be most pronounced when all the stitches are knitted at the same stitch size. Lengthening some of the slip stitches will keep the edges under control, as will staggering the effect, as shown in the chart above.

Bridging to Increase Stitch Size 15

Weaving Slip Stitches

Step 1. After a bridged row to increase the size of every alternate group of seven stitches, place the needles holding those stitches into HP for the next two rows so that two long floats lie across each block of needles in HP. Insert a transfer tool under these floats to remove the first stitch from its needle, as shown in the photo.

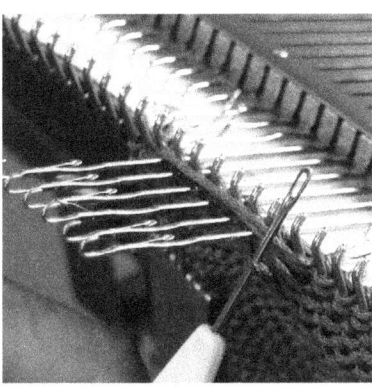

Step 2. Carefully draw the transfer tool under and away from the floats so that the stitch can be replaced on its needle, trapping the float on the knit side of the fabric.

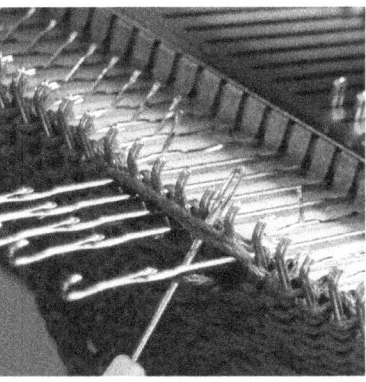

Step 3. The floats remain on top of the second needle for now, but you'll weave it behind the third stitch by removing and then replacing that stitch on its needle.

Step 4. The first, third, fifth, and seventh stitches in this group have been removed from and then replaced on their needles to trap the floats on the knit side of the fabric.

Step 5. Do not remove the stitches on the three needles remaining in HP, but do release the floats lying across their shafts so that they lie across the purl side of those stitches. To do this, move each needle back slightly in its slot so that you can use the tip of a transfer tool to coax the floats over the latch and off the needle. These floats will look exactly like slip stitches that the carriage might have formed on the purl side.

Step 6. The first pair of floats have been woven through the seven needles in this block of the design. The next row will be a bridged row to increase the size of the same seven stitches, which will remain in HP for the following two rows. The next weaving sequence alternates, so that the stitches that were behind/in front of the slip floats in the previous repeat will be in front of/behind them.

Pattern Variations

Enlarging some of the stitches in a fabric gives you increased options for manipulating stitches and creating new patterns. My previous book, *Hand-Manipulated Stitches for Machine Knitters*, contains lots of stitch patterns that require enlarged stitches, so refer to that volume for more ideas. You'll also probably come up with some of your own once you start experimenting with this method.

For starters, try varying the direction in which you manipulate the stitches, the number of stitches you work with, and the number of plain rows between manipulations. Some stitch patterns will benefit from more relaxed stitches, and others will require slightly smaller enlarged stitches to create surface texture or tension.

Swatch 2: Slip stitches weave from front to back throughout this fabric. The groups of needles that form the pattern are placed in HP for two rows. The yarn floats or slips over seven needles at a time (but don't think of these as tuck stitches). Then, every other float is eased off its needle so it lies on the purl side of the fabric, without moving the stitch that was originally on the needle. The alternate slips are moved to the knit side of the fabric by removing each stitch from its needle with a transfer tool and replacing it behind the float.

CHAPTER 3

Bridging Manually

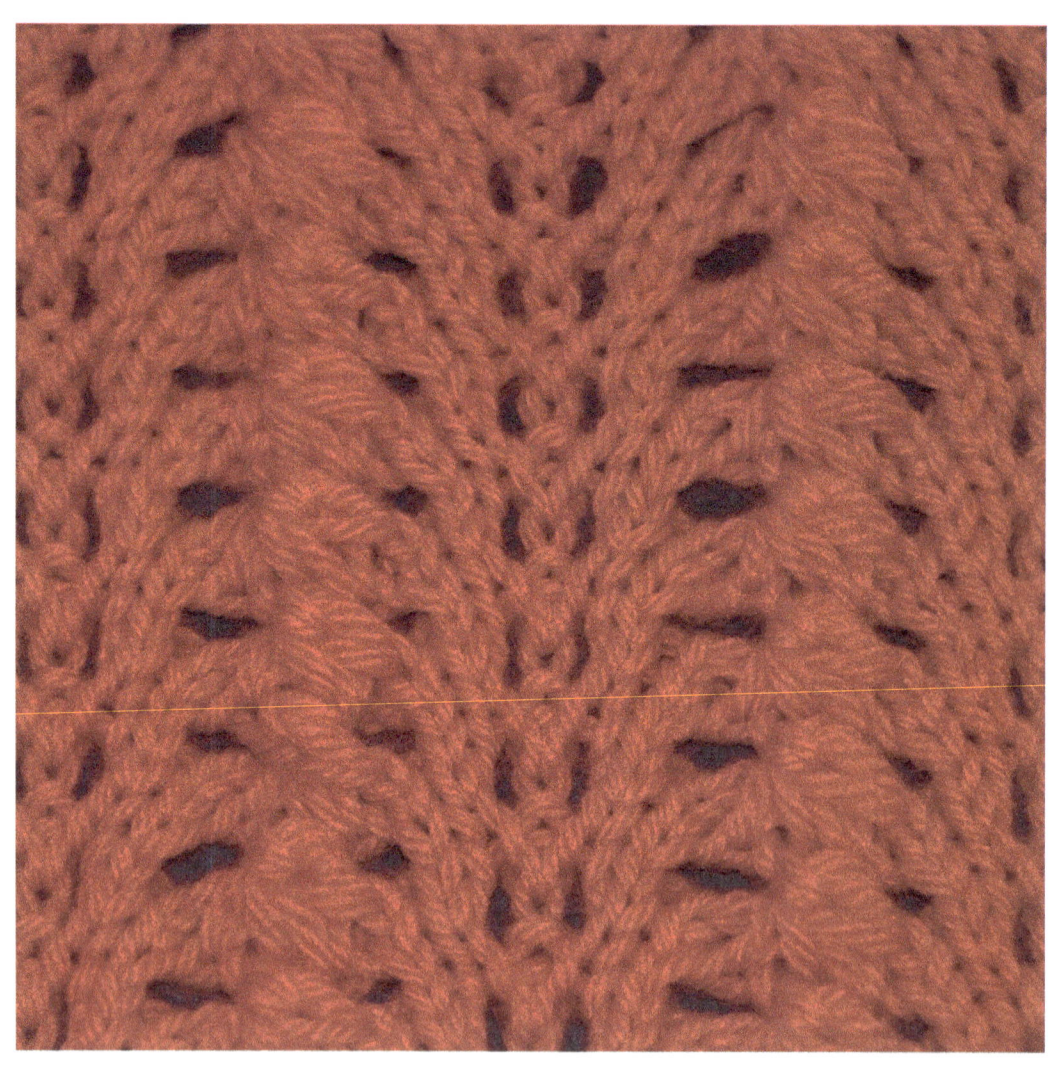

Bridging with the stitch dial to change stitch size will help you work many hand-manipulated stitches that you might have struggled with in the past. If, however, you are already knitting the background fabric at the top of the stitch dial, or if you need really, really huge stitches, the stitch dial will be of no further use to you. In those cases, you need to take manual control of the needles.

The stitch-dial setting on the carriage will remain the same throughout the process. Specific needles are "hand-knitted" back to NWP or HWP to form really huge stitches.

Hand-Knitting Large Stitches

To hand-knit a stitch, simply lay the yarn over the open hook of the needle. Use the needle butt (or bump) to move the needle back in its slot so that the old stitch slides over the closed latch and a new, elongated stitch forms as you pull the needle all the way back to NWP or HWP, as shown in the photo below.

Needles knitted back to NWP may be left there, close to the back rail, so that NWP becomes an alternative HP. You need to be certain that the needles you knit back to NWP are tight against the base of the slot, otherwise they are liable to start knitting again—and the elongated stitches can cause quite a mess. I keep my fingers on the butt of each needle I have knitted back as I knit the next one.

Pushing needles all the way back to NWP creates really huge stitches. When I don't need stitches quite that large, I lay a long, 1/4 in. to 3/8 in.-thick dowel or barbecue skewer across the back of the bed, in front of any non-working needles, and knit the needles back to HWP instead. You don't have to use the dowel, but it makes it easier to form stitches that are all the same size. You *must*, however, remove the dowel and place these needles in regular (forward) HP or WP before you knit any additional rows, because this adjusted position is not a "legitimate" needle position on any machine!

Also, remember that bridges only knit once, so the serpentine arrows on the charts simply represent the backing-up motion of the car-

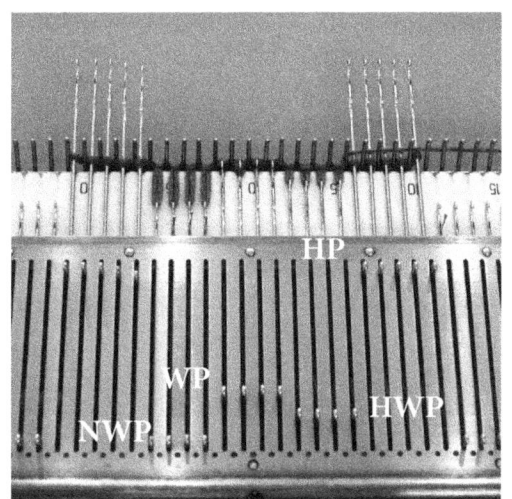

This photograph illustrates HWP and NWP position needles in relation to those in WP and HP.

Manually Knitting to NWP
Begin with the carriage at the right end of the bed, set to hold needles in HP.

Turn off the row counter. The stitch size should be set as for the background fabric. Bring all needles to HP except the first bridge on the carriage side.

*Knit one row. Manually knit the next group of needles back to NWP and leave them there; hold the bridge needles just knitted by the carriage and return the carriage to the right end of the bed. The needles that you hand-knitted all the way back to NWP do not need to be moved because they are, in effect, in a rear holding position.

Place the next group of bridge needles into UWP.**

Repeat * to ** across the entire row.

Complete all special-effect stitches, turn on the row counter, advance it by one row, and work to the next bridge row.

riage, not extra rows. To differentiate these arrows from those arrows that show the carriage path for bridging when the carriage controls stitch size, I have shown the manually knitted needles with a zigzag line. As when changing the stitch dial, the enlarged row precedes the row in which the action will take place. In other words, enlarge stitches in one row, then manipulate and knit them in the next.

Knitting with Beads

You can easily add beads to your machine knitting, although they often distort the surrounding fabric as the stitches snug together to make room for them. To avoid this distortion, I usually enlarge any stitches that will hold beads or paillettes. In the beaded cables shown in Swatch 3, there's a single enlarged stitch per cable, every six rows, for threading a "crystal" bead. The enlarged stitch also offers a little crossing ease for the 3x3 cables (which, in this sample, are divided by plain knit stitches with a reformed tuck on either side). I use the following method when beading:

Cast on and knit one row, ending COL.

Knit five rows and then reform as tuck stitches the stitches on needles 3, 10, 12, 19, 21, etc. With COR, set to hold needles in HP, hold all needles except for the first four on the carriage side. Knit one row.

Manually knit the next needle back to NWP, hold the bridge needles just knitted, and return COR.

*Place the next eight needles in UWP and knit one row.

Manually knit the next needle back to NWP, hold the bridge needles just knitted, and then return COR.**
Repeat * to ** to the end of the row.

Place a bead on each of the enlarged stitches, as shown in the photos on page 22.

Cross the cables so that the group of three stitches that includes a beaded stitch is returned to the needles first. (There's no point in hiding the beads on the back of the fabric!)

If you leave needles in HP after crossing cables and use your carriage levers to knit them back automatically, remember to reset the carriage to hold before working the next bridged row.

Swatch 3: The "crystal" beads seem to float on the surface of the cables, without distorting any of the stitches. The latched-up tuck stitches at each side of the cables adds a light, open texture to the fabric.

Beaded Cables

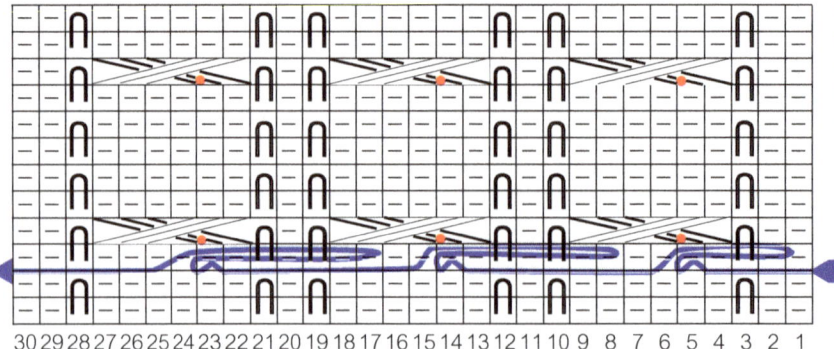

Only a single stitch in each 3x3 cable is enlarged to hold a bead, which is indicated by a red dot.

Slanted Stitch Design (swatch 4)

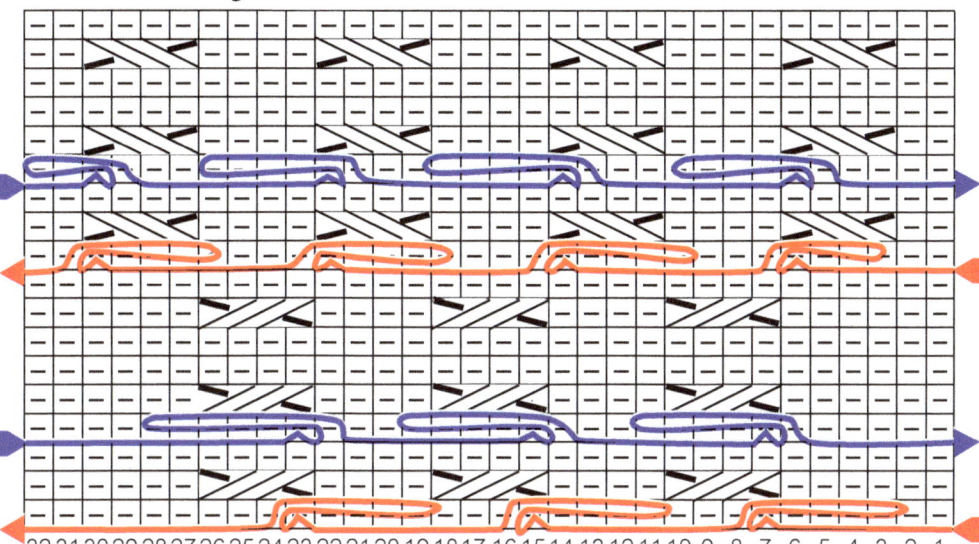

The red serpentine arrows show the bridging path from right to left. The blue arrows indicate the path from left to right. Whenever there is an odd number of rows in a pattern repeat, the bridged rows will alternate right and left, and the path it follows will change.

Swatch 4: This fabric features a single enlarged stitch for each cable crossing. In this case, the cables are crossed as 1x3 cables every three rows. The single, enlarged stitches cross to the front of the fabric and negate any cabled effect. Instead, the pattern is one of large, diagonal stitches.

Bead Knitting Tools

Adding beads or paillettes to your machine knitting is really quite simple. You'll just need to have a latch tool that will fit through the holes in the beads. Check the sewing notions counter for a hosiery/knit repair needle, which is a very tiny latch tool that works well with most small beads. Needles from fine-gauge sock-knitting machines also work very well, but are a little harder to come by. You can also use a thin, steel crochet hook, but if you plan to do a lot of beaded knitting, I'd recommend purchasing one of the fine-latch needles. Usually, you can hang very large beads with a standard-gauge latch tool or crochet hook.

Knitting a Beaded Cable

Step 1: With bridge needles in HP and bead needles in NWP, the last bridge at left is in UWP, ready to complete the bridged row.

Step 2: Bring each of the needles that will be used for beading to HP. Load two or three beads onto the shaft of the beading tool. Then catch the first stitch that will be beaded in the hook of the tool. Slide the needle back to WP so that the stitch closes the latch as it slides over the needle and onto the tool. Then slide one bead off of the tool and onto the stitch.

Step 3: Use the beading tool to lift the stitch back into the hook of its needle, leaving the needle in WP.

Step 4: With a pair of 3-prong transfer tools, remove the cable stitches from their needles. First place the three right-hand stitches on the left needles; then place the three left-hand stitches on the right needles. Repeat this step for all the other cables in the row.

Step 5: To reform stitches as tuck stitches, insert the latch tool into the base of a column of stitches and drop the stitch from its needle so that it runs and forms a ladder. Push the tool forward so that the first stitch slides behind the latch and the latch is open. Then, insert the latch tool under the next two bars of the ladder, but only catch the second bar in the hook of the tool, as shown here. Pull back on the tool so that a new stitch is formed and the skipped bar becomes a tuck stitch.

Wrapped Stitches

At first glance, the fabric shown in Swatch 5 looks like a cable variation, but the effect is actually created by one enlarged stitch, positioned alternately at left or at right, which wraps around the center three stitches. On the bottom half of the swatch, the same groups of three stitches are continuously utilized, while the top of the swatch shows alternating repeats.

Swatch 5: Although this wrapped-stitch design looks like an elaborately braided cable, it has more depth and texture than most cables.

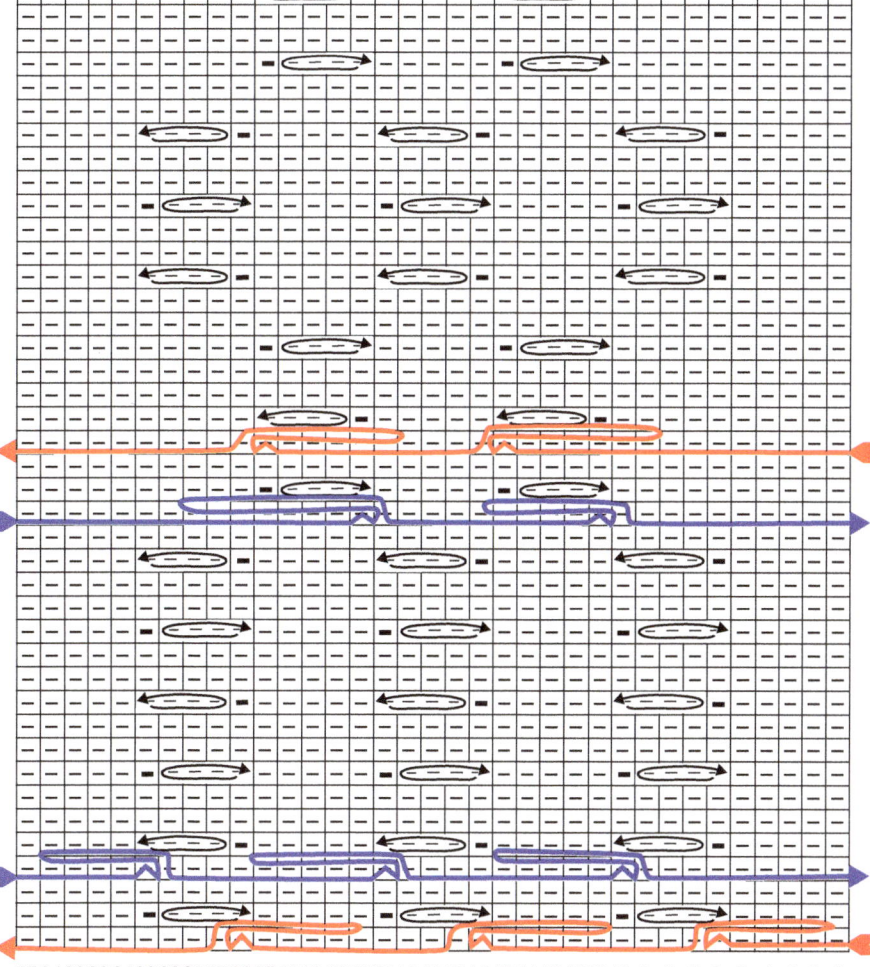

The same groups of three stitches are alternately wrapped by a stitch at the left or right of each group, indicated by the black arrows. The red and blue serpentine arrows reflect the difference in bridging from the left end or right end of the bed.

Wrapped-Stitch Design

Step 1. After bridging the preceding row, as shown on the chart on page 23, remove the center three stitches in each group with a 3-prong transfer tool, holding the tool slightly away from the edge of the bed. Use the latch tool to remove the enlarged stitch (at left in this photo) and pull it to the right between the stitches on the transfer tool and the edge of the bed.

Step 2. Return the stitches on the transfer tool to the same needles from which they were removed.

Step 3. Return the stitch on the latch tool to its needle.

Step 4. The enlarged stitches encircle the adjacent group of three stitches, gathering them slightly. There will usually be a small gap at the edge of special effects like this one. You can either minimize the gaping by latching up adjacent stitches or accept it as part of the fabric design.

Making Chinese Knots

Chinese knot stitch (Swatches 6 and 7) is a stitch pattern that weaves enlarged stitches through each other. The chart shows the bridged rows for working four-stitch Chinese knots, separated by 10-stitch bridges and with the placement of the knots staggered every six rows.

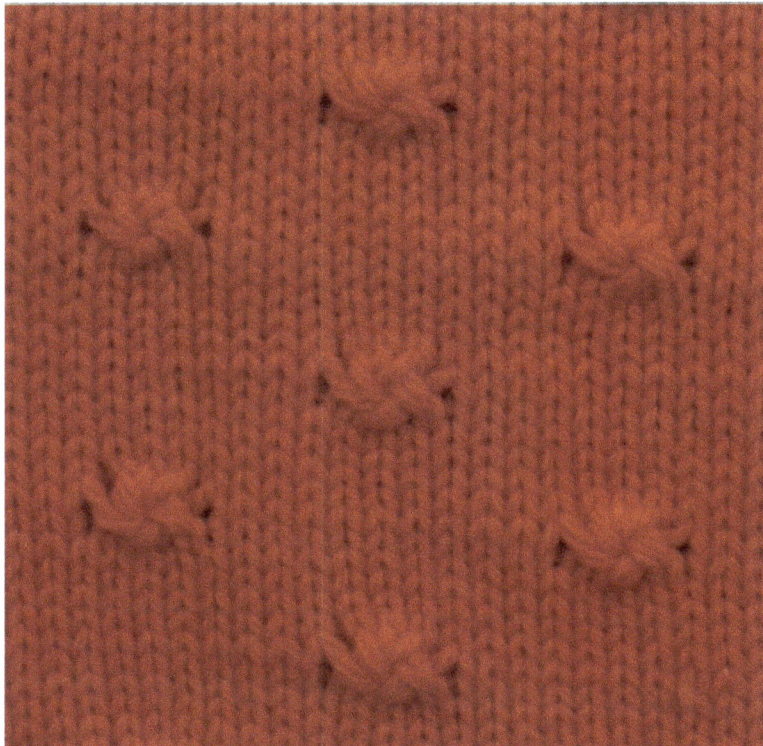

Swatch 7: Like many hand-manipulated techniques that rely on stitch movement, Chinese knot stitch tends to leave small gaps at the edges of the motif. If they are bothersome to you, you can reform the four knot stitches the row before and after forming the knots as well as a bridge stitch at each side. This adjustment adds a little extra work, but it does make the knots stand out even more crisply against the background fabric.

Swatch 6: Chinese knot stitch has always been a personal favorite of mine. It produces a raised texture that does not add bulk or draw in the fabric. Although two pairs of stitches trade needles, as for a cable, the finished effect is not at all like a cable.

Chinese Knots

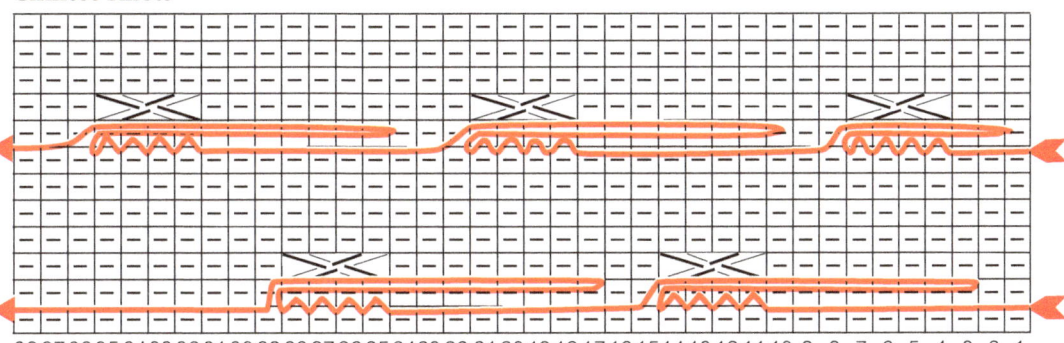

All four stitches in each group are enlarged, as shown by the red serpentine arrows. An even number of rows per repeat means that the bridging row is always worked from right to left.

Knitting the Bridged Row

Begin COR, set to hold needles in HP, with the stitch size set as for the background fabric. Turn off the row counter.

Bring all needles to HP except the first 10 on the carriage side. Knit one row. Manually knit the next four needles back to NWP. Place the 10 bridge needles into HP and return COR. Four needles remain in NWP.

*Place the next group of 10 needles into UWP. Knit one row. Manually knit the next four needles back to NWP, place the 10 bridge needles into HP, and move COR.**

Repeat * to ** to the end of the row, knitting the final bridge over the last 10 needles at left. Turn on the row counter and advance it by one row. Form the Chinese knots according to the steps shown below and at right.

Forming the Knots

Step 1. Bring all four of the enlarged stitches for each knot to HP. Weave a latch tool through the first two stitches at right and catch the third stitch in the hook of the tool, as shown here.

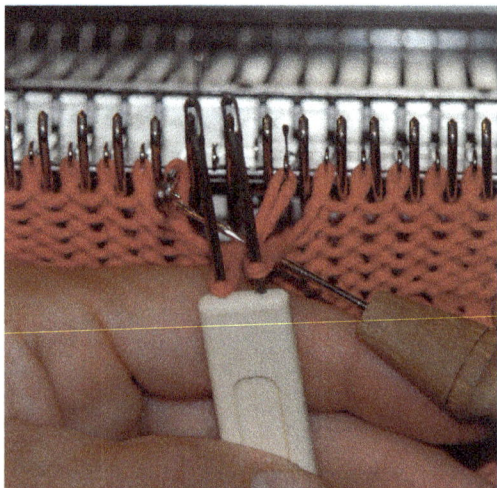

Step 4. Weave the latch tool through the two stitches on the transfer tool and catch the fourth stitch in the hook of the latch tool.

Step 2. Release the third stitch from its needle and pull it through the first two stitches.

Step 3. Remove the first two stitches from their needles with a 2-prong transfer tool. Then deposit the stitch from the latch tool onto the hook of the first needle.

Step 5. Pull the latch tool to the right and deposit the stitch on the latch tool onto the hook of the second needle.

Step 6. Transfer the two stitches from the tool onto the two empty needles at the left of the group.

Open Effects

Many fabrics actually utilize several different manipulations to create more complex looking patterns. The open-effect fabric shown in Swatch 8 features groups of five enlarged stitches that are grouped, twisted, and transferred. The techniques are shown in the photos below and at right. The reformed stitches between each group are optional, but they add a little extra definition to the pattern.

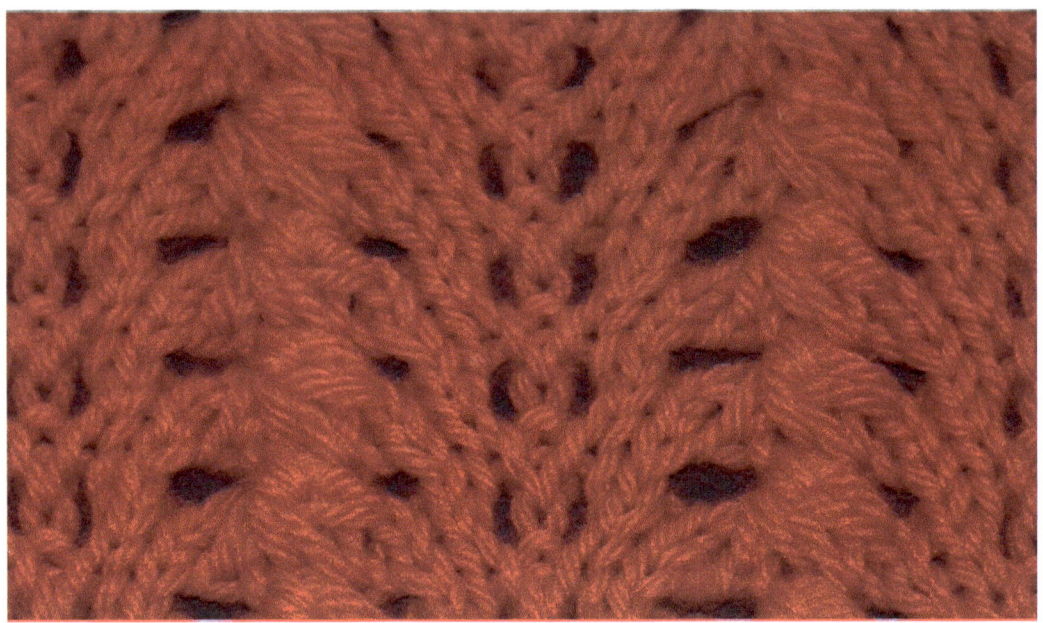

Swatch 8: At a quick glance, this fabric almost looks crocheted.

All five stitches in each repeat are enlarged in the row preceding the manipulations. Before knitting the next row, they are all twisted together, leaving two empty needles at each edge. The empty needles are filled with transferred stitches. The spacing of the effect requires an uneven number of rows per repeat, so the direction of the bridged row alternates throughout.

Open Stitch Effect

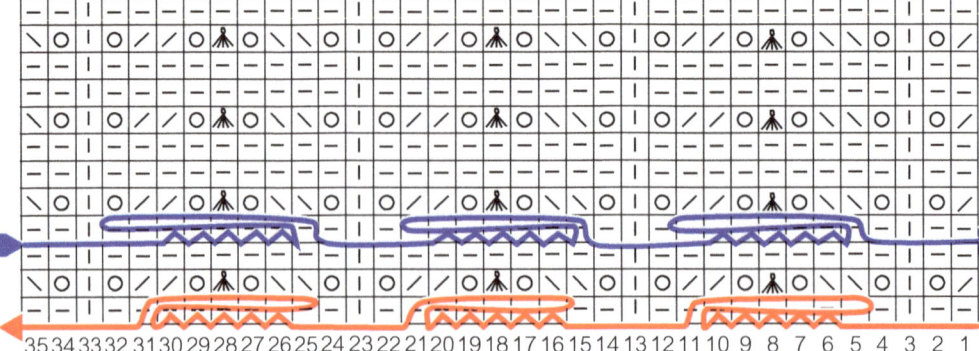

Creating an Open Effect

Step 1. The first group of pattern stitches are twisted together and replaced on the center needle. For clarity in the photograph, I put the bridge needles on each side of the group in WP, but when you're knitting, the groups of needles alternate between HP and NWP.

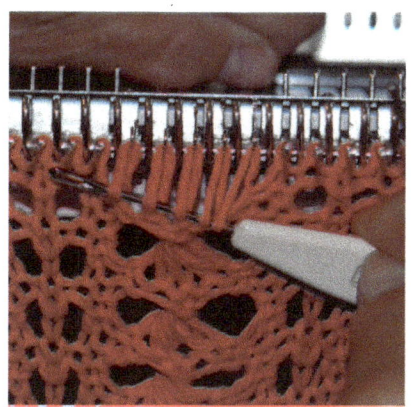

Step 2. Carefully push all five enlarged stitches to HP and then catch the stitches on a single-prong transfer tool. Push the needle butts back to release the stitches onto the tool.

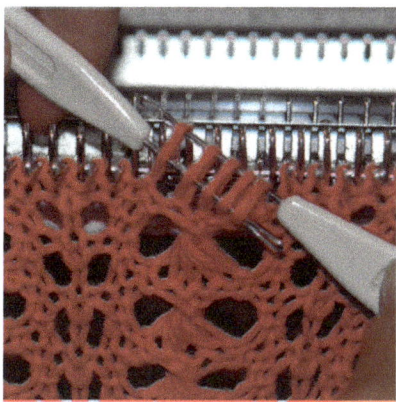

Step 3. Insert a second transfer tool from above and then remove the first tool.

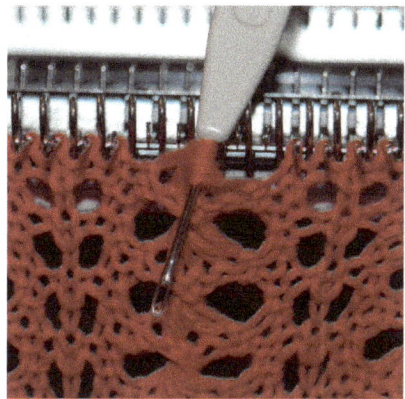

Step 4. Rotate the transfer tool 360 degrees (left) and deposit all five stitches in the hook of the center needle (right).

Step 5. When you have twisted all of the 5-stitch groups, there will be pairs of empty needles on each side of the twisted bundle of stitches.

Step 6. The twisting is complete.

Step 7. Use a 2-prong transfer tool to move the first and last two stitches in each group over by one needle.

Step 8. Then knit two rows. Prior to knitting the next bridged row, you can latch up the center bridge stitch.

Step 9. Because of the transfers and the eyelets they created two rows back, the ladder will drop, forming a loop. If you tug on the ladder, all of the stitches will drop, and the reformed column of stitches will appear as plain purl stitches on the front of the fabric. If you tug gently and retain the loop, however, the column of stitches will form a V as it branches over the adjacent eyelets.

CHAPTER 4
Bridging to Add Rows

The bridging technique is also an effective way to add extra rows to stitches on specific needles to create special effects, such as more-dimensional cables, popcorns, nops, and a variety of trims, edgings, and textured stitches. With these bridging applications, the same rule holds: *Bridges only knit once.* The other, non-bridging groups of needles—those that hold the special-effect stitches—may, however, knit many extra rows of stitches of the same size. Only the extra rows provide ease and/or texture. Note: In all of the examples in this chapter, the serpentine arrows indicate the extra rows that are worked over specific needles—not the backing-up motion of the carriage as they indicated in previous charts for modifying stitch size with the stitch dial or by manually knitting stitches.

In all bridging, the bridged rows are only worked prior to the cable or other special rows; the rows between are knitted normally. When working lots of extra rows on a small group of needles, you must either move the weights regularly or use your fingers to keep a little tension on the stitches. I sometimes also poke a transfer tool through the work, one row below, and then use the tool to tension the stitches.

Raising Cables

Because machine-knit cables can sometimes look a bit flat when compared to their hand-knit cousins, I often add a couple of extra rows to some of the needles. The extra rows have nowhere to go but up and off the surface of the fabric, creating pronounced texture. It makes no sense to hide that texture on the back of the fabric. When crossing cables, the stitches that are returned to the needles first are the stitches that show on the knit face of the fabric. Therefore, you need to be clear about which direction you are crossing the cables and which needles should knit the extra rows.

Swatch 9: was knitted from the chart below, which shows two columns of 3x3 cables with a 10-stitch bridge between them and 5-stitch bridges at each edge. Although I did enlarge the stitches in both columns, I intentionally did not cross any cables at left so that the extra rows would be easy to see in the photo.

3 x 3 Serpentine Cables

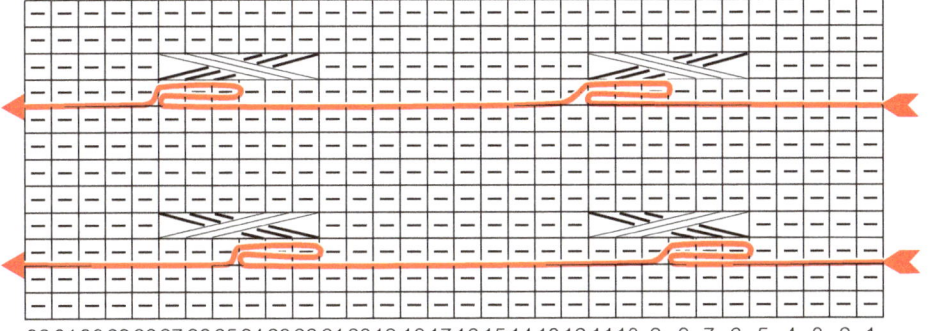

These cable crossings alternate right and left, which will produce a serpentine or open cable, with six rows between each crossing. The arrows indicate the extra rows worked.

Left-Cross Cables

Begin with COR, set to hold needles in HP.

Hold all needles except the first 11 on the carriage side (the first five bridge needles and all six cable needles). Knit one row.

Hold the five bridge needles and the first three of the cable needles.

*Knit one row on the remaining three needles (left half of the cable). COR.

Return the next 10 bridge needles and the following 6 cable needles to UWP and knit one row to the left.

Hold the last 3 needles of the previous cable, the 10 bridge, and the first 3 right needles of the current cable.**

Repeat * to ** to the end of the row.

Cross all cables, returning the left half of each cable to the machine first so that the extra rows are on the knit face of the fabric.

Combination Cables

Swatch 10 combines both left- and right-cross enlarged cables to form a wishbone cable, shown at left in the photo, and an X and O cable (or Hugs and Kisses cable), shown at right. With combination cables like these, it is important to know which stitches cross left and right (in other words, which stitches return to the machine first) and then to bridge accordingly.

Both of these cables result from combining a pair of 3x3 cables. The chart shows a wishbone cable at right and an X and O cable at left. There is a 10-needle bridge between them and 5-needle bridges at each edge. The red arrows show the same carriage path for the wishbone cables throughout the chart and also for the first two cable crossings of the X and O cable. The second two cable crossings (X and O) require different bridging, however, as shown by the blue arrows.

When I work a cable like this X and O cable, I tend to think "cross out-out-in-in," which is exactly what the darker lines in each cable cross are indicating, as the pairs alternately cross away from and then toward each other for two repeats. The third and fourth X and O crossings will strain the stitches somewhat (even with the extra rows), so I usually push those needles to HP and then back to UWP before knitting the row to keep needles from jamming the carriage.

Right Cross Cables

Begin with COR, set to hold needles in HP.

Hold all needles except the first 8 on the carriage side (5 bridge needles and the first 3 cable needles). Knit one row.

Hold the 5 bridge needles. *Knit one row on the remaining 3 needles (right half of the cable). COR.

Move the next 16 needles to UWP (the remaining 3 cable needles, 10 bridge needles, and the first 3 needles for the next cable).**

Knit one row to the left. Hold the first 13 needles. Repeat from * to ** to the end of the row.

Cross all cables, returning the right half of each cable to the machine first so that the extra rows are on the knit face of the fabric.

Bridging to Add Rows 35

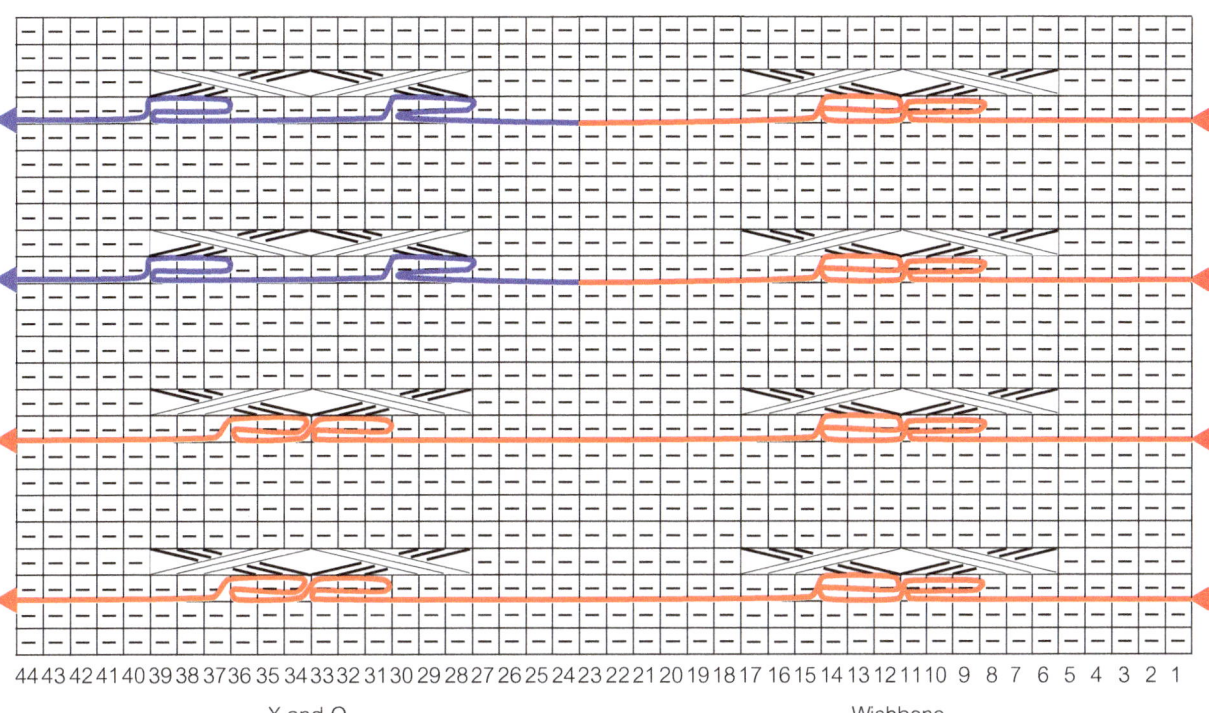

The paired cables at right (wishbone) consistently cross away from each other. The paired cables at left (X and O) alternate two crossings toward each other and two away from each other. The extra rows, as indicated by the arrows, are worked on the stitches that will return to the needles first, adding greater depth to the surface of the cables. Because different sets of stitches are returned to the needles first for the two crossings, the bridging arrows are different.

Swatch 10: Wishbone cables (left) and X and O cables (right) look surprisingly different from each other when you consider that there are only two cable crossings that differ in every 24-row repeat.

Crossing Combination Cables

Begin COR, set to hold needles in HP.

Hold all needles except the first 11 needles on the carriage side (the first bridge and the first left-cross cable). Knit one row. COL.

Hold eight needles at right (the first bridge and half of the cable needles). Knit one row. COR.

Move to UWP the next three needles at left. Knit one row. Hold three needles at right (second half of previous cable). Knit one row over remaining three needles. COR.

Move the next 19 needles to UWP (the next three needles of this cable, the 10-stitch bridge, and the entire next cable). Knit one row. COL.

Hold 16 needles. Knit one row over remaining three needles. COR.

Move next three needles to UWP and knit one row. COL. Hold three needles at right.

Knit one row over remaining three needles. COR.

Move next eight needles to UWP and knit to the end of the row.

Cross all cables so that extra rows are on the knit face of the fabric. Knit five rows and then repeat exactly for the second crossings.

Begin COR, set to hold needles in HP. The blue arrow repositions the bridging for the third and fourth crosses of the X and O cable because the cables now cross toward each other.

Hold all needles except the first 11 needles on the carriage side (the first bridge and the first left-cross cable). Knit one row. COL.

Hold eight needles at right (the first bridge and half of the cable needles). Knit one row. COR.

Move to UWP the next three needles at left. Knit one row. Hold three needles at right (second half of previous cable). Knit one row over remaining three needles. COR.

Move the next 16 needles to UWP (the next three needles of this cable, the 10-stitch bridge, and the first three needles of the next cable). Knit one row. COL.

Hold 13 needles. Knit one row over remaining three needles. COR.

Move next nine needles to UWP and knit one row. COL. Hold six needles at right.

Knit one row over remaining three needles. COR.

Move next five needles to UWP and knit to the end of the row.

Cross all cables so that extra rows are on the knit face of the fabric.

Popcorns and Nops

Popcorns and nops are quite similar, except that popcorns include lifted stitches and nops generally do not (although they often benefit from wrapped adjacent needles). They both form little bumps on the surface of the fabric, with popcorns appearing more regular and defined than nops usually do.

Knitting Popcorns

The fastest popcorns to knit are worked over two or three stitches for eight rows, as they were for the fabric in Swatch 11. This proportion seems to work for most machines and most yarns. I always work popcorns this way when knitting lots of popcorns across a row. In addition to the serpentine, bridging arrow, the chart below shows that the first row of stitches for each popcorn are lifted to the needles above.

At the extreme, the ties in Swatches 12 and 12a on the next page were knitted over 40 rows, but the method is exactly the same.

Swatch 11: The popcorns at the bottom of this swatch were knitted on two needles, as shown in the chart. The popcorns at the top were worked over three needles.

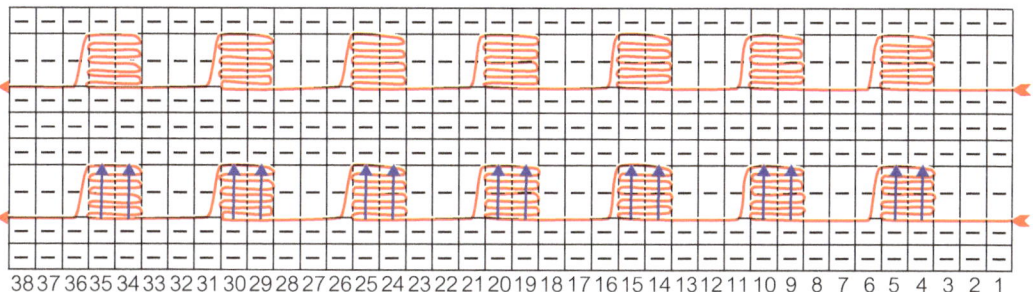

This chart illustrates 2-stitch popcorns, but you would follow the same procedure to make 3-stitch popcorns and the bridges can always be wider. I usually lift the first row of each popcorn before knitting the next one, but you might find that you prefer lifting them all at the end of the row. Make sure you keep tension on the stitches while you knit, or they will drop easily.

38   Chapter 4

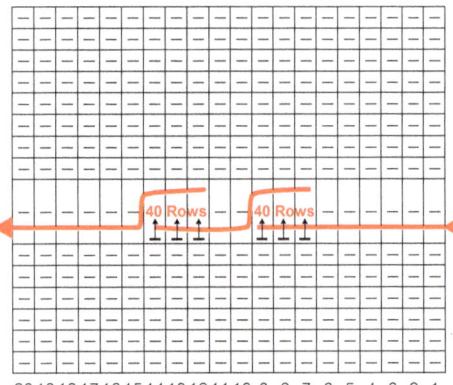

Popcorns are usually knitted for just 6-8 rows, but by working lots of rows you form large loops on the surface of the fabric. After knitting 3 stitches for 40 rows, the first row of each strip is lifted onto the needles above to create a large loop.

Although you can use a single or 2-prong transfer tool to lift the first row of each popcorn. I use a 2-tool method that eliminates poking around to find the stitches later. This method, shown in the photo series at right, guarantees that all of the popcorns are lifted from the same row and it also provides tension on the popcorn stitches while I knit the extra rows. For clarity in the photo, I've moved some of the needles back to WP, but you don't have to bother doing that. Larger popcorns require "borrowing" needles, as described on page 77, which involves a lot more work, so I use that method less often.

Swatch 12: Completed 40 row loops/ties.

Basic 2-Stitch Popcorns

Begin COR, set to hold needles in HP.

Hold all needles except the first three bridge needles and the first two popcorn needles. Knit one row. Hold the bridge.

*Knit seven more rows over these two needles.

Move the next three bridge needles and the next two popcorn needles into UWP and knit one row.

Lift the first row of the popcorn onto the needles and place them in HP. Hold the bridge.**

Repeat from * to ** to end of row.

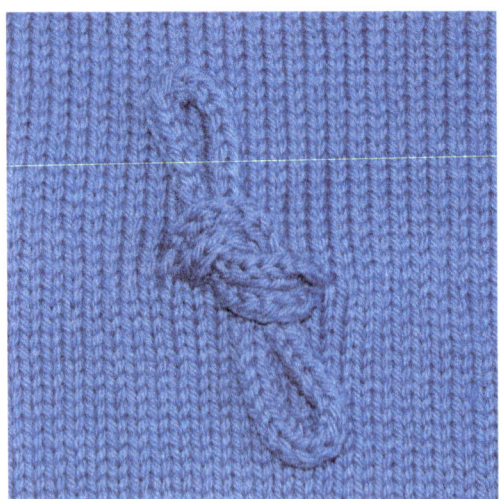

Swatch 12a: Knotted loops. Ties like these provide the closure for the cardigan on page 90.

Two-Tool Method for Lifting Popcorns

Step 1. Before you knit the extra rows for each popcorn, insert a transfer tool from above to catch the purl bumps of the stitches in the needle hooks.

Step 2. Tip the tool forward, toward you, and use it to provide tension on the stitches while you knit the extra rows for the popcorn.

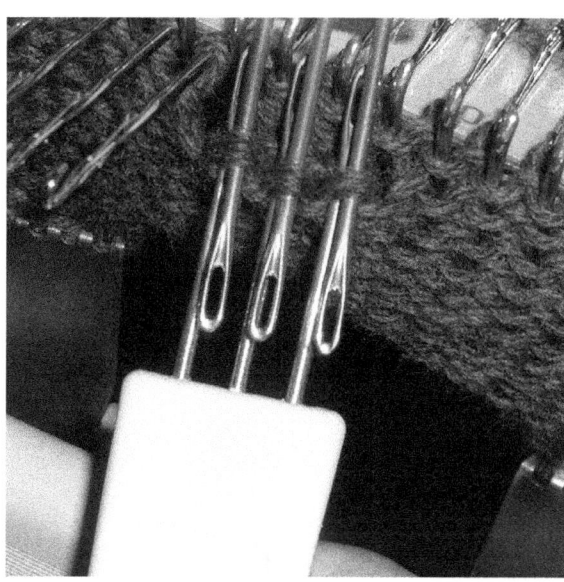

Step 3. Return the tool to its original downward-facing vertical position and insert a second tool through the same stitches from above.

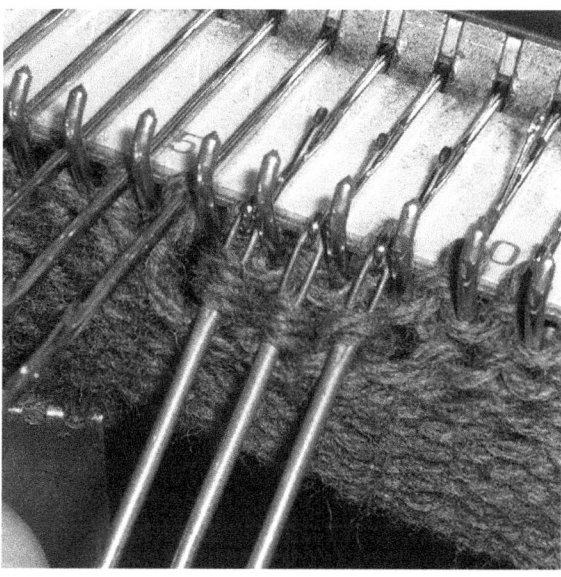

Step 4. Remove the first tool. Use the second tool to lift the purl bumps onto the needles to complete the popcorn.

Knitting Nops

Nops are very interesting texture accents that are structurally stable—which means they don't stretch out or disappear as the fabric is handled or finished. Swatches 13 and 14 have an allover nop pattern that was knitted for eight rows on three needles, with three bridge needles between them. An adjacent needle was wrapped every third and sixth row of each sequence, as indicated by the X on the chart below. Nops also take on a whole new personality when the fabric is felted, as you can see in Swatch 14.

Nops can be wrapped every row or have no wrapping at all. Without wrapping, they do not pop up quite so far from the surface of the fabric. The size of the bridge—or the lack of one—will also change their appearance. With allover patterns like this one, rather than turning the row counter off and on, I count repeats, which are easier to keep track of than rows. Note that this chart is very similar to the popcorn chart except that, instead of lifting stitches, you wrap adjacent needles.

Step by Step Nops
Begin COR, set to hold needles in HP.

Hold all needles except the first three bridge needles and the first three nop needles. Knit one row and then hold the bridge.
*Knit two rows, wrap at left.

Knit three rows, wrap at right.

Knit two rows. COR.

Move the next three bridge needles and the next three nop needles into UWP and knit one row. Hold the completed nop and the bridge.**

Repeat * to ** to end of the row.

Knit two rows over all needles. COL. Set carriage to hold needles in HP and repeat as shown by the blue serpentine arrow on the chart.

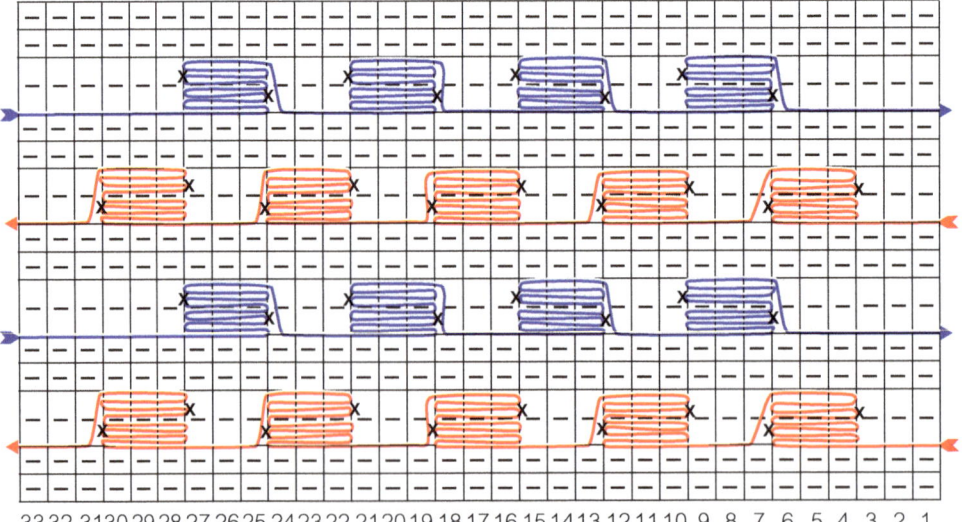

Red and blue serpentine arrows illustrate the different bridging sequence required by staggering the placement of the nops and by beginning on either the left or the right end of the carriage.

Swatches 13 and 14: Both of these swatches were knitted from the same chart, but the swatch in the photo at right was felted.

Seashell Nops

While basic nops tend to look like soft popcorn bumps on the fabric, it is also possible to knit shaped nops. Working short rows (or partial knitting as some manuals call it) enables you to unevenly or gradually build up extra rows on specific needles. You might be more familiar with short rows as they are generally used in patterns to shape shoulder slants at the edges of a fabric or sock heels mid-row. When short rows are worked from one side of a nop, they build up at an angle and the resulting nops look, to me, like tiny seashells. I incorporated seashell nops into the body of the fabric with four rows between each repeat, as shown in the chart on the following page. (There is also a seashell border/insertion on page 171 of *Hand-Manipulated Stitches for Machine Knitters* that uses short rows to modify the shape of the nops.)

Note that the repeats begin alternately from the left and right sides. Also, at the end of each repeat, the edge stitch in the first row of the repeat is lifted onto the needle above, which helps define the shape and diminish the gap at the edge of each shell, as you can see in Swatch 15 at right.

Working with the same chart, but eliminating the lifted stitch and working only two rows (instead of four) between alternating repeats, you can transform the seashell effect into a

Swatch 15: The seashell shape in the fabric below is defined by working four rows between repeats and by lifting the edge stitch in the first row of each repeat.

Swatch 16: In the photo at right, only two rows are worked between repeats and the lifted stitch is eliminated, transforming the seashell nops (swatch 15) into a corded ruffle.

corded ruffle, as shown in Swatch 16 at left. The stitches lie perpendicular to the background stitches, and the ruffle seems to float on the fabric surface.

The appearance of this pattern would change again if, rather than lifting the edge stitch of each seashell, you simply wrapped the adjacent needle every so many rows, worked all of the nops from one side only, or changed the number of stitches in each nop and the short-row sequence.

Nop variations are endless, and each attempt leaves me wondering "What if I. . . ." I also chose to vary the placement of the nops, working the same short-row sequences as for

Seashell Nops

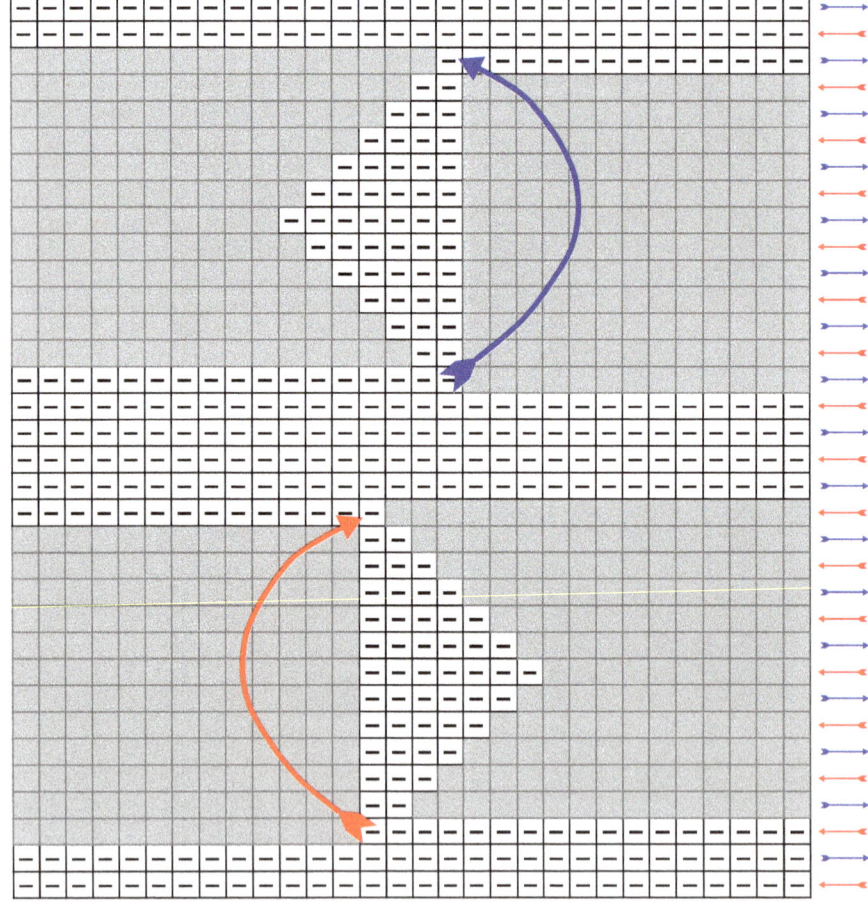

The red and blue arrows indicate which stitches to lift onto which needles. The grey shaded area represents needles that are in HP while each of the edge seashells is short-rowed.

the seashells, and came up with the ruffled edging in Swatch 17, at right. Positioning the shaping at the edges of the fabric forces the seashells to remain open; the extra rows create the ruffle. I also latched up the tenth stitch from each edge of the fabric to help set the ruffle apart from the body of the fabric. I was so delighted by these two ruffled effects that I combined them in a single sequence for the Ruffled Scarf pattern on page 118.

Swatch 17: This integrated ruffle can be worked at the edges of a scarf, shawl, or afghan—and it minimizes the amount of finishing that the piece requires later.

Ruffled Edging

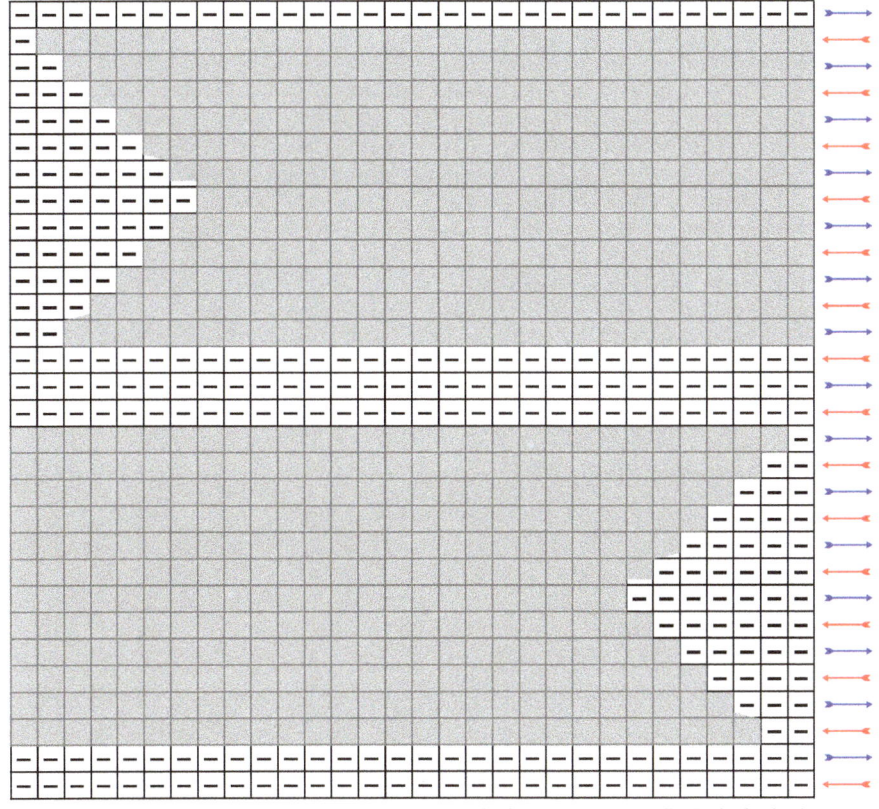

The short-row sequences are identical to those at the center of the seashell chart except that they are worked at the edges of the fabric.

Swatch 18: The ruching rows in this fabric stack up vertically, causing the lower edge of the fabric to curve.

Wrapped Ruching Sequence

Begin with COR, set to hold needles in HP.

Hold needles 21–30, knit to the left, and wrap the yarn around needle 21.

Hold needles 1–10, knit to the right, and wrap needle 10.

*Place needles 21 and 22 in UWP, knit, place needle 22 in HP.

Place needles 9 and 10 in UWP, knit, place needle 9 in HP.

Knit to left, hold needle 21.

Knit to right and hold needle 10.**

Repeat from * to **.

Place needles 21–30 in UWP and knit to left. Knit three rows across all needles and then repeat the entire sequence for the next section.

Ruching stacked vertically.

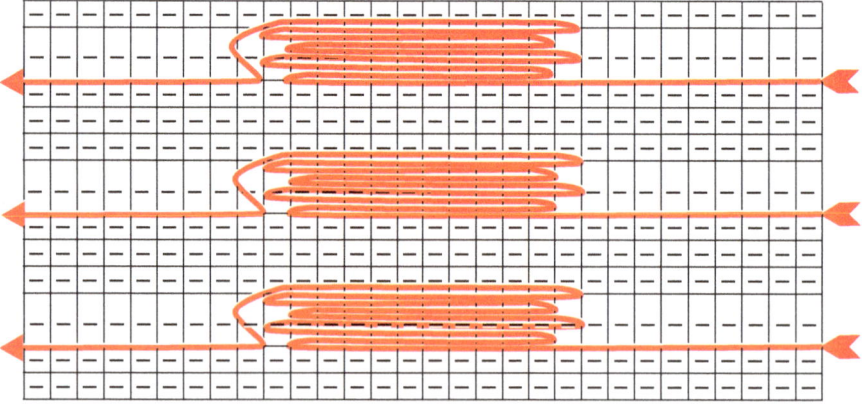

Ruching

Ruched fabrics are usually created by lifting stitches from rows below and hanging them on the needles above. They can, however, also be knitted by working extra rows in specific arrangements. Ruching this way causes the fabric to pucker in predictable—and often surprising—ways that I tend to think of as Nops Gone Wild!

Swatches 18, 19, and 20 were all produced by working eight extra rows over groups of 10 needles. The placement of those rows differs from one swatch to the next. The fabric in Swatch 18 stacks the rows vertically so that the same needles are always worked; the fabric in Swatch 19 shifts the rows five needles to the left. Both of these patterns have three plain rows between each bridged repeat. There is only one plain row in Swatch 20 so that, visually, the ruched shapes seem to merge.

The ruching in all three of these fabrics was worked the same way--with both ends of each section wrapped to prevent gaping holes at the edges. This method staggers the wrapping over a couple of needles at each edge, which also helps soften the edges of the ruching. The directions that follow are specific to the needle numbers in the chart for the vertical column of ruching, shown at left, but once you have worked through a couple of repeats, you should be able to carry the logic over to the other samples—and beyond—to create your own designs.

Swatch 19: With four plain rows between each repeat, the texture shifts over five needles in each successive repeat.

Ruching rows offset by five needles.

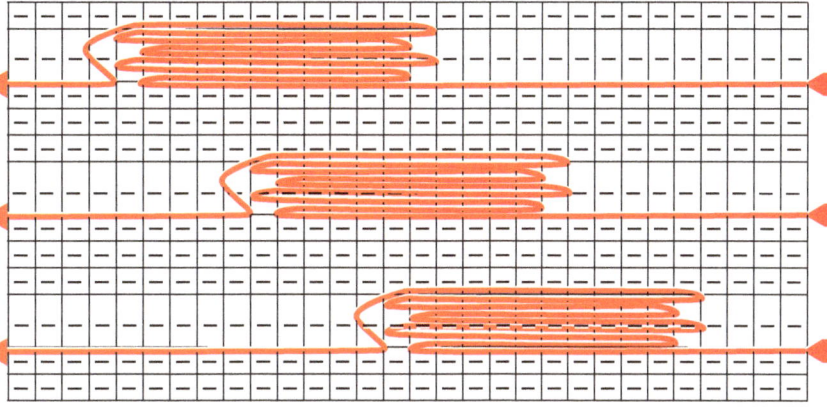

46   Chapter 4

Swatch 20: The texture in this swatch is much more interesting than the texture in the other ruched swatches, because the repeats, with just one row between them, seem to melt into each other, forming a complex allover texture. As with the other samples, the lower edge of the fabric curves.

Ruching with a single plain row between each repeat.

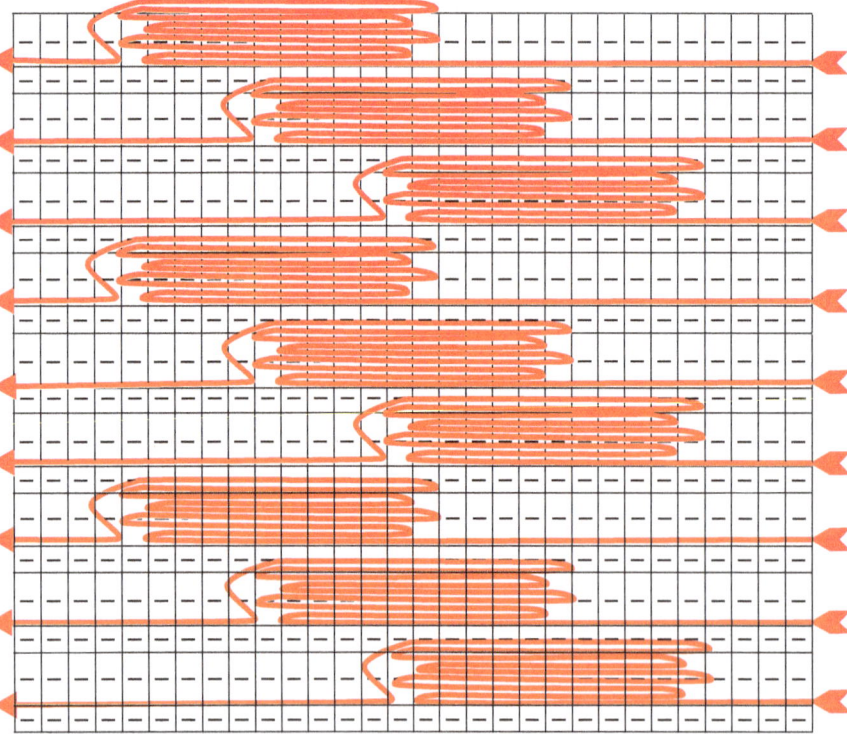

Short-Rowed Textures

These next two samples feature short rows (or partial knitting)—rather than extra rows over the same number of needles, as in the previous samples. The short rows look like little sock heels in the middle of the knitting. The two fabrics are knitted with nearly identical methods; one is finished with lifted stitches, and the other is finished with a cable crossing. The 3-D triangle short-rows down to a single needle so that it has a nice sharp point. The Stegosaurus cable works down to two needles for a rounder effect.

3-D Triangles

While adding an interesting allover texture, the triangle method can be used to knit pocket flaps, trim, or an alternative to the popcorn. For variations, think about changing the size and spacing of the triangles or lifting only some of the stitches. Worked on the lower edge of a garment, 3-D triangles create an interesting hem. The triangles in Swatch 21 are seven stitches wide, with three-stitch bridges between them.

Knitting 3-D Triangles

Begin COR, set to hold needles in HP.

Hold all needles except the first three bridge needles and the first seven triangle needles. Knit one row. *Hold the bridge needles and the left most triangle needle. Six needles remaining in WP.

(Knit one row. Hold one needle on carriage side.) Repeat (to) until only one needle is in WP. Knit one row. COL.

Then return one needle on carriage side every row until all six needles are work-ing again. COR. Move one needle on the carriage side, next bridge and next seven triangle needles to UWP. Knit one row to left.

Lift each of the seven stitches from the first row of the triangle onto the needles directly above them and leave them in HP.

Place the next three bridge needles and the next seven triangle needles into UWP and knit one row to left. **
Repeat from * to **.

Swatch 21: Because these triangles have only three plain rows between each vertical repeat, they stand away from the surface. A single triangle would lie flat against the fabric.

3-D Triangles

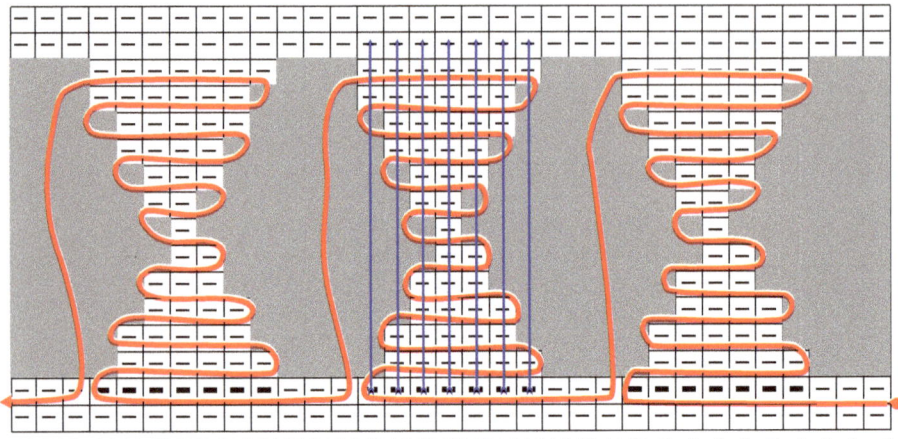

The blue arrows indicate which stitches to lift after each triangle is short-rowed. You can wait and lift them all at the end of the row, but it is easier to just complete each one as you go.

Swatch 22: The cables on the left-hand side of this swatch are right-cross cables. Notice how they slant to the right. The cables on the other side are left-cross cables, which slant to the left. The center cables slant alternately left and right.

Knitting Stegosaurus Cables

Begin COR, set to hold needles in HP.

Hold all needles except the first six bridge needles and the next six cable needles. Knit one row and then hold the bridge needles.

*Wrap one needle at left.

(Knit one row. Bring one needle to HP on carriage side) five times until one needle remains and COR.

Knit two rows on this single needle.

(Return one needle to UWP on carriage side and knit one row) four times until one needle remains in HP at right edge of cable.

Move this last needle, the next bridge (five needles) and the next cable group (six needles) to UWP and knit one row. COL.

Cross a 3x3 cable on the group just short-rowed. Hold the bridge**. Repeat from * to **. Latching up a stitch at each side of the cable helps define the texture. You can reduce the gap at each crossing by catching an edge loop, as shown in the photo at right.

Stegosaurus Cables

This cocky cable is almost identical to the 3-D triangle except that each sequence is finished by cable crossings instead of lifted stitches. I find it easiest to cross all of the cables when I finish knitting the row. You can change the final appearance by varying either the size of each section, the direction of the cable cross, or the number of rows between repeats, but—in every variation—these cables always stand up crisply and provide serious texture.

When latching up the stitches at each side of the Stegosaurus cable (Swatch), catch half of an edge stitch from the cable. Do not latch this loop. Just let it slide behind the latch of the tool and treat it as a tuck stitch. The loop won't show on the front of the fabric, but it will reduce the gap at each side of the cable.

Stegosaurus Cables

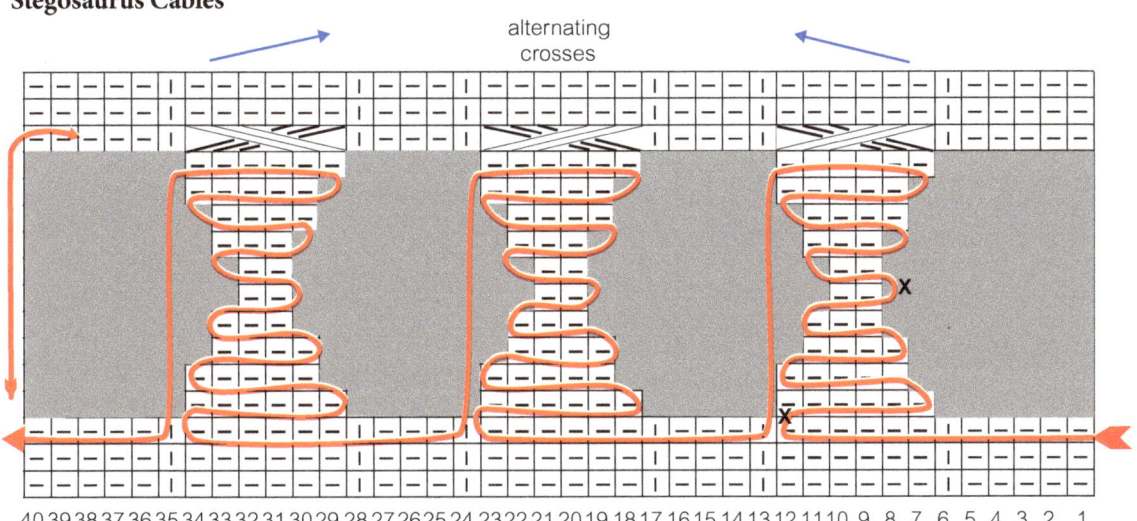

Latched-up stitches on each side of the cable columns help the cables stand away from the background fabric.

Zig-Zag Trim

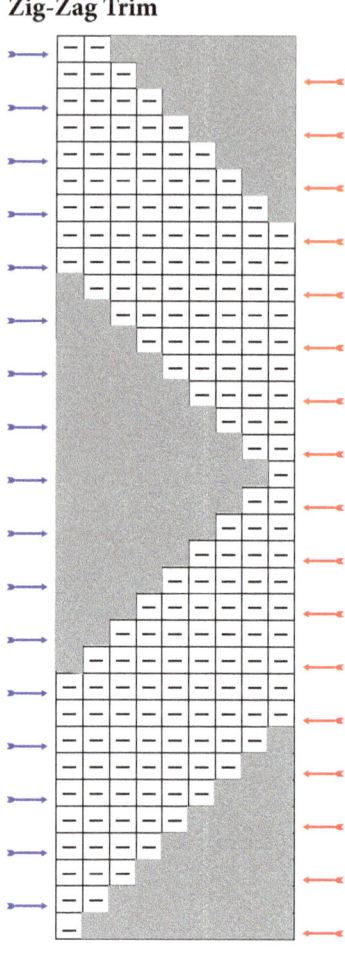

9 8 7 6 5 4 3 2 1

Because one needle is held or returned to work every row, the wrapping is automatic. The repeats begin alternately from the left and right, and the last completed "zig" or "zag" always points to the side from which it started—which helps you keep track of the repeats if you are interrupted.

The chart above shows the short row progression and the direction each row is worked.

Zigzag Trim

With scrap yarn, cast on nine stitches. Knit some rows, hang a weight, and end COR. Change to main yarn and knit one row to the left. Set carriage to hold needles in HP.

To begin a strip with a straight end (rather than angled):
Hold needles 1–7 and knit one row. COR.
Now follow the chart:
*Hold needle 8 and knit one row. COL.
Move needle 8 to UWP and knit one row. COR.
At the beginning of the following rows, return one needle to UWP until all needles are working again and COL.
Knit one row to begin next repeat COR.
Hold one needle at left every row until only one needle remains in WP and COR.
At the beginning of the following rows, move one needle back to UWP until all needles are working again and COR.
Knit one row to begin next repeat COL.**
Repeat * to * for desired length of trim.

Bridged Fills

Sometimes you bridge extra rows not to add texture, but to fill in or level off a previously knitted shape. For example, you can knit a zigzag trim and then hang the trim sideways on the machine to act as the cast-on or lower edge of a sweater. Unless you fill in the "zigs," however, the knitting will pucker where the trim joins the body, and the whole effect will be lost. So, before you can begin knitting the sweater body, you need to build up the negative spaces in the trim.

This trim can be knitted over as many needles as you want, although usually you will work with an odd number of needles. Depending on the gauge of your machine, you can also use this method to knit delicate rickrack to sew onto a garment or work wide strips for a scarf or really wide strips to join for an afghan.

Block the finished strip and use safety pins or yarn to tag the points of the zigs (or zags) along the edge you want to rehang on the machine. The ratio of stitches to rows (for stockinette) is generally about two to three. To make the fabric in Swatch 23, each section was knitted over 17 rows, and I picked up 13 stitches between each of the tags.

Each short-row sequence begins at the point of one section and widens to fill the negative triangle shape. The last row of one triangle knits with the first row of the next, so there are no plain bridges here.

To use this trim-and-fill method for a scarf or the lower edge of a garment, begin the strip on the first row of the chart and end with the last row of this 34-row sequence. I have purposely split the left-side sequence on the chart to ensure that the ends of the strip knit straight and line up evenly with the edges of a garment or scarf. In practice, one repeat will simply flow into the next as you work, and the only half-repeats will be at the beginning and end of the strip. (I usually begin and end these strips on waste yarn so that I have the option of grafting the ends together when I finish the garment.)

If you need to adjust the number of rows in order to fit the strip to the number of stitches at the lower edge of a sweater, for example, you might need to work the strip wider or narrower. This width adjustment will change the number of rows required for each repeat. It goes without saying that you need to swatch the whole process in advance to make sure that everything meshes just as you would like.

Swatch 23: The zigzag trim is shown here as a lower band, but it would also make an excellent edging for cuffs or for a sideways-knitted cardigan.

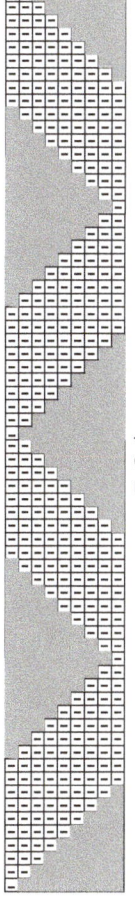

← end last repeat here

Beginning and ending rows for zig-zag trim with straight ends

Bridged Fill

Note that the first row is knitted from left to right across all of the needles before the short-row bridging begins on the right. This single row acts as a "smoothing" row, so that the two fabrics are joined with a crisp line between them.

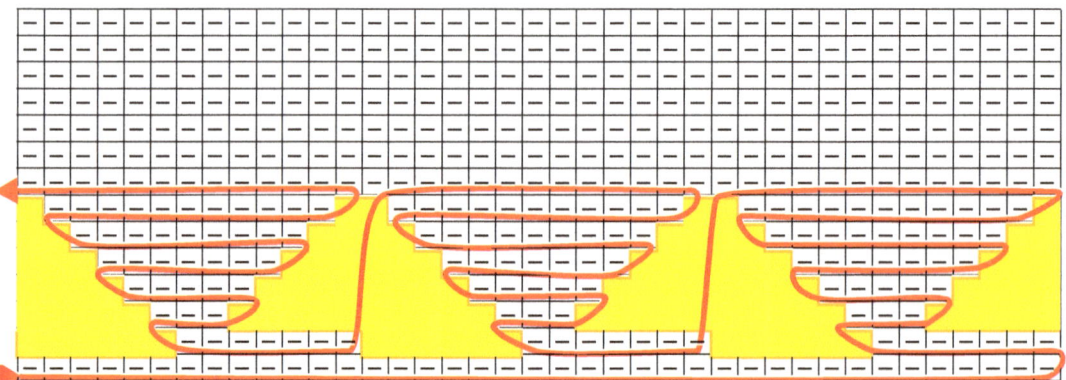

Bridged Fill - Step by Step

Knit a smoothing row across all needles from left to right.
COR and set to hold needles in HP.

*Hold needles 8–39. Knit one row.

Move needle 8 to UWP and needles 1–5 to HP. Knit one row. COR.

Move needles 5 and 9 to UWP. Knit one row.

Move needles 10 and 4 to UWP. Knit one row. COR.

Move needles 11 and 3 to UWP. Knit one row.

Move needles 12 and 2 to UWP. Knit one row. CR.

Move needle 1 and needles 13–20 to UWP and knit one row. COL. Hold needles 1–18.**

Repeat the sequence from * to **, moving one needle into UWP every row on each side, as before.

Oversized Cables

The large cables shown in Swatches 24 and 25 were worked exactly the same way, except that the tighter column of cables in Swatch 24 was worked with only two rows between repeats, while the more standard column of cables in Swatch 25 was worked with nine rows between repeats.

This giant cable pattern is quite straight forward. You bridge the extra rows much as you would for any of the previous examples. There is, however, an extra detail to manage when crossing the cables. If you study the charts on the next four pages, you will see that, in each pattern, there is a long float of yarn from the last row of the right half of each cable to the first row of the left half. You have to make sure that, when you cross the second group of stitches from right to left, they pass under that float before you place them on the needles—otherwise, the float will show on the front of the fabric. The steps shown in the photos on page 56 illustrate the process.

The cables in Swatch 26, the third sample in this series, look like links of chain because of the placement of the cable crossings. As an allover pattern, this pattern would resemble a giant basket weave. To make it, you would cross all of the stitches in a row as adjacent cables, crossing in the same direction. The cables in the next crossing row would cross in the opposite direction, and their placement would stagger the placement of the preceding and following rows. I refer to this row placement as splitting pairs.

For example, in the first row of cables, needle groupings A and B, C and D, E and F would cross to the right. In the next cabled row, groupings B and C, D and E, etc., would cross to the left. Splitting pairs and alternating the direction of the crossings are the basic techniques for creating braided and woven cable effects.

Swatch 24: Closely spaced right cross cables

Closely Crossed Giant Cables

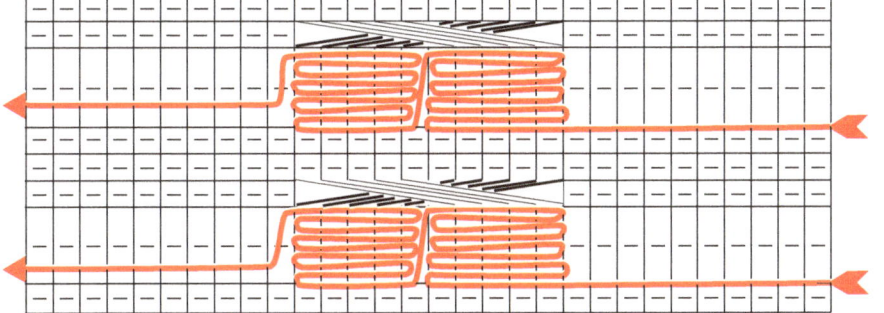

With only two rows between repeats, these cables have a tighter, almost knotted appearance, rather than a typical cabled look.

54   Chapter 4

Swatch 25: All of these cables are also left-cross cables. If , instead, they alternated right and left with each repeat, they would produce a serpentine or open cable.

These cables are managed exactly like those in Swatch 24, on the previous page, except that there are enough rows between each repeat to define the shape of the cabled column of stitches. I manually reformed two stitches on each side of the cable and two at the center to help the cable stand out from the background. To avoid gaps where the cables cross, I caught half an edge stitch from the side of the cable and treated that loop like a tuck stitch while latching up the adjacent stitches.

Giant Left Cross Cable

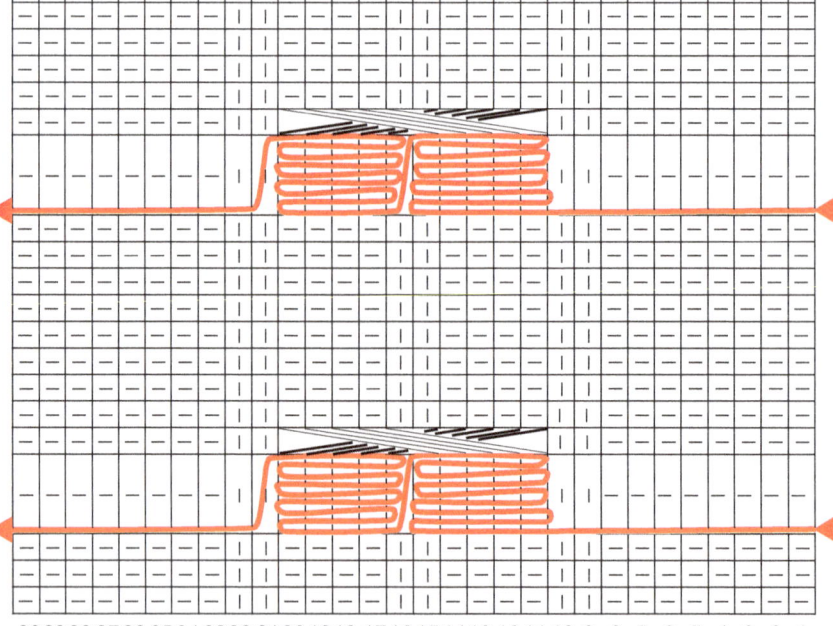

Bridging to Add Rows   55

Swatch 26: This staggered placement of single cable crossings, crossed in alternating directions, could easily be expanded to produce an all-over giant basket weave.

Alternating Cross Cables

To make the pattern in Swatch 26, the placement of the cables simply shifts by five needles with each repeat, and the number of rows between each repeat reduces to just one. The linked-chain effect is the result of alternating the direction of the cable crossings, a standard technique for producing woven or braided cable effects.

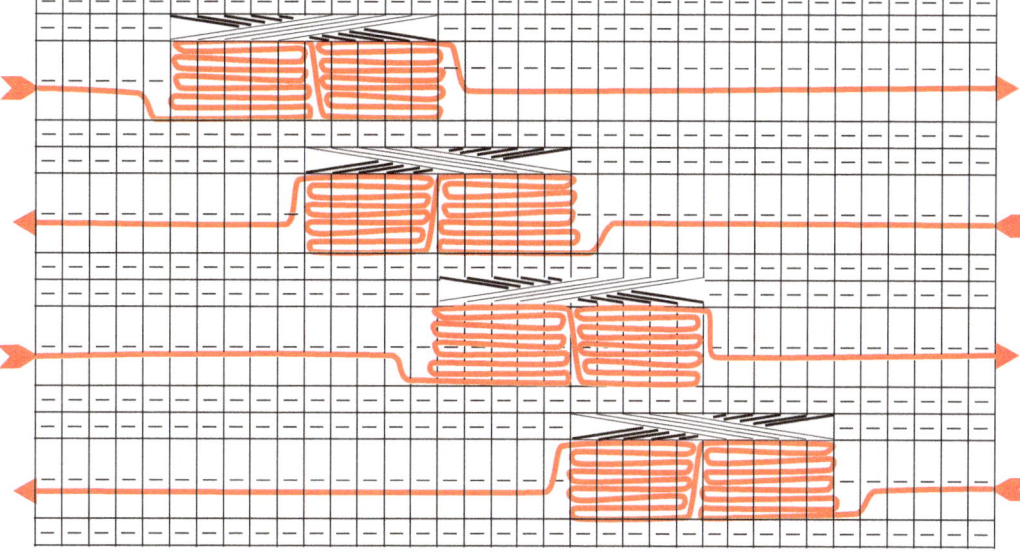

Crossing Giant Cables

I have moved all of the needles back into WP to make the photographs easier to read. You will find it easiest to handle the four tools if you make sure all the latches are open before you begin replacing stitches on needles.

Step 1. Complete the bridged row.

Step 2. Remove each group of five cable stitches on a 2-prong and a 3-prong tool (or use a 5-prong tool if you have one). Keep in mind that this two-tool maneuver looks more awkward than it actually is.

Step 3. Hold the right pair of tools off to the side to replace the five left-hand stitches on the right group of needles, one tool at a time.

Step 4. When you move the right group of stitches to the left needles, make sure you reach below the float that spans those five needles as you hook the transfer tools onto the needle hooks.

Step 5. After you have crossed both groups of stitches and replaced them on the needles, pick up the purl bump from the edge stitch at the left and right edges of the cable; if you don't, a small gap will open there.

Step 6. Before knitting the next row, drop the long float from the hooks of the five needles at left so that the float just lies across the back of the fabric

Triple-Crossed Horizontal Cables

For years, I have struggled to produce a truly horizontal cable, without relying on insertions. The sample shown in Swatch 27 represents years of trial and error! The chart shows familiar bridging sequences, although the only knitted-once bridges are at each edge of the fabric. Adjacent groups of three needles are knitted for 12 rows, except for the second group from the right and the last group on the left. Those two groups are knitted for eight rows because they interlace only twice; the others cross three times. It is especially important to keep tension on the stitches when knitting so many extra rows.

This cable appears braided because the paired groups of stitches that cross each time are split from one crossing to the next and the direction of the crossings alternates. That is, for the first crossings (for example) groups A and B and groups C and D cross to the left. For the second crossings, B and C cross to the right. Braided cables are always knitted by splitting pairs and alternating the crossing direction.

When the bridged row is complete, cross all of the enlarged groups as 3x3 right-cross cables (except needles 34–36). Then, rather than knitting a row, cross the alternating cables as left-cross cables, followed by a row of right-

Swatch 27: The horizontal cable at the bottom of the swatch is worked against a plain knit background, while the sample at the top is outlined by a ridge of garter stitch.

Horizontal Cable

There are no bridge stitches at all between the enlarged sections. The stitches actually cross three times before the next row is knitted.

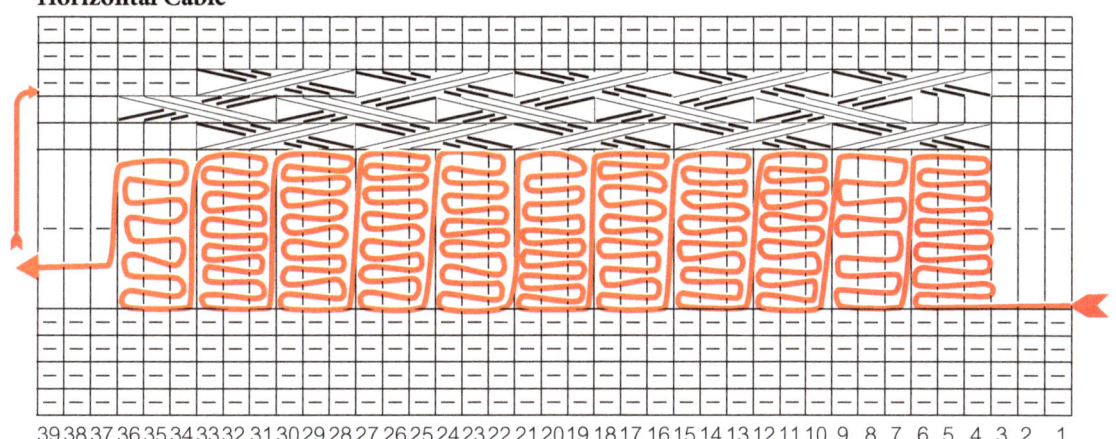

cross cables. The cables actually cross three times before you knit the next row! Just make sure you always pass the second transfer tool under the long float before replacing those stitches on their needles, as shown in the photos below and at right.

I have moved all of the needles into WP to make the process easier to see in the photographs. In this case, however, having the needles in WP also makes it easier to perform the multistep operation of producing a horizontal cable, so I am suggesting that you do the same.

Step 1. After you have completed the bridging row, use a transfer tool to move all of the needles into WP.

Step 2. Begin making right-cross cables with the first two groups at the right (excluding the edge bridge). Make sure the transfer tool reaches under the long float before placing the three left stitches on the right needles.

Step 3. When you have crossed all of the groups for the first time, the floats are all on the back of the fabric. If any of the floats are caught in the hooks of the needles, gently lift them off so that they fall to the back of the fabric.

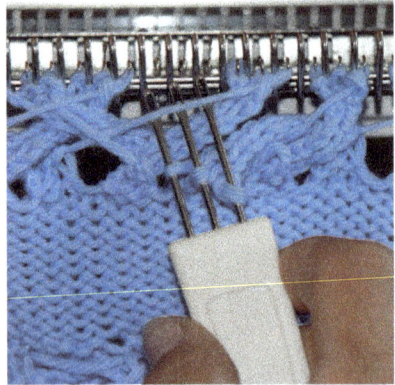

Step 4. Beginning with the first group on the left (excluding the bridge), make left-cross cables across the row. Again, make sure the transfer tool reaches under the float before placing the three right stitches onto the left needles. The last group on the right does not cross this time.

Step 5. After the second set of crossings, the floats are still on the back of the fabric. The split pairs and the direction of the crossings are easy to see.

Step 6. Beginning with the first group on the right, work right-cross cables across the row. Again, make sure the second tool passes under the long float.

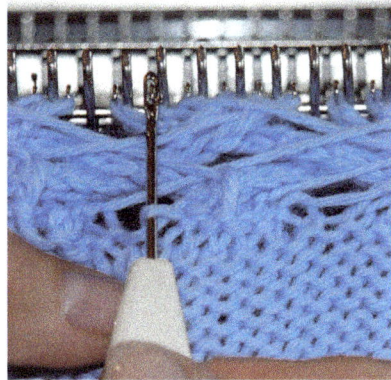

Step 7. When you have crossed all of the cables for the third time, pick up the purl bump from the first row of each cable and hang it on the needle directly above to prevent any gaps along the side of the cable.

Step 8. When you have closed all the gaps by hanging a purl bump from each cable, bring all of the needles to UWP to continue knitting across all the needles.

Swatches 28: Horizontal cable against a background of purl stitches.

Creative Innovations

Bridging to add extra rows opens all kinds of possibilities for creating highly textured stitches on the knitting machine. I have presented many of the possibilities in this chapter, but these techniques barely scratch the surface of all that is possible. Think in terms of the basic variables—like numbers of stitches and rows, direction, progression of movement, wrapped and unwrapped edge stitches, short-rowing. Then combine those variables with the variables of lifting, twisting, crossing, weaving, and wrapping stitches. You're bound to discover all kinds of new patterns and effects.

Sometimes pattern variations are obvious; other times you will need to experiment and play a little at the machine. Try to keep good notes as you work. If you know what you did and can repeat it again, it becomes a pattern—otherwise, it was just an attractive one-time mistake.

CHAPTER 5

Bridging with the Free Yarn

For lack of another name, I have always referred to the yarn between the first working needle and the carriage yarn feeder as the "free yarn." Most knitters are aware of this free yarn only when knitting the end of a row, where the yarn is apt to cause loops at the edges if there are tension problems. With bridging, you can work with the free yarn at any point across a row, without having to depend on separate strands that require finishing later on. So, for starters, you can add wrapped, beaded, fringed, knotted, or crochet details at will!

Wrapped Stitches

Swatch 29 shows a simple wrapped-stitch pattern made by bridging with the free yarn. The serpentine arrows in the second row of the chart below are interrupted by a scroll symbol that indicates wrapping. The method is detailed at right.

Wrapping Stitches

Begin with the COR, set to hold needles in HP.

Hold needles 4–21. Knit one row. COL.

With a 3-prong tool, remove the stitches from needles 4–6. Snugly wrap the free yarn around the stitches three or four times, passing the yarn between your hand and the tool so that it encircles the stitches, not the tool.
Return the stitches to their needles and bring all of the needles to HP. Move COR.

Move needles 7–10 to UWP and knit one row. COL.

Remove the next three stitches and wrap as before. Return the wrapped stitches to their needles, place all of the needles in HP, and move COR.

Repeat across the row. Work three rows across all needles and then repeat the bridged/wrapping row, staggering the placement as shown in the chart.

Wrapped Stitches

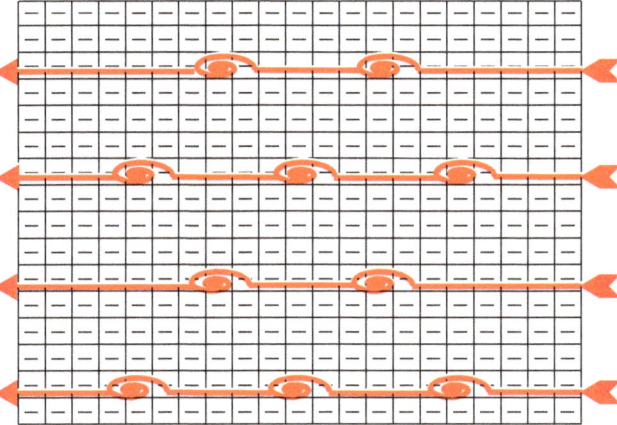

This chart shows a staggered placement of wrapped stitches; you could just as easily stack the stitches vertically or on the diagonal for a different effect.

Swatch 29: Make sure you wrap the stitches tightly enough to gather them together, or you'll dilute the effect.

Forming French Knots

To form a row of tight little French knots, similar to those in the bottom row of Swatch 30 at left, transfer every fifth stitch to the adjacent needle, as shown in the chart. Put empty needles in NWP and follow the steps illustrated below. Needles in HP are used to form equal-sized loops for twisting.

Step 1. Begin COR, set to hold needles in HP. Hold needles 6–29. Knit one row. COL. Wrap the free yarn around needles 6–9 four times, as shown in the photo.

Step 2. Manually knit needle 6 twice to secure the loops.

Step 3. Use a latch tool to remove the wrapped loops from the needles. Do not remove the actual stitches from these needles.

Step 4. Rotate the latch tool twice to tightly twist the loops together.

Step 5. Deposit the loops on the empty needle (needle 5). Use the free yarn to manually knit needle 5 once to secure the twisted loops. Place needles 1–5 in HP and move COR. Place needles 6–9 in UWP and knit to left. Repeat the wrapping sequence, using needles 11–14, hanging the twisted loops on needle 10.

French Knots and Pussy Willows

Swatch 30 shows a different kind of wrapping that produces tight little French knots (center and bottom rows) and pussy willow catkins (top row). I used a different wrapping method to form the loops in each row, as shown in the chart below. The bottom row of French knots was worked by wrapping the yarn around adjacent needles to form the loops. The loops in the knots in the middle row were formed by wrapping from the hook of a needle to a hand-held latch tool. The pussy willow catkins in the top row were made with a circular hand-knitting needle. In each case, the wrapped loops were tightly twisted and returned to the needles. In order to form loops of the same size within each wrapped bundle and from one bundle to the next, you'll need some sort of gauge. It might be as simple as lining the latch tool up with a specific row of completed knitting and holding it there while you wrap—or you could wrap around a ruler or your fingers to size the loops.

Swatch 30: The row of pussy willow catkins in the top row were crossed like cables in order to create a diagonal texture on the face of the fabric.

French Knots and Pussy Willows

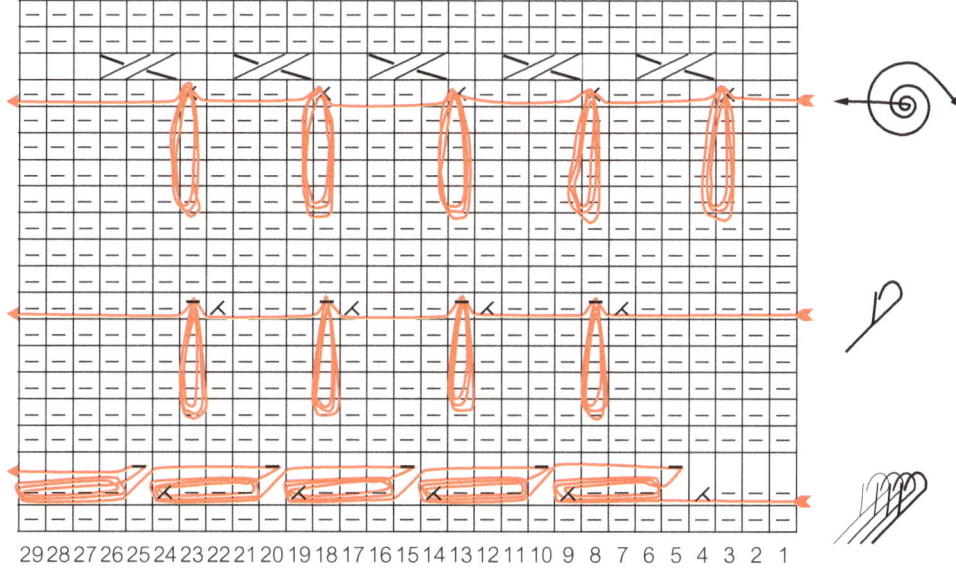

The transfer of stitches to adjacent needles produces an eyelet, through which the wrapped texture can be pushed to the knit side of the fabric. When the twisted loops are placed on the empty needle they function as a stitch on the needle and prevent an eyelet from forming.

To form the loops for the type of knots shown in the middle row of the swatch, you'll wrap from the empty needle in each repeat to a hand-held latch tool as shown in the two photos below. Wrap the yarn four times and then knit the needle back manually twice to secure the loops. Because the loops are wrapped onto the latch tool, it is a simple matter to twist and place the loops onto the needle and then knit it back. The tricky part here is to keep the latch tool the same distance away from the needle as you form each of the loops. I find that, with this method, my loops aren't quite as regular as they are when I work either of the other two methods—but try it and decide for yourself. At the very least, you'll get an introduction to some new uses for basic hand tools. If you are a crocheter, you might want to try wrapping onto a crochet hook and then, rather than twisting, use the loops to begin a crochet detail midrow.

When wrapping from the hook of a needle to the latch tool, hold the tool firmly so that all the wraps in each group are of uniform length.

Manually knit back the completed wrapping twice to secure all the loops.

Making Pussy Willows

The pussy willow cattails, shown in the top row of Swatch 30, are finished a little differently from the French knots, although the wrapping is basically the same. I transferred every fifth stitch to an adjacent needle, beginning with the fourth needle, and put empty needles in NWP.

I like this method because poking the circular needle through the fabric at intervals almost guarantees even loops. I also prefer twisting all of the loops at the end of the bridged row instead of stopping each time, as is necessary with the other methods. In the following photos, I moved the needles from HP to WP to make the process easier to read in the photographs.

Step by Step Pussy Willows

Step 1. Begin COR, with carriage set to hold needles in HP.

Step 2. Hold needles 5–29 and knit one row to left.

Step 3. Poke a circular hand-knitting needle through the fabric four or five rows below the needle catching the loops to prevent the needle from shifting as you wrap. Wrap the free yarn four or five times, from the tip of the circular needle to needle 3.

Step 4. Poke the tip of the needle through the fabric again so your hands are free and manually knit the loops twice to secure them. Place needle 3 and the bridge needles in HP and move COR.

Step 5. Place needles 5–8 in UWP and knit to left. Pull the circular needle through the previous wrapping enough to poke it through the fabric under needle 8. Repeat the wrapping procedure.

Step 6. Bridge your way across the row, wrapping as indicated on the chart. The circular needle alternately pokes through the fabric [below the needles being wrapped] and holds groups of wrapped loops. COL.

Step 7. Use a latch tool to remove the first group of loops from the circular needle.

Step 8. Twist the latch tool twice and then hold it to the side as you move the stitches from needle 5 and 6 onto a 2-prong tool.

Step 9. Move the transfer tool out of the way so that you can hook the latch tool onto needle 6 to deposit the loops.

Step 10. Return the two stitches on the transfer tool to needles 5 and 4.
You might need to keep a finger on the twisted loops to make sure they do not pop off the needle while you are completing this unusual cable crossing. The crossing simply makes it possible for the pussy willow to lie across the front of the stitches.

Steps 1 - 6

Step 7

Step 8

Step 9

Step 10

Chapter 5

Fence Knitting

The pattern in Swatch 31 is made with an embroidery technique called fence knitting. I knitted only three columns with this technique in order to clearly illustrate the effect, but the possibilities are endless if you vary the placement and size of the loops. Unlike the fence knitting method described in my previous book—which incorporates a separate strand of yarn and uses the purl side as the right side of the fabric—the technique I describe here uses the free yarn and puts the patterning on the knit side of the fabric. Because you work with the free yarn, there are no ends to finish later.

Free-Yarn Fence Knitting

This free-yarn method of fence knitting creates the patterning on the knit side of the fabric, but you can also use it for fabrics that have the purl side as the right side. In that case, while you are working, you have the advantage of seeing exactly where the loops will fall and how they will look on the finished fabric.

Swatch 31: In fence knitting, the size of the loops is limited only by practicality. If they loops are too large, they are apt to get caught and pulled during a garment's regular wear.

Fence Knitting

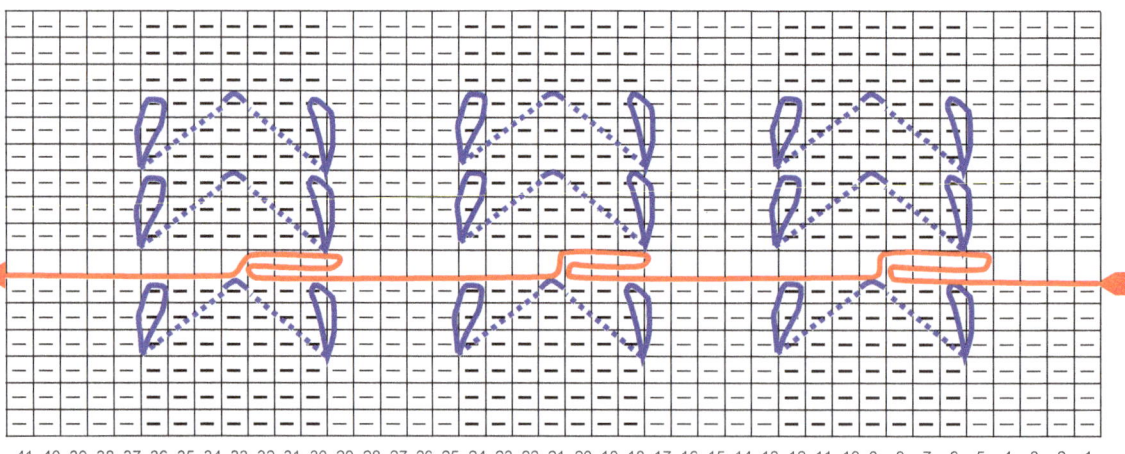

The dotted lines indicate the placement of the free yarn on the knit side of the fabric. The serpentine arrow represents the backing-up motion of the carriage.

Step by Step Fence Knitting

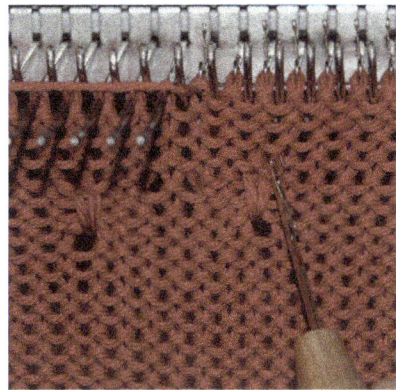

Step 1. Begin the patterned row with COR, set to hold needles in HP.

Step 2 - 3. Hold needles 9–41 and knit to left. Insert a latch tool between needles 6 and 5, three rows down.

Step 4. Bring the hook of the tool through the fabric to the right of needle 9 and catch the free yarn in the hook.

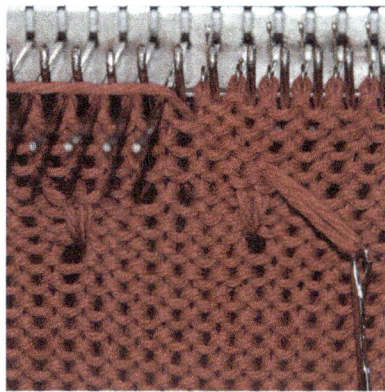

Step 5. Pull a loop through to the back of the fabric with the latch tool and . . .

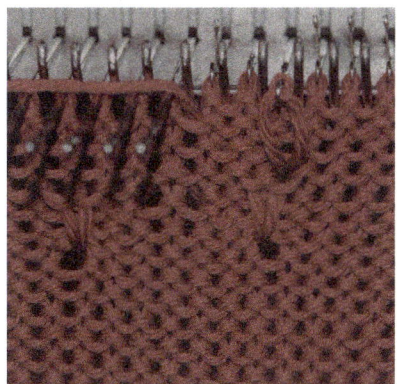

. . . .hang the loop on needle 6.

Step 6. Insert the latch tool between stitches 12 and 13, three rows down to the left of needle 9.

Step 7 - 8. Pull a loop through to the back of the fabric and hang it on needle 12. Hold needles 1–8 and move COR. Move needles 9–20 to UWP and knit to left to begin next repeat. Knit three plain rows between each patterned row.

Midrow Cast-On and Bind-Off

Swatch 32: By casting on and binding off midrow, you can vary the width and length of the decorative sections at will. The resulting strips can be steamed flat or allowed to curl, depending on the effect you prefer.

Perhaps the most useful thing about working with the free yarn is that it provides you with the capability to bind off and cast on stitches in the middle of a row. This approach has obvious, practical uses for buttonholes, pocket slits, or armholes in one-piece garments. It also has decorative potential. (For an example of a twisted insertion made with midrow techniques, see *Hand-Manipulated Stitches for Machine Knitters*, page 167.)

The fabric shown in Swatch 32 features a column of slits that are formed by binding off stitches in one row and immediately casting them back on in the next. I chose a vertical arrangement, but you could just as easily randomly place different-sized slits all over a sweater surface to produce a fashionably distressed look.

The samples shown in Swatches 33 and 34 also feature binding off and casting on midrow, but additional rows are knitted between those rows to form large ladders instead of slits. The resulting floats make most of these large ladders impractical for garment fabrics unless they are finished with needle weaving, as shown in the photos on the following page. The floats of the ladder form a little "loom" for needle weaving—a great way to use up odds and ends of yarn or small amounts of a delicious yarn you just can't resist (or can't afford more than one ball of!). Needle weaving is also an excellent way to use really chunky yarns that might be too heavy to knit on your machine.

The cast-on and bind-off methods you use can become decorative methods that contribute to the design of even a simple fabric like this one.

Knitting Slits

To work the bind-off row, begin COR, set to hold needles in HP.

Hold needles 6–19. Knit one row to left.

Bind off needles 6–14 (with a latch tool or transfer tool). Place the empty needles in NWP. Move COR.

Place needles 15–19 in UWP and knit to left.

COL and needles 1–5 are in HP. Bring empty needles 6–14 to HP.

Knit one row to right

Use the e-wrap method or the latch tool to cast on needles 6–14. Leave needles in HP. Bring needles 15–19 to HP and move COL.

Move needles 1–5 to UWP and knit to right.

Swatch 33: Large ladders are formed by knitting extra rows between midrow cast-ons and bind-offs. Full-fashioned decreasing and increasing shape the sides of this circle.

Circle and Square Ladders

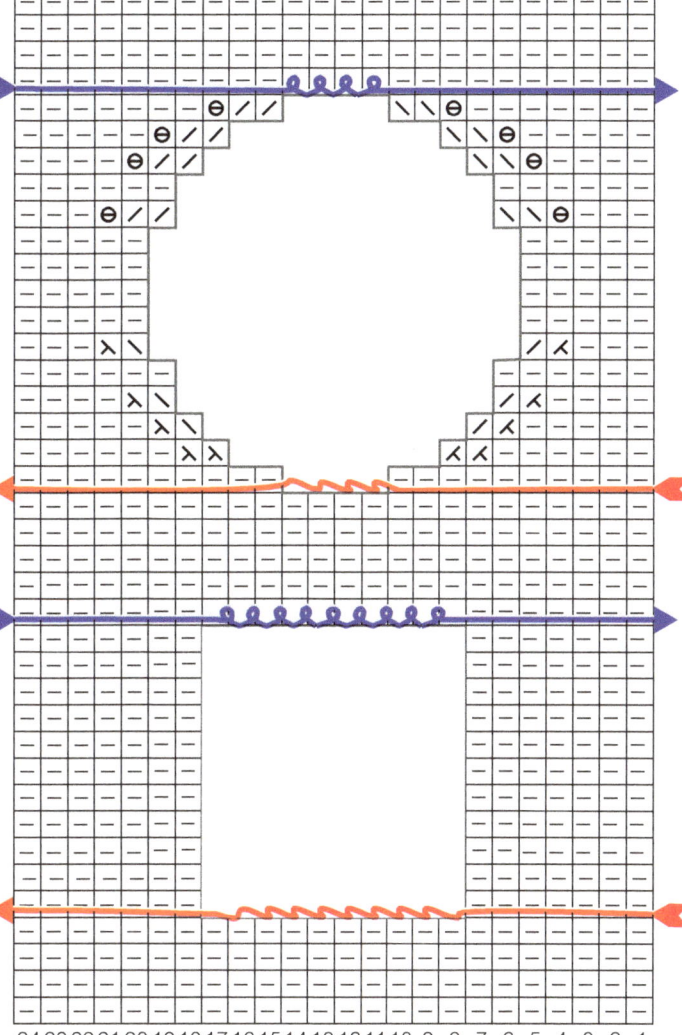

The chart on the previous page shows a square pattern at the bottom. The bridged rows in that pattern are worked exactly like the slits in Swatch 32 except that the empty needles remain in NWP for 10 rows before you cast on and begin knitting them again. The circle pattern also uses conventional decreasing and increasing, but it is a little different because it requires a bridged bind-off and cast-on in the first and last rows—as do the two triangles in the chart on the facing page. The diamond in that chart requires no bridging.

Swatch 34: The curved sides of the circle were woven with short rows to gradually fill in the shape. By weaving over two, under two, the weaving yarn packs closely to completely cover the strands of the ladder. If you wanted the ladder strands to show, you could weave over one, under one.

Diamond and Triangle Ladders

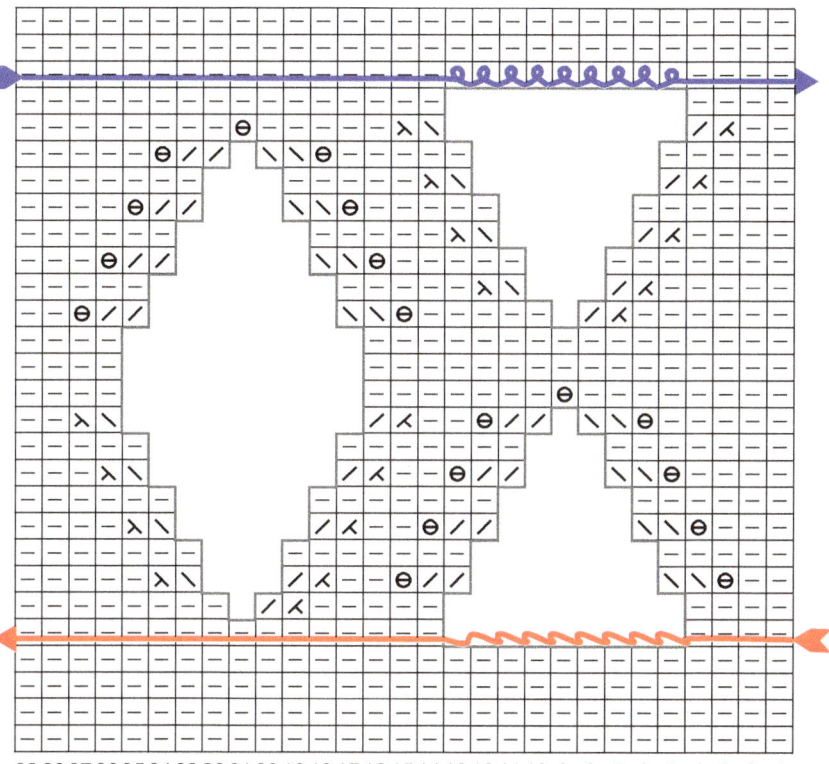

The bottom of the first triangle and the top of the second were the only places that required bridging and midrow binding off or casting on. All of the other increases and decreases were worked full-fashion with a 2-prong transfer tool. I chose to fill empty needles by picking up the purl bar of an adjacent stitch. If you choose not to pick up the bars, the eyelets that would form might add an interesting touch to the fabric design.

Swatch 35: Diamond and triangle ladders offer all kinds of design potential and opportunities to incorporate unusual yarns that might not be suitable for your knitting machine.

CHAPTER 6
Combining Methods

Combining Methods 73

There are some bridged effects that require a combination of the methods, discussed in the previous chapters, for increasing stitch size, adding extra rows, and accessing the free yarn. Some of the many possible design effects I'll discuss here include the Lazy Daisy stitch, knotted ties, twisted eyelets, 5-stitch popcorns, 3-D flowers, and petal clusters.

Lazy Daisy Stitch

Lazy Daisy stitch, shown in Swatch 36 at right, is one of my favorite stitches for open, lightweight fabrics. I think it looks best when each border of "daisies" is outlined by garter stitch, as in the top two rows, but I have also shown it without the garter outline in the bottom row.

The bottom border pattern in the chart features a 1-stitch bridge between each group of enlarged stitches. In this case, I find it easiest to dispense with bridging and just hand-knit the whole row, working some needles back to NWP and others to WP. The other two border patterns show several bridge stitches between each daisy. For those, I use the manual

Swatch 36: All of these daisies are worked over five stitches, but you could make larger daisies, too. The number of stitches you wrap is determined by the gauge of the machine you are working on, the type of yarn, the number of rows between borders, and the size of the bridges.

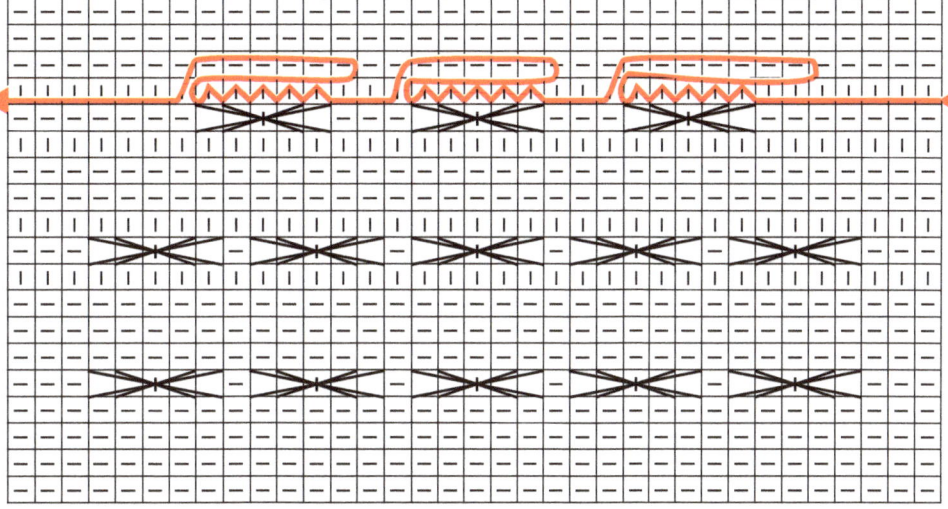

Lazy Daisy Stitch

bridging method, knitting some stitches by hand and knitting the bridge stitches with the carriage.

Because garter bars, which are used to turn over the work, are currently difficult to come by, I have included directions in the appendix (page 154) for creating a pretty slick, make-do garter bar, conceived by machine knitter, Colleen Smitherman. I'm not sure that I'd want to work an entire sweater in garter stitch with this nifty little gadget (or even with a metal garter bar), but it works quite well for working accents like the garter borders for Lazy Daisy stitch. The alternatives would be either to reform the entire row of stitches before and after each row of daisies or to scrap off and rehang twice to form each garter ridge. As you can see from swatch 36, the decorative effect is almost lost when the garter rows are eliminated.

To work the Lazy Daisy stitch with three stitches between each daisy:

Knit up to one row before the border. Remove the work on a garter bar and turn. Knit one row and turn again.

With COR and set to hold needles in HP, *hold all needles except for the first three bridge needles on the carriage side.

Knit to the left, then hold the three bridge needles. Manually knit the next five needles all the way back to NWP and leave them in NWP.** Repeat * to ** across the row.

With COL, hold all needles except the first bridge on the carriage side. The needles that were knitted back to NWP can remain there. *Knit the first bridge and then place those needles into HP.

Remove the first group of five enlarged stitches from their needles, using both a 2-prong and a 3-prong transfer tool (or a 5-prong tool if you have one).

Wrap the free yarn snugly around the stitches at least five times and then return them to their needles. Put those needles into HP, place the next bridge in UWP and repeat from * to ** across the row, ending with a bridge.

Knit one row, then turn with the garter bar (twice).

Make sure you wrap the stitches tightly. If the wrapping is too loose, the daisies will look sloppy. For ease of handling, I usually hold the two transfer tools on top of each other, as shown in the photo. In order to wrap the free yarn under the stitches on the tool, you need to pass it between the tools and your hand. Be consistent in wrapping clockwise or counterclockwise so that all of your daisies look the same.

Knotted Ties

Knotted ties produce a great surface texture. You can also incorporate them into the front of a cardigan to make a built-in closure.

Swatches 37 and 38, shown below, were worked by bridging up to the three needles for the first tie, knitting 20 rows, binding off the stitches, and pushing the strip through to the knit side of the fabric. After lifting the first row of the strip onto the needles, I placed the needles in HP and bridged to the three needles for the second tie.

Because these ties are only three stitches wide, the knitting tends to curl to form what looks like an I-cord, so it is very easy to hide the yarn tails at the bound-off ends. You could, of course, actually knit the ties as I-cords by setting the carriage to knit in one direction and slip in the other only when you are working the ties. Longer or wider ties might enable you to try some fancy knotting or special effects—like a beaded fringe, for example.

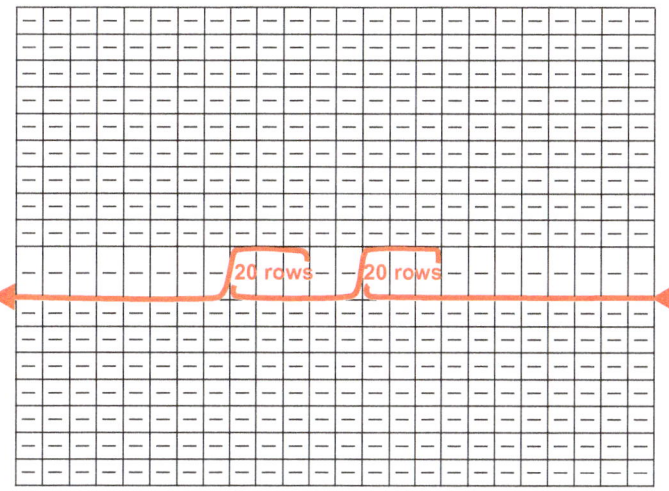

Swatches 37 and 38: Fancy knots, like the one at right, may require long ties. You could work shorter, unknotted ties as an interesting fringe-like texture or lace them through eyelets in the fabric. Although they look like I-cords, these ties were knitted in stockinette, which curls when it is worked this narrow. If the width of the ties increases, the bridge between each tie also needs to be wider.

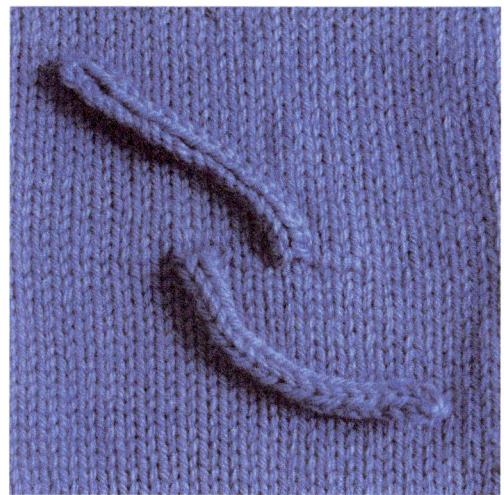
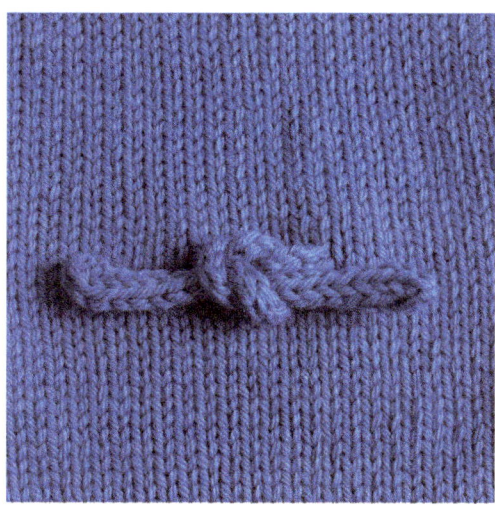

Twisted Eyelets

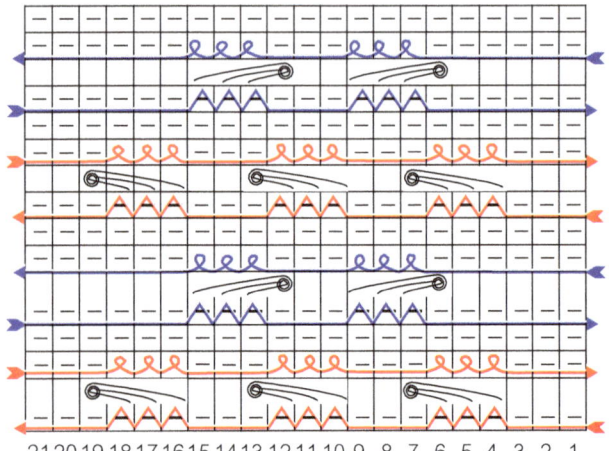

21 20 19 18 17 16 15 14 13 12 11 10 9 8 7 6 5 4 3 2 1

Before the e-wrap bridging row is knitted, the twisted stitches are returned to an adjacent needle that already holds a stitch.

Twisted Eyelets

The twisted eyelet fabric in Swatch 39, shown below, combines the techniques of manually enlarged stitches and midrow casting on. The serpentine arrows on the chart indicate which needles need to be knitted all the way back to NWP in the first patterned row and cast-on with e-wrapping in the next. The enlarged stitches are twisted before the e-wrap row is worked. Because the pattern requires bridging from both sides, I have used red arrows to illustrate the sequences that start on the right end of the bed and blue arrows for those that start on the left. Please note that I have placed some needles in WP to make the photographs easier to read.

The first row of the repeat is complete once you have twisted all of the enlarged stitch groups and placed them on the adjacent needles. The next row is a bridge row, with the carriage stopping so you can e-wrap the empty needles; for the following row, you knit all of the needles in the row.

Swatch 39: This pattern is an eye-catching combination of eyelets, dancing blocks of stockinette, and pussy willow cattails. The little rectangles of knit stitches between the twisted eyelets seem hinged together. Space-dyed yarns that have a fairly short repeat are a good choice when making a fabric like this.

5-Stitch Popcorns

Popcorns worked over five needles, like those in Swatch 40, are larger and considerably rounder than those worked on just two or three needles. If, however, you work 5-stitch popcorns with the method described on page 37 for 2- and 3-stitch popcorns, the end results would be more like narrow pin tucks than popcorns. In order to work 5-stitch popcorns, you need to "borrow" some needles.

The chart on the next page shows 5-stitch popcorns that have nine stitches between them—even though, at first glance, it looks as though the bridges are only five stitches wide. This bridging row is worked a little differently than most because it combines the processes of accessing the free yarn and knitting extra rows.

Before starting the bridged row, remove the stitches shown in bold (2–6, 12–16, etc. on the chart) from their needles and place them on a stitch holder. I like using a circular hand-knitting needle that is long enough to extend across the width of the knitting, leaving several inches to spare at each end. I bring the required needles to HP. Then I poke the tip of

Swatch 40: Five-stitch popcorns are larger and rounder than 2- or 3-stitch popcorns—and knitting them requires a combination technique.

Twisting Eyelets

Step 1. After enlarging all the required groups of stitches in the first row, remove one set of enlarged stitches onto a latch tool.

Step 2. Twist them two full rotations.

Step 3. Place the stitches on the adjacent needle at left or right, according to the chart. Place the three empty needles in NWP.

Making a 5-Stitch Popcorn

Step 1. Referring to the chart below, remove all of the stitches shown in darker print [2–6, 12–16, etc.], onto the circular needle and place the empty needles in NWP

the circular needle through the stitches, one by one, while pushing each needle back to NWP and sliding the stitches onto the length of the circular needle, as shown in the photo at left.

When I have removed all of the stitches, I poke the ends of the circular needle through the fabric to anchor it, to make sure it can't slip out of the stitches. If the yarn is at all slippery, I put rubber needle tips on the ends as extra insurance. In any case, you want to make sure that the circular needle is held down and out of the way as the carriage moves across the bed. If the circular needle gets caught in the carriage, you can damage the carriage, some machine needles, or the fabric. Once you have emptied all the needles you will need to borrow, follow the steps shown in the photos at right.

5-Stitch Popcorns

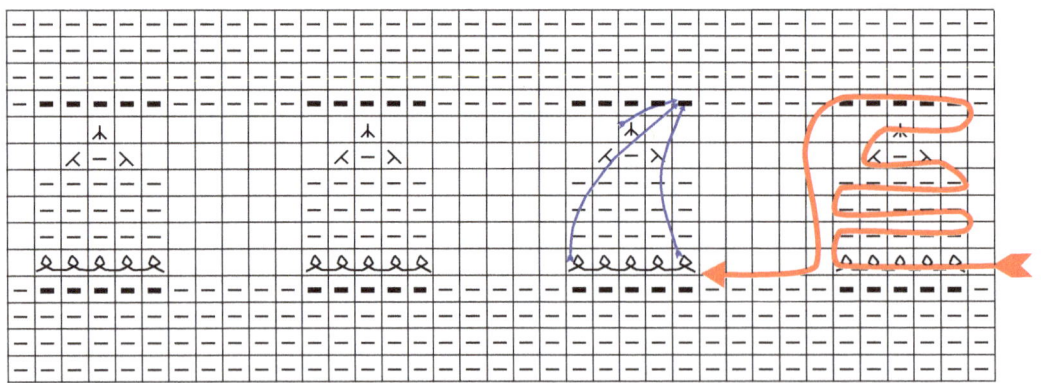

Each of the popcorns is bridged and lifted, as illustrated on the second popcorn on this chart.

Step 2. Begin with the COR, set to hold needles in HP. Hold all needles except the first bridge at right (needle 1). Knit to left and then hold the bridge. *COL. E-wrap the first group of empty needles (2–6) from right to left

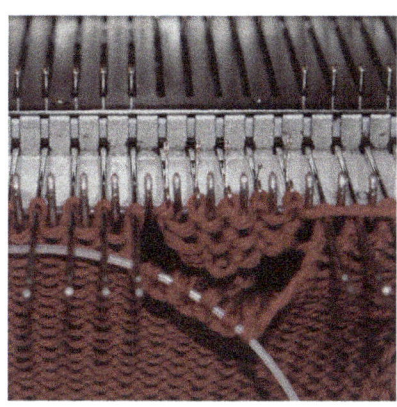

Step 3. Put the e-wrapped needles into UWP and then knit three rows, ending COR.

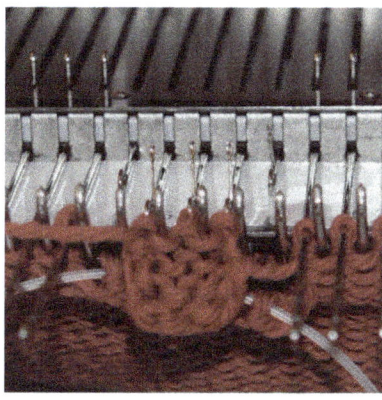

Step 4. (Decrease one stitch at each edge. Knit one row.) twice to reduce to three stitches and then a single stitch.

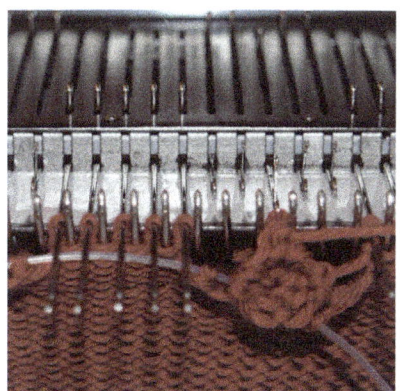

Step 5. The knitting has been reduced to a single stitch.

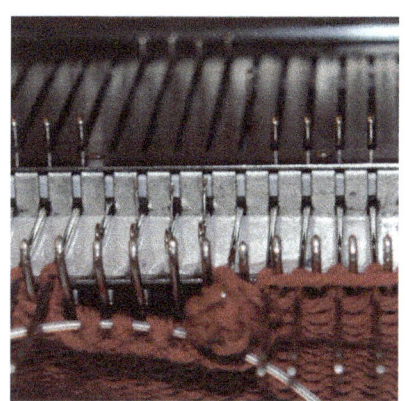

Step 6. Move the single stitch from the center needle (#4) to the right-edge needle (#2). Use a single-prong transfer tool to pick up the first and fifth stitches in the fist row of the popcorn (as shown by the blue arrows on the chart) and also place these stitches on the right-edge needle. Manually knit the needle once.

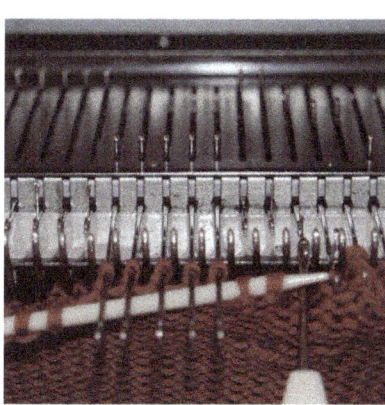

Step 7. Push the popcorn to the knit side of the work. Return the first group of stitches on the right end of the circular needle to needles 2–6, trapping the popcorn on the right side. **

Move the next bridge (needles 2–11) into UWP and knit one row to left. Repeat the sequence from * to ** across the row, returning stitches from the circular needle after knitting and lifting each popcorn.

3-D Flowers

The method for making the three-dimensional flowers in Swatch 41 is very similar to the method for making 5-stitch popcorns—but there are a couple of important differences. First of all, the stitches for the flowers are not removed from the borrowed needles all at once. The flower petals are knitted for five rows before they are decreased to a single stitch, and the first row is not lifted onto the needles. Also, although the single remaining stitch is moved to one side, it is not always placed to the right. If it were, the petals would not all radiate smoothly from the center of the flower.

With this method, only one group of stitches is removed at a time, so I use a somewhat shorter circular needle (16 in.). If the circular needle is too long, it is clumsy to manage.

Please note that when knitting the petals on the right half of the flower (shown with the red arrow on the chart on the next page), the stitches that are removed from their needles are knitted before the petal is worked. When knitting the petals at left (shown with the blue arrow), those stitches are knitted after the petal is worked. The last stitch of all right-side (red) petals is moved to the leftmost needle of the group; the last stitch on the left side (blue) is moved to the rightmost needle of that group. There is a short float that anchors each petal to the background fabric. This alternating bridgework takes that float into account so that each of the petals lies flat and the float drops to the back.

Also, when you return stitches from the hand-knitting needle to the machine needles, make sure you do not twist the stitches. I ease the stitches toward the end of the circular needle and then insert a single-prong transfer tool through one stitch at a time, returning each to its original needle. There are times when you can simply hold the hand-knitting needle in front of the bed and poke each latch needle through a stitch, but this method is too cumbersome when you are dealing with such small groups of stitches.

You may want to embellish the center of each flower with beads, wrapping, or a popcorn. You could also work solid-colored flowers on a background fabric of two-rows-per-color striping, although the petals and flower would need to be much larger in order to be proportionate to the two extra rows worked between each bridged, petal-producing row.

Instead of the diamond petal placement I used to produce these daisy-like flowers, you could work the petals to the left and right of a latched up "stem" stitch to make large sweet peas or other vertical flower effects. For design variations that do not radiate from a central point (as a daisy does), you may not need to alternate the red and blue methods. If you choose not to alternate, all of the petals will slant in the same direction and lie on the fabric in the exact same way.

Swatch 41: Each of these flower petals is simply an un-lifted 5-stitch popcorn variation. You could embellish the centers of the flowers with beading or popcorns.

Knitting 3-D Flowers

Begin COR, set to hold needles in HP. Hold needles 9–19.

Knit one row to left. Remove stitches from needles 4–8.

E-wrap the five empty needles from left to right and then manually knit the same needles back to WP. Hold all needles to the right of them.

Knit four more rows, ending COL.

Decrease one stitch at each edge and knit one row.

Decrease one stitch at each edge, move all three stitches to needle 8. Move needles 9–11 to UWP and knit one row. Leave COL.

Push the petal cleanly to the right side and then return the original stitches to needles 4–8. All needles are in HP.

Remove stitches 12–16 from their needles.

E-wrap the empty needles from right to left.

Knit five rows. Ending COR.

Decrease one stitch at each edge and knit one row.

Decrease one stitch at each edge and move all three stitches to needle 12. Knit one row. COR.

Push the petal to the right side and then return the original stitches to their needles and knit one row over needles 12–19.

Knit one row over all needles to begin the next bridged/petal row from the right.

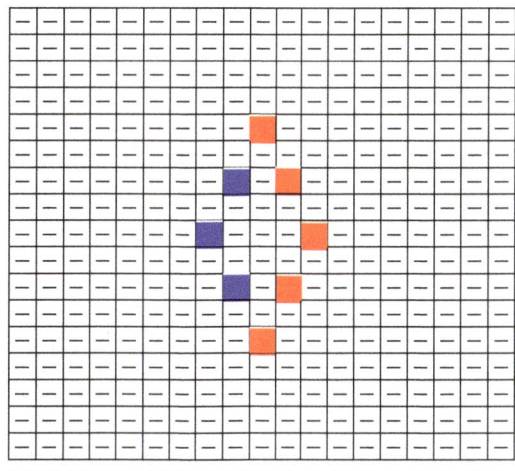

This chart only shows the placement of each petal, not the bridging and knitting procedure. Those petals shown in red are knitted a little differently than those shown in blue, as described in the directions in the text.

3-D Flowers

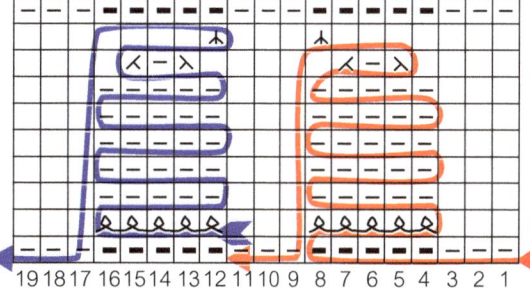

This chart shows red and blue arrows in the same row and specifically represents the third row of flower petals with knitting and bridging directions.

Petal Clusters

If you want to place the petals in clusters, you do not need to observe the left and right chart directions. You can work all the petals the same way, as they were in the example at left. The method for borrowing needles, however, does change a little bit.

Before I reduced the last three stitches of the petal into a single stitch, I moved them all to the last needle at left. Then I placed the next two bridge needles at left into UWP so that all three needles knitted with the next pass of the carriage. I returned five stitches to the borrowed needles to complete that petal.

Next, I removed the last three stitches of the previous petal and the two bridge stitches just knitted to borrow their needles for the next petal. Although you are borrowing some of the same needles, it is simpler to return the stitches to their needles as you complete each petal and before removing the next group of five. (Believe me, if there were a reasonable way to deposit three stitches while leaving two on the stitch holder, I would have found it.) As you are returning the stitches to the borrowed needles, knitting the last stitch from the stitch holder through the stitch on the needle (the last stitch of the reduced petal) reduces some of the bulk on the needle and makes it easier to borrow the needle for the next repeat.

Swatch 42: Clustered petals.

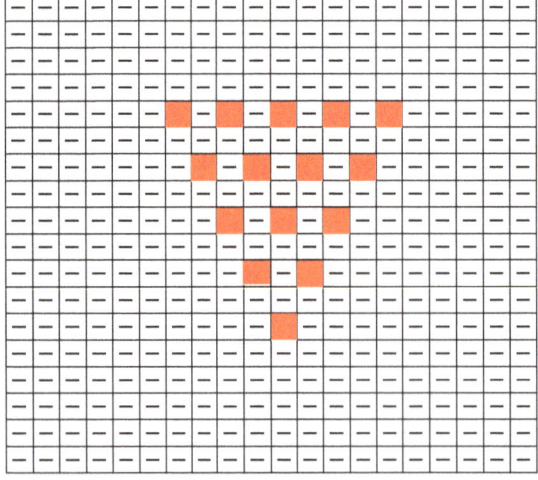

A triangular placement of the petals yields luscious grapelike clusters, all worked as right-side (red) petals.

PART TWO
Knitting the Patterns

All knitters have favorite methods for knitting and finishing their knits. Please read through this introduction before you begin knitting any of the projects so that you have a clear understanding of why I suggest some of the methods that I do.

Knitting patterns usually offer specific techniques, new ways of doing things, or special details. When I look at new patterns in magazines or books, rather than looking for garments I want to copy exactly, I try to evaluate what that book or pattern can teach me. I hope you will approach the patterns in this book with the same open-minded enthusiasm!

About Your Machine

All of the projects in this book were knitted on a midgauge (6.5mm) machine, but many could have been knitted on a bulky/chunky (8–9mm machine.) I don't think that any of the yarns I've used will knit properly on a standard-gauge machine. Midgauge machines have 150 needles. Most bulky/chunky machines have only 110, which may limit the sizes you are able to knit, although you may be able to make minor changes to the garment—like adding a side gusset or changing the gauge—to accommodate the size limitation.

As I mentioned earlier, I change the sponge bars in my machines about once a year to maintain good needle tension in the bed. I also religiously clean and oil the bed and carriage before I start a project. Every machine manual discusses oiling, and I can't overemphasize the importance of this step—even for plastic hobby beds—in keeping your machine moving smoothly.

It is always important to replace damaged needles, but especially so when working hand-manipulated stitches. If needles are out of alignment, it's more difficult to use the transfer tools and more likely that you will drop stitches (usually at the least opportune time).

If you have any problems with your machine, make sure you send it to a reputable repair center. If you do not know of a center nearby, check online sites or chat groups to get recommendations. I would advise you not to attempt servicing a machine yourself unless you have service manuals and have been trained to make repairs. I have saved all the manufacturer's boxes for my machines so I could pack them up to ship for repair if necessary.

The All-Important Schematic

The first decision you face when knitting a garment is deciding which size to make. The schematic will show you the garment's finished measurements and is a more reliable guide than the designer's designation of small, medium, or large. All patterns should include wearing ease, and the heavier the yarn, the greater amount of ease required for a comfortable fit.

Compare the schematic measurements to your own measurements. Determine whether the sleeves will be the right length, whether you want the neck higher, etc. Make only those changes that you feel comfortable making. You can make many alternations simply by adding or subtracting rows or stitches, but sometimes you will have to consider gauge carefully, for example, to redistribute increases and decreases or recalculate short rows. Be certain that any changes you make to stitches and rows will not adversely affect repeats in the pattern.

Altering patterns can be tricky if you do not have a firm understanding of gauge and how it works in defining a garment's size and shape. There are several excellent computerized charting programs available (Designaknit [DAK] and Garment Designer, to name two. See page 165.) These programs make it quite easy to refigure garment shapes in different gauges—a small investment that yields great versatility. They are especially useful for recalculating the spacing of increases and decreases. Many machines also have charting attachments (built in or available as an accessory) that "read" quarter-, half-, or full-scale drawings of garment pieces and provide row-by-row directions. Although these attachments are not exactly cutting-edge technology, they work extremely well.

I'm a real fan of garment schematics. I think of the schematic as a road map to the pattern, and I'll create one from the written text if the book or magazine doesn't supply one. Once you've set up your machine for whatever pattern you intend to use, all you really need are the row counts and the numbers of stitches to increase, decrease, or put into holding position. A clear schematic puts that information at your fingertips.

I usually make a copy of the schematic and then enlarge it enough to fill an entire sheet of 8 1/2 x 11-inch paper. I use a yellow highlighter to mark all the information that refers to the size I am knitting. I also highlight the text directions, because multisized patterns can be confusing to follow. Read through the text directions and transfer any information that doesn't already appear there onto the schematic. For example, many hand-knitting patterns do not show increases and decreases on the schematic. Because the schematic is usually all I have next to me when I knit by machine, I like to include all that information on the schematic itself.

The schematics in this book include lots of information. Because the measurements are provided in inches only, I have included supplemental schematics with metric measurements in the appendix on page 142. Please note that when charting garments, it is always necessary to round off some of the measurements—half-stitches just don't work, and most of us don't want to deal with fractions other than 1/2 or 1/4 inches– so there is a little "wiggle room" built into the measurements I've provided.

After I've tweaked the text and the schematics, I pull out a calculator and "knit" the garment on paper. I enter the number of stitches I am supposed to cast on, subtract armhole shaping, and compare the number of stitches the pattern says I should have at that point with the number on my calculator. Then I follow through with the shoulder or neckline shaping to make sure I am scrapping off or binding off the right number of stitches for each shoulder and that the stitch count for the neckline is correct. I check both the front and back to ensure that the pieces match up properly and also to ensure that I understand what the pattern is directing me to do. Finally, I double-check the sleeve increases and the cap shaping, if any.

The time I spend with the calculator can catch any mistakes there might be in the pattern. More often, it eliminates misunderstandings on my part and, ultimately, saves me hours of knitting time, which I might have wasted if I had needed to rip out rows or start over. Be sure to double-check your knitting instructions, especially if you download patterns from the Internet, because, very often, those patterns have not been checked by anyone but the designer—and we are often blind to our own mistakes.

Swatching

No matter what I am knitting and no matter how many times I have used a particular yarn, I always make a gauge swatch. I knit as large a swatch as necessary to include any textured stitches that might affect gauge. I also use the gauge swatch to practice any special trims or techniques in the pattern. Then I wash the swatch and dry it exactly as I plan to wash and dry the sweater to see the finished effect and to account for any shrinkage. The yarn quantities listed in patterns seldom include enough yarn for swatching, so make sure you purchase extra yarn so you can knit generous-sized swatches. I usually allow a couple of extra ounces when I purchase yarn on cones; if using skeins, I always buy one extra.

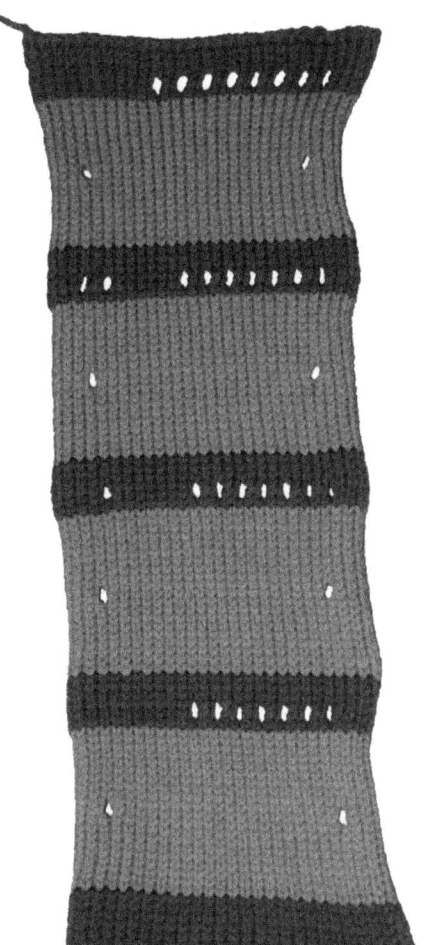

This swatch shows four different stitch sizes (7, 7., 7.., and 8), as indicated by the eyelets in each section of scrap knitting. I've also made eyelets 20 stitches apart, half way up each 20 row section to eliminate pesky counting when it comes time to measure the swatch. Having all of the stitch sizes together helps me evaluate which stitch size comes closest to matching gauge.

When knitting swatches, I usually cast on 30 stitches (at the center of the bed), knit 6–8 rows of scrap, and then change to the main yarn. After knitting 10 rows, I move the 11th stitch at each side of zero to the adjacent needle and leave the empty needle in WP so that it casts back on to form an eyelet. When I measure my swatches later, I always know that there are 20 stitches between the eyelets (and 20 rows between the scrap), so I don't have to bother counting. After the eyelets, I knit another 10 rows, followed by more scrap knitting.

I begin and end every swatch with waste yarn. I usually make a strip of swatches and separate each section with scrap knitting. The swatch strip enables me to compare swatches and to come as close as possible to matching gauge. Sometimes the swatches differ by one "dot" on the stitch dial; other times by a full stitch size. When I try several stitch sizes in a strip of swatches, I generally mark each section with eyelets between the swatches. If I have worked a swatch at stitch size 7 plus 2 dots, for example, I make 7 eyelets at left and 2 more at the right.

When I swatch specific patterns, the pattern itself dictates how many stitches and rows I knit, but I usually make much larger swatches than I do for stockinette or other allover stitches. If you decide to knit larger swatches, make sure you keep notes specifying exactly how many stitches there are between the eyelets and how many rows there are between the bands of scrap knitting.

Keeping it All Straight

There are two things I always do when knitting hand-manipulated patterns. I mark the numbered tape on the front of the bed with red, yellow, and black grease pencils (also called China markers). I use the different colors to mark the position of cables or bridges or pattern repeats. The markings help me avoid miscounts, which can cost dearly in time spent ripping out mistakes. I can wipe the marks right off the tape with a tissue when I am done with them. (And if they start to look grimy, I simply replace the numbered strip.)

I also make endless "cheat sheets," which I keep next to me while I work. Sometimes I write or print out a list of all the row numbers. Then I circle the numbers of the rows where I need to cross cables or underline the numbers of rows where I increase, decrease or do something else. I use left- and right-facing arrows to indicate knitting direction and check marks to represent latch-ups. When working complex patterns, I never knit a row without checking my charts first. I've even been known to photocopy multiple copies of the same chart so that I can cross out rows as I knit them.

Whenever possible, I try to coordinate the direction in which I cross cables (for example) with the side of the bed where the carriage is. Then I know, without checking charts, that if the carriage is on the right, the cable should be crossed as a right cable. Sometimes, I hang yarn tags to identify the stitches I need to pick up later or to indicate matching points for seams. Relying on the numbered bed and the row counter is always much more accurate than measuring later.

Scrap Knitting

I use scrap knitting wherever I can. Casting on with scrap provides an edge onto which I can hang weights to facilitate knitting a particular edging or to spare a fragile yarn. Sometimes, after the scrap knitting, I cast on for a finished edge, but often I wait until the garment is done. Then I apply a trim or band or rehang the edge and work down.

I scrap off necklines, rather than binding off in steps, because I think this method produces the smoothest necklines. I like to eliminate bulk in shoulder seams so I always scrap off the shoulder stitches. I take care of binding off both the front and back shoulder stitches as I join the seam, as described on page 162.

Short Rows

Also called partial knitting, short rows are a great asset to good finishing. When you join two garment pieces together, you eliminate bulk by retaining live stitches by short-rowing rather than binding off. For example, if you bind off slanted shoulder stitches, the binding off produces stair-step edges, and those edges will add extra bulk when joined in a seam. Necklines are also smoother when short-rowed.

In order to shape garment pieces with short rows, you need to be able to leave specific needles in HP. If you are also bridging for patterning, however, you will not be able to rely on the levers to bring needles back into WP without disrupting the short-row shaping. In this case, you will need to manually nudge the needle butts into UWP so they can resume knitting as required.

Sometimes I shape a shoulder or neckline with short rows and then, if I need a bound-off edge, I bind off all the stitches at once. Otherwise, I usually just knit one row of the main yarn across all the short-rowed stitches to produce a "smoothing row" and then scrap off. You can always bind off the stitches later, but, if you decide you want live stitches instead, it is tedious to undo a bound-off edge without dropping stitches in the process.

Finishing

I have included finishing instructions for most of the patterns in this book. If you have a finishing method you prefer, however—and you fully understand what the pattern is directing you to do and why—do not feel bound by my instructions. There are lots of ways to finish knits, and the end goal is usually always the same: perfect seams, minimized bulk, and good drape. I combine hand- and machine-finishing techniques. I especially like joining live shoulder stitches on the machine because it produces firm seams with minimal bulk.

Knitters often skip the process of blocking, but I am convinced that proper blocking makes garment pieces easier to handle and to match up perfectly. I use blocking wires, laced through edge stitches and pinned to a fabric-covered board, to shape every piece. My board is covered with several layers of old blankets and a gridded cloth that makes it easy to count inches and block to size. I use a steam generator iron, which I hover about 1/2 inch above the fabric and which produces lots and lots of steam. (For suppliers of blocking wires and gridded cloths, see Sources of Supply on page 165.) When possible, I weave in yarn tails while I am knitting to avoid finishing them later. To weave in tails, bring 8–10 edge needles to HP. Weave the yarn tail over and under the needle shafts and then either set the carriage to knit the needles back to WP or place them in UWP. The ends will be securely woven in and will not show on the knit side of the fabric. If the purl side is the right side or if there is a lot of bridging or other holding going on, I do not use this method, but it is a real time saver.

You can also facilitate finishing by using full-fashion increases and decreases whenever possible. They retain the same stitch along the edge of the fabric, which makes it much easier to join a straight seam. These methods are always explained in knitting machine manuals.

When changing colors or adding a new a new yarn, weave the ending yarn tail over and under edge needles in holding position. Hold the tail of the new yarn while knitting the next row and then repeat the tail-weaving with the end of the new yarn. Later on, the tails are clipped close and require no further finishing.

Tied Up in Style Cardigan

This oversized, cropped cardigan is knitted from cuff to cuff with short-rowed gores that add extra swing. The upper sleeve seam is joined with a knitted-on I-cord, which is also used to finish all of the garment edges. The double rows of slits on each front and the ties on the left front are bridged to form a unique and interesting closure.

Sizes:
Oversized S (M, L, XL) with finished chest measurement 40 (44, 48, 52)" and finished length 19.75 (20.25, 21, 21.75)" (Garment is shown in size Large.)

Yarn:
Trendsetter Yarn's Merino 8 (100% extra fine superwash/preshrunk merino wool) with 98 yards/90 meters per 1.75 ounce/50 gram ball, 11 (13, 15, 16) balls color #2001 (Linen)

Stitch Size:
9 or to obtain gauge

Gauge:
18 stitches/26 rows = 4"

Machine:
Model garment was knitted on the Studio/Silver Reed SK860, a 6.5mm midgauge machine. The yarn is suitable for a 9mm chunky/bulky machine, although you will need to adjust the garment length (the number of stitches) for the two larger sizes for a 110-needle bed.

Notes
(1) Begin and end the garment pieces on scrap knitting. Pre-knit six "rags": three with 22 (24, 28, 32) stitches for the body increases, one with 20 stitches for back collar and two with 10 stitches for front collars. To knit a rag, cast on the required number of needles with scrap yarn, knit 5–6 rows, and scrap off with a contrasting scrap yarn. Knit all rags before starting the garment pieces. I usually bind off all scrap knitting just to be safe. (2) Each gore adds 2" to the lower edge of the sweater. (3) The back collar extension is twice as wide as the front collar extensions because it will be folded to the inside to stand up and offer greater support at the back neck. (4) Some row counts are continuous, while others begin anew from RC 000; this information is always noted in the text but not on the schematics. (5) Cast on 40 needles to the right of zero for all pieces to allow enough needles at left and right for sleeve, body, and collar increases.

Back

With scrap yarn, cast on 23 stitches and knit some rows. COR. Change to the main yarn and knit to RC 102 *at the same time* increasing 1 stitch at left edge (only) every 5th row twelve times, every alternate row ten times and every row twenty-two times. 67 stitches. End COR. RC 102.

At the left edge, increase 22 (24, 28, 32) stitches for the body by hanging the pre-knit rag. RC 000.

Knit to RC 41, COL, to begin shaping first short-row gore. Turn off the row counter, set the carriage to hold all needles in HP, and hold all needles except the first 20 on the carriage side. Knit, wrap, and knit back (KWK). (Return next 20 needles to UWP, KWK) twice. (Hold 20 needles, KWK) twice and then turn on the row counter and resume working across all needles.

At RC 45 (51, 59, 65), with COL, hang the 20-stitch rag at right for back collar.

At RC 81 and 121, repeat short-row gore. *At the same time*, at RC 86 (92, 100, 106) scrap off 20 collar stitches.

At RC 132 (144, 160, 172), scrap off 22 (24, 28, 32) body stitches at left. RC 000.

Knit to RC 102 *at the same time* decreasing 1 stitch at left side (only) every row twenty-two times, every alternate row ten times, and every fifth row twelve times. Scrap off the remaining 23 stitches.

Right Front

Work the same as the back through sleeves, single gore, and to RC 45 (51, 59, 65) to hang 10-stitch rag for front collar. 99 (101, 105, 109) stitches. At RC 20, shape the one short-row gore on the front.

At RC 74 (80, 88, 94) and 80 (86, 94, 100), work one row of bridged slits as follows: With

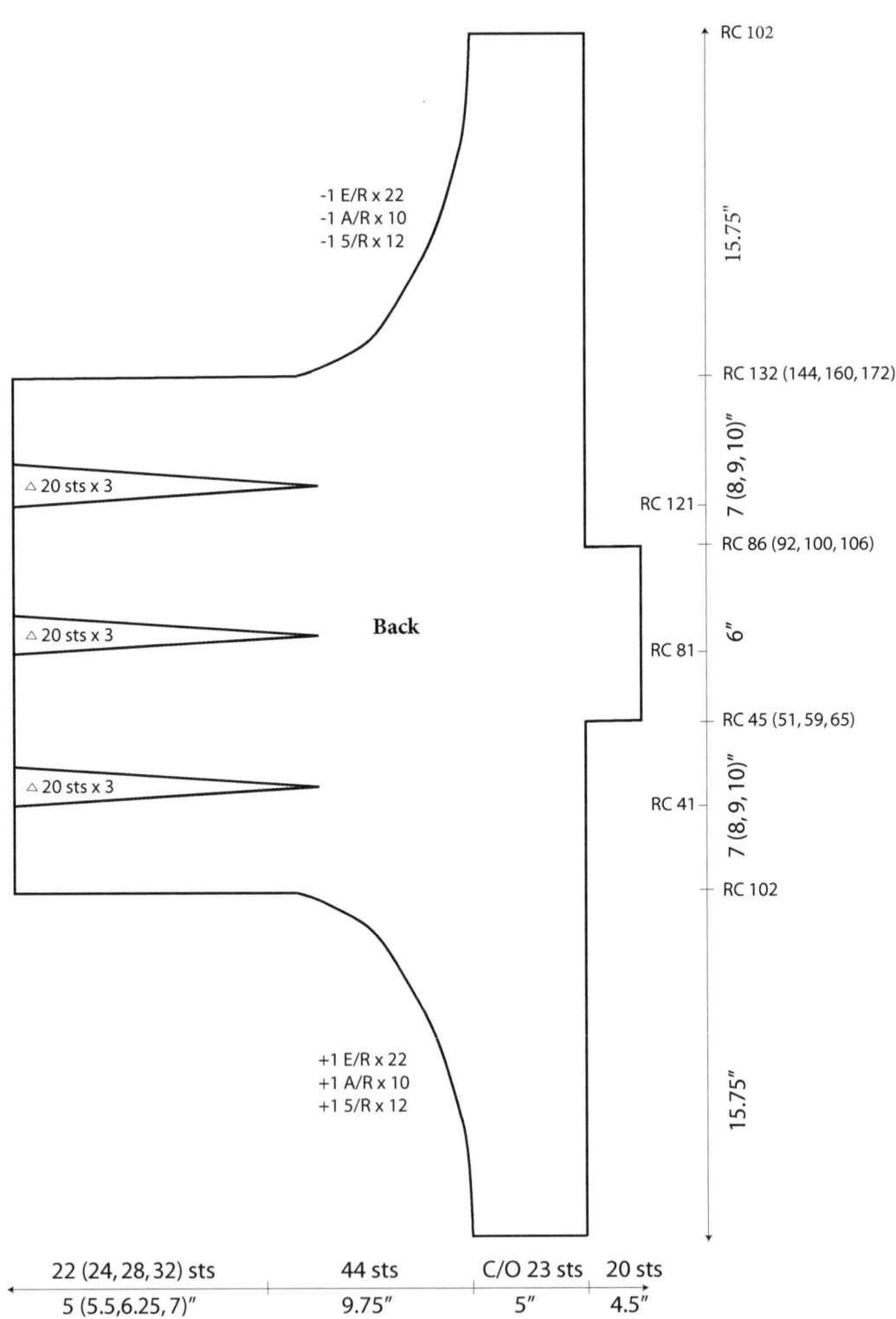

COR, set to hold needles in HP. Hold all needles except first 6 on carriage side. Knit and leave COL. *Hold bridge and use the free yarn to bind off the next 9 stitches. Put the empty needles in NWP and return COR. Bring next 3 needles to UWP, knit, and leave COL. ** Repeat from * to ** across row, ending with a 9 (11, 12, 7) stitch bridge, which remains in WP.

COL, bring all empty needles to HP. Knit to the right, then use the free yarn to work crochet *cast-on over the first/next group of 9 empty needles, hanging the last loop on the next needle. Move COL and place the next group of 3 bridge needles into UWP. Knit 1 row across the bridge** and repeat from * to ** across the row, ending with a 6-stitch bridge. (See page 68.)

Knit 4 rows across all needles and then repeat the bind-off and cast-on rows for the slits. End with 4 rows stockinette and scrap off all 99 (101, 105, 109) stitches.

Left Front

Work as for right front, reversing the shaping so that the sleeve increases are on the right and the collar on the left. Hang scrap for collar when COR at RC 44 (50, 58, 64). At RC 54 (60, 68, 74) and at RC 58 (64, 72, 76), work two 3-stitch ties. (See page 38.) Position the first tie 27 (29, 33, 37) stitches from the right edge and the second tie 21 stitches to the left of the first.

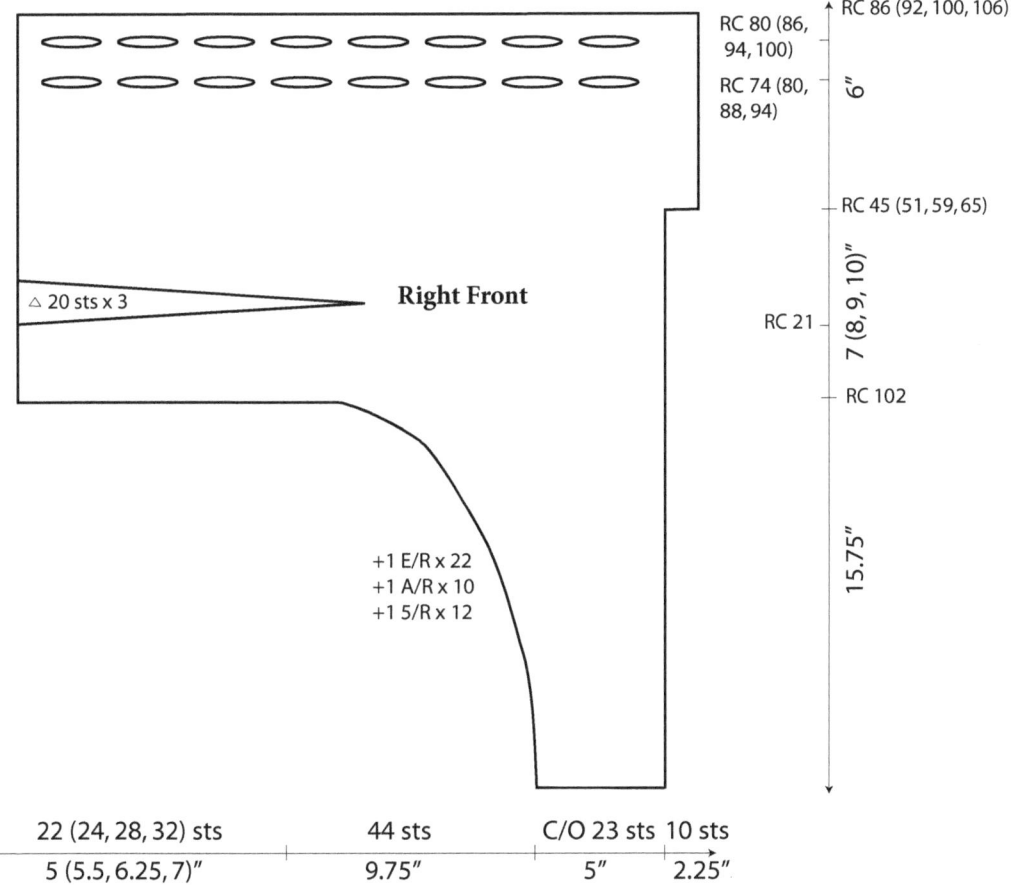

Join-as-you-knit I-cord edging runs up the shoulder seam to the lower edge of the stand-up collar.

Work the ties by bridging as follows: With COR and set to hold needles in HP, hold all needles except the first 30 (32, 36, 40) on the carriage side. Knit 1 row to left. Hold first 27 (29, 33, 37) needles and work 49 more rows on the 3 needles that remain in WP, ending COR. Pick up the stitches from the first row of the tie and hang on the needles directly above, pushing the length of the tie through to the right side of the fabric. Place the next 21 bridge needles and the next 3 tie needles into UWP and knit to left. Hold the bridge and the 3 needles used for the first tie. Complete the second tie and then bridge to the end of the row.

AT RC 74 (80, 88, 94) and RC 80 (86, 94, 100), work the slits as for the right front. End with 4 rows of stockinette and scrap off.

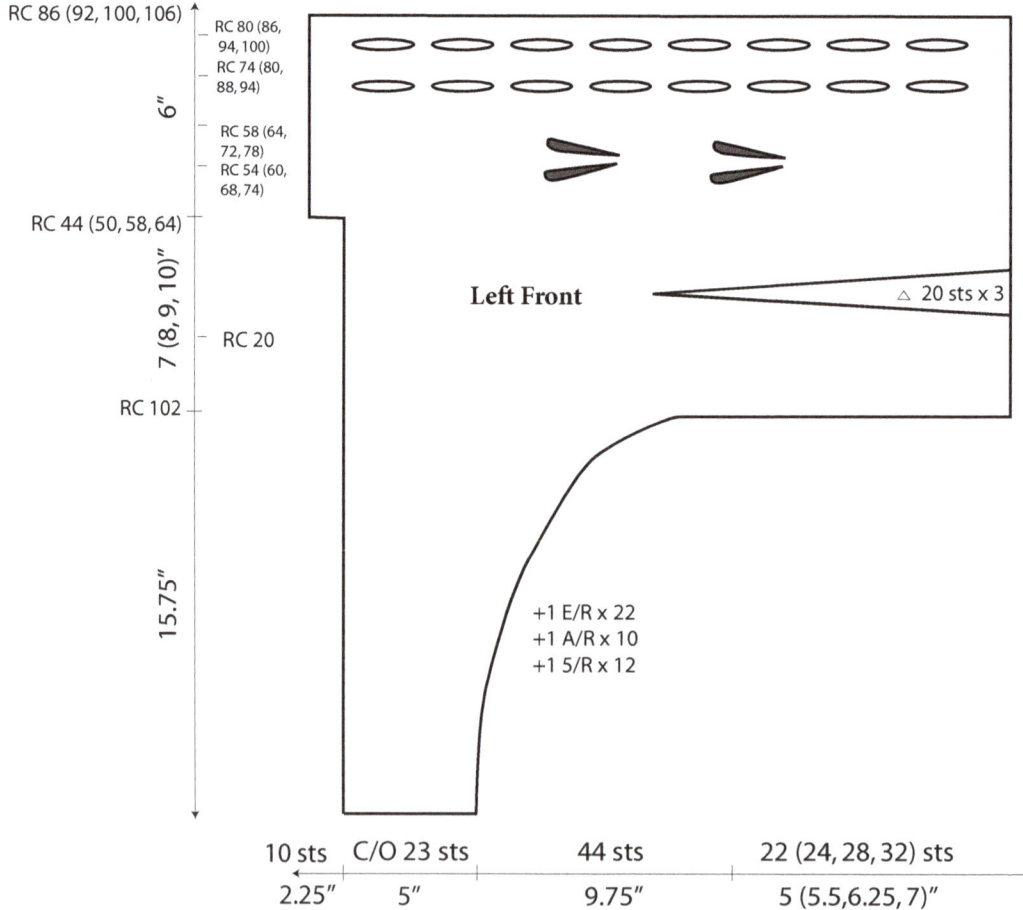

Finishing

Work in all yarn tails and block all pieces to size. Press scrap knitting flat.

Join the upper sleeve seams with join-as-you-knit I-cord edging.

Turn the back collar to the inside, folding back the scrap knitting to expose the live stitches. Fold back the scrap knitting on each front collar and graft the front collar edges (see page 164) to the back collar, working through 2 stitches together on the back. The back collar, once doubled, is the same height as the fronts.

Fold back scrap knitting at sides and graft side seams. Use mattress stitch (see page 163) or single crochet to join the sleeve seam and the remainder of the side seam.

Beginning at the undersleeve seam, work join-as-you-knit I-cord edging on each cuff. Beginning at one side seam, work I-cord around all lower, front, and collar edges. Smoothly join the two ends of each cord and then work a second row of I-cord along the edge of the first, picking up a full stitch every row (2 passes).

Join-As-You-Knit I-Cord Edging
When knitting I-cord edging, every two passes of the carriage results in only one knitted row. When the directions instruct you to knit 2 rows, it will be necessary to make 4 carriage passes. When working this edging to join the sleeve seam, only pick up one loop from each sleeve edge; for all other edges, you should pick up both loops of an edge stitch.

Cast on 3 stitches with scrap yarn and knit some rows, ending COR. Change to main yarn and set carriage to knit in one direction and slip in the other. Knit 2 rows (4 passes). With the right side of the fabric facing you, hang the first edge stitch of the garment on the leftmost needle. Knit 2 rows (4 passes), skip the next edge stitch, then hang the following edge stitch on the leftmost needle and knit 2 rows. Continue picking up every other edge stitch and knitting 2 rows (4 passes) until the entire edge has been worked. Cut the yarn and thread it through all 3 stitches to bind them off and gather them together. Where ends of a cord meet, fold back the scrap knitting (at the beginning end) to graft the live stitches over the gathered end as invisibly as possible.

For the sleeve seam: Pin fronts to back with wrong sides together. To compensate for the slight differences in the front and back of the trim, work the left sleeve seam from cuff to neck (not including the collar edges) and the right sleeve seam from neck to cuff. Work I-cord edging, picking up every stitch but only one loop from each edge (1 front loop and 1 back loop) every 2 rows (4 passes), alternating with every row (2 passes) so that the seam does not stretch and can support the weight of the garment.

For the garment edges: Work with the right side of the fabric facing you. When picking up cuff stitches from the scrap, pick up one stitch every row (2 passes), then pick up 2 stitches together every 5th row (10 passes) to slightly reduce the edge. For front, collar, and lower edges, pick up one stitch every row then every alternate row. You will be able to tell if the pickups are too close or too widely spaced by looking at the work and will be able to correct the edge by knitting fewer/more rows between pickups. Also, you may not need to pick up every (full) stitch along selvage edges, but you do have to pick up every live stitch from the scrap yarn.

Pairs of bridged ties lace through slits for a novel closure.

Loopity Lou Hat

This textured extravaganza is just the thing to get you through the frostiest winter with a smile on your face. This hat features popcorns, stegosaurus cables, a looped ruffle, a short-rowed crown, and an I-cord topknot. Some of the sections are scrapped off and then rehung, stitch by stitch, as the next section is knitted. There's a lot going on, which makes this an interesting knitting project for intermediate knitters.

Size:
One size (adult) with lower band measuring 18–19" (relaxed)

Yarn:
Worsted weight, approximately 5 ounces. Samples are shown in Cascade 220 (100% wool with 220 yards/200 meters per 3.5 ounce/100 gram skein) and Noro Kureyon (100% wool with 110 yards/100 meters per 1.75 ounce/50 gram skein)

Stitch Size:
7 (midgauge) or 5 (chunky/bulky) to obtain gauge (Changes to stitch size noted in the pattern refer to midgauge machines.)

Gauge:
5 stitches/7 rows = 1" in stockinette

Machine:
Model hats were knitted on a Studio/Silver Reed SK860, a 6.5mm midgauge machine, but pattern is also suitable for a chunky/bulky machine.

Notes
(1) The pattern is written for worsted-weight yarns. Working with DK (at the appropriate stitch size) will result in a finer gauge and a smaller, child-sized hat; Aran/heavy worsted weights will produce a coarser gauge and larger, adult-sized hat. Adjust stitch sizes according to yarn and machine used. (2) A ribbed band can be substituted for the hem, but the hat will be very deep, and you might want to eliminate one of the popcorn borders. (3) To reduce the risk of losing stitches as you handle and rehang the work, bind off all scrap knitting. (4) This pattern lends itself to use of a variety of yarns (a good way to use up odd bits), but can also be worked in a single color. Color changes are not specified in the directions. (5) When picking up the base of each popcorn, you can use a single-prong transfer tool, but you might need to do a lot of poking around. See the two-tool method illustrated on page 39. (6) When knitting the popcorns or the stegosaurus cables, it is important to keep some tension on the working stitches so they do not jump out of the needle hooks. Pull down gently with your fingers or a transfer tool. (7) For more information, see page 37 for popcorns and page 48 for stegosaurus cables.

Band

With scrap, cast on 94 stitches and knit some rows. Change to the main yarn and knit the inside of the hem with 2 rows at stitch size 5, then 4 rows at stitch size 4. Knit the next 2 rows with stitch size 5, turning the work over with a garter bar after each of these 2 rows. Now work 2 rows at stitch size 4, followed by 4 rows at stitch size 5. Hang the hem by folding back the scrap yarn at the cast-on edge, picking up and hanging each of the live stitches in the hook of a needle. To reduce bulk, as you hang each stitch, manually knit it through the stitch on the needle. Knit 1 row.

Popcorn Border 1

Change color and, beginning with the COR and set to hold needles in HP, knit 2 rows. Hold all needles except the first 6 on the carriage side. Knit 1 row to the left and hold 3 needles opposite the carriage. All remaining bridges in the row will be 2 stitches wide and all popcorns 3 stitches. Use your fingers or a transfer tool to help tension the fabric below the 3 needles that are working and *knit 5 rows over these 3 popcorn stitches, ending COR. Move the next 5 stitches at left (2 bridge stitches and 3 popcorn stitches) to UWP and knit 1 row to the left.

Hang the popcorn you just knitted by picking up the 3 stitches at the base of the popcorn. As you deposit the stitches in the hooks of the needles, bring the needles to HP and then bring the 2 bridge needles next to them to HP so that only the next 3 popcorn needles are working.** Repeat from * to ** across the entire row. Scrap off all 94 stitches.

Stegosaurus Cables

With scrap, cast on 12 stitches. Change to main yarn and knit 1 row from left to right. Set the carriage to hold needles in HP. With the wrong side of the hat facing you, *pick up 1 stitch from the scrapped-off popcorn stitches and hang it on the left edge needle every row, four times. COR.

Pick up a stitch from scrap and then hold 3 needles at left. Knit to left and manually wrap the 3rd needle. Hold 3 needles at right, knit 1 row, bring 1 additional needle to HP. Then (knit 1 row, hold 1 needle on the carriage side) three times. Knit 3 rows over the 2 working needles, ending COR.

Use your fingers or a tool to pull down on the stitches and provide some tension. (Return 1 needle on the carriage side to UWP and knit 1 row) three times. Return 1 needle at left and 3 needles at right to UWP and knit to right. Return 3 needles at left to UWP and knit 1 row. Pick up 1 stitch from scrap and hang it on the left- edge needle.

Cross a 3x3 cable on the center 6 stitches and knit 1 row to right.** Repeat from * to **, alternately crossing the cable left and right. Scrap off.

The stegosaurus cable is flanked by rows of popcorns — the top row of popcorns is half hidden by the loopy ruffle.

Popcorn Border 2

With wrong side facing you, pick up 94 stitches along the edge of the stegosaurus border and repeat the popcorn border with another color. Scrap off.

Ruffles

Cast on 6 stitches. With the wrong side of the hat facing you, pick up the edge of the previous popcorn border once per ruffle sequence, alternately picking up 1 stitch and then 2 stitches from the scrap. Begin COL, set to hold needles in HP.*Knit 1 row, pick up 1 stitch from scrap and hang on the left needle. Hold 2 needles at left and knit 10 rows on the remaining 4 needles. Return the 2 needles at left to UWP, knit 1 row, and then pick up 2 stitches from the scrap and hang them on the left-edge needle.** Repeat from *to ** until all of the stitches have been picked up from scrap. Scrap off.

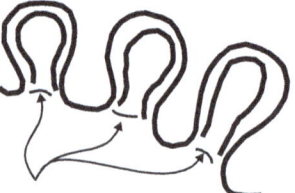

Every time the carriage is on the right, you need to pick up a stitch at the base of a ruffle loop as shown by the arrows.

Crown

Whenever COR, pick up the edge stitch that lies across the open base of one ruffle section (see drawing above). All holding of or returning needles to UWP takes place when COL. Wrong side of hat is facing you.

Cast on 20 stitches with scrap and then change to main yarn and knit 1 row from left to right. COR and set to hold needles in HP. Pick up 1 stitch at the base of a ruffle loop and hang it on left-edge needle. Knit 1 row. *Hold 5 needles at right, knit 1 row, and manually wrap. Pick up base of 1 ruffle and hang at left.

Knit 1 row.** Repeat from * to ** until there are only 5 needles working. Then, whenever COL, return 6 needles at right to UWP, knit 1 row, and return the last needle to HP (automatic wrap) at the same time; whenever COR, pick up ruffle stitch to hang on left-edge needle.

Ideally, you should pick up 6 ruffle loops in each complete short-row sequence. It will take 11 sequences to complete the crown. Count the number of ruffles before you begin. If there are more than 66, plan to double up at intervals. If there are fewer than 66, pick up the same ruffle a second time to ensure that the short-row sections and the picking up end together when the crown is complete. As you near the end of the crown, count the remaining ruffles one more time so you don't end up having to fudge it all in the last few rows! These ruffles are so dense that the spacing will look fine if you stagger the doubled-up ruffles. Scrap off the completed crown.

Twisted Edging

The top edge of the crown is finished with a narrow strip of twisted stockinette. Cast on 4 stitches with scrap. Change to main yarn and *(knit 1 row. Pick up 1 edge stitch from crown) twice. Knit 3 rows and then twist the hat 360°, skip the next edge stitch, and hang the following edge stitch.** Repeat from * to ** to end. Scrap off.

I-Cord Topknot

Set the carriage to knit in one direction and slip in the other to knit as many I-cords as you can fit along the lower inside edge of the twisted edging. Pick up 4 stitches–or anything that looks like a stitch—and knit 10–12 rows of I-cord edging (20–24 for larger topknots), threading the end of the yarn through all stitches to gather them off. For striped I-cords, cut a strand of a contrasting color and use it to e-wrap the left edge needle every row. This is the same e-wrap you would use to cast on with, except that in this case the yarn is wound around only one needle and there is already a stitch on that needle.

Finishing

Work in all the ends of the I-cords and trim. Then begin at the top of the hat and, using dangling yarn tails, finish your way to the band, joining the ends of each section. Where possible, graft the ends together from the scrap (see page 164) and use mattress stitch (see page 163) for the selvage edges so that the back seam is nearly invisible.

I run a double strand of ravel cord through the inside of the lower hem and tighten it snugly before I wash the finished hat to prevent it from stretching out of shape while it is wet. Washing will help the wool "bloom," to fill out the stitches. It also helps trap the yarn tails so they don't work loose.

The short rowed crown is circled by ruffles and topped with I-cords. The black cords have a gold stripe running through them where a second color e-wrapped the edge needle every row. The crown stitches, like those in the stegosaurus cable lie perpendicular to the popcorn borders.

Faux Crochet Cardigan

Raglan styling, garter stitch accents, and crochet-like patterning add up to an ultra-wearable cardigan. The front bands stop short of the lower border, creating a separation at the lower front edges. The stitch pattern would also work nicely for a collar above (or instead of) the garter stitch neckband.

Sizes:
S (M, L, XL, XXL) with finished chest measurement 38 (42, 45.5, 49, 53)" and back length 23.5 (24, 24, 24.25, 24.5)" (To alter the length, add or subtract rows above the lower border and before armhole shaping. Garment is shown in size L.)

Yarn:
Knit Picks City Tweed DK (55% Merino Wool, 25% Superfine Alpaca, 20% Donegal Tweed with 123 yards/112 meters per 1.75 ounce/50 gram ball), 10 (11, 12, 13, 14) balls color #CH98 (Enchanted)

Stitch Size:
6 or to obtain gauge

Gauge:
22 stitches/28 rows = 4" in stockinette

Machine:
Model garment was knitted on the Studio/Silver Reed SK860, a 6.5mm midgauge machine.

Notes
(1) Bridging is used to manually increase the stitch size for the openwork border and to work the buttonholes in the right-front band. (2) There are four rows of garter stitch at the beginning of each garment section and after each of the openwork borders. If you do not have a garter bar, hand-knitting these rows is the fastest alternative. If you do not hand-knit (no purling required), you will either have to forego these accent rows or remove the work on scrap and rehang after each row. This approach is slow, but quite doable. (3) Work all of the raglan decreases as two-step decreases with a 3-prong tool. Move the 4th stitch from the edge onto the 3rd needle and then move in the 3 edge needles. (4) The openwork stitch is easiest to do when the work is lightly weighted, as the weight minimizes the possibility that the yarn will split. (5) Use a grease pencil to mark the pattern repeats on the bed to reduce counting mistakes. The patterning on the back will begin and end with 5 plain stitches at each side for all sizes, as will the fronts for sizes S, L, and XXL. The fronts for sizes M and XL will have 3 plain stitches at the center-front edge and only 2 stitches at the side. Center the patterning on the sleeves.

Back

With scrap yarn, cast on 105 (115, 125, 135, 145) stitches and knit some rows, ending COR. Change to the main yarn and e-wrap to cast on from left to right. Thread the carriage and set to stitch size 6. Knit 2 rows. (Remove the work on a garter bar, turn, and knit 1 row) four times. Knit 2 rows.

Work 8 repeats of the openwork pattern. Every 10th stitch is dropped down and latched up as a tuck stitch. Do this latching up after each four-row repeat to catch any errors before you get too far beyond them. Follow the border with four rows of garter stitch (ending with the purl side of the work facing you as usual).

RC 000. Work stockinette stitch to RC 64 to begin shaping raglan armholes. RC 000. At the beginning of the next two rows, bind off 5 (5, 5, 5, 5) stitches. Then make full-fashion decreases at both ends of the row as follows: every row 0 (0, 8, 16, 23) times, every alternate row 26 (34, 30, 27, 24) times, and every third row 4 (0, 0, 0, 0) times. At RC 66 (70, 70, 72, 74), scrap off the remaining 35 (37, 39, 39, 41) stitches.

Fronts

Work two fronts with reversed shaping. With scrap, cast on 55 (60, 65, 70, 75) stitches. Work as for the back through armholes to RC 51 (55, 55, 57, 59) with COL to shape front neck with short rows, *at the same time continuing the armhole decreases*. Set the carriage to hold needles in HP. Hold 5 (6, 7, 7, 8) needles at neck edge. KWK. Then hold 3 stitches once, 2 stitches three times, and 1 stitch twice. At RC 66 (70, 70, 72, 74), cut the main yarn, leaving a tail three times the width of the work. Rethread with scrap yarn and scrap off the 4 needles remaining in WP. Rethread the carriage with the tail of the main yarn and knit 1 smoothing row across all 16 (17, 18, 18, 19) front neck stitches before scrapping them off.

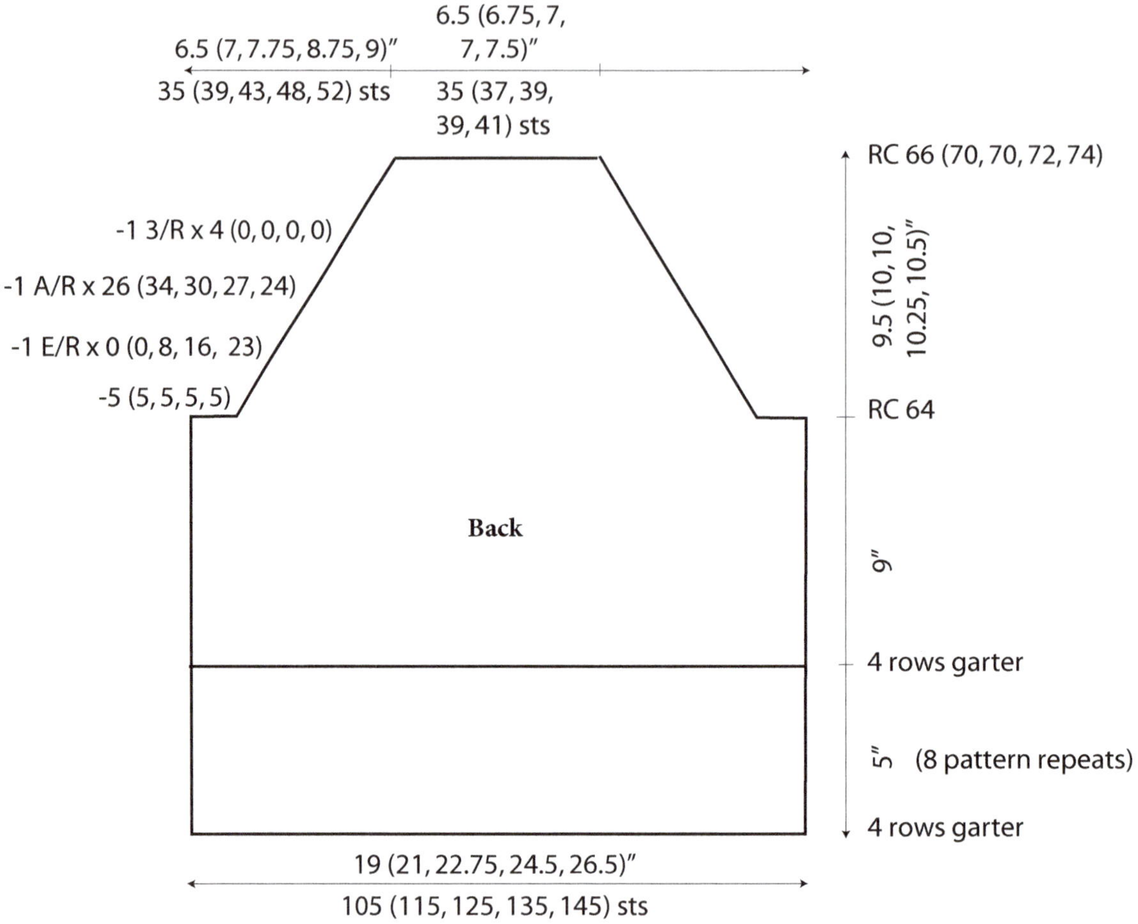

6.5 (7, 7.75, 8.75, 9)"
35 (39, 43, 48, 52) sts

6.5 (6.75, 7, 7, 7.5)"
35 (37, 39, 39, 41) sts

RC 66 (70, 70, 72, 74)

9.5 (10, 10, 10.25, 10.5)"

-1 3/R x 4 (0, 0, 0, 0)
-1 A/R x 26 (34, 30, 27, 24)
-1 E/R x 0 (0, 8, 16, 23)
-5 (5, 5, 5, 5)

RC 64

Back

9"

4 rows garter

5"   (8 pattern repeats)

4 rows garter

19 (21, 22.75, 24.5, 26.5)"
105 (115, 125, 135, 145) sts

This pattern is similar to the one shown on page 28 except that there are 3 rows between each bridged row, which means that all bridged rows begin from the right. Also, only a single stitch at the edge of each repeat is moved over to the next needle after each group of 5 stitches is twisted. This variation facilitates latching up the tuck stitches.

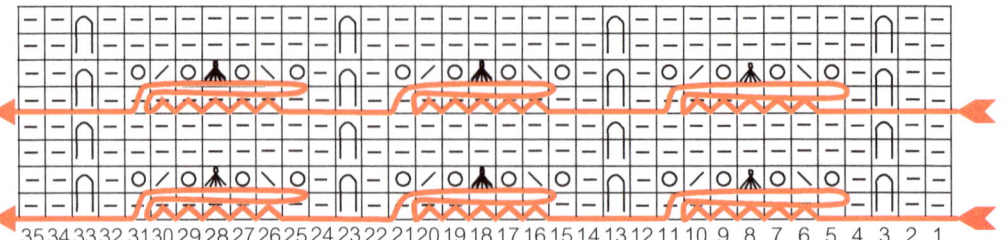

Sleeves

With scrap, cast on 44 (44, 50, 50, 50) stitches and work garter rows, 4 pattern repeats, and the ending garter rows, as for other pieces.

RC 000. Knit stockinette to RC 106, increasing 1 stitch every third row 0 (0, 0, 0, 14) times, every fourth row 0 (4, 9, 24, 15) times, every fifth row 2 (17, 13, 1, 0) times and every sixth row 15 (0, 0, 0, 0) times. 78 (86, 94, 100, 108) stitches.

RC 000. Shape raglan armholes as for other pieces. At RC 66 (70, 70, 72, 74), scrap off the remaining 8 (8, 8, 4, 4) stitches.

Finishing

Work in all ends and lightly block all of the pieces. Sew all four raglan seams with mattress stitch (see page 163), working one full stitch from each edge. Then complete side and sleeve seams.

For the neckband:
All live stitches are picked up by folding back the scrap knitting. Do not remove any scrap knitting until the band is complete and you have checked the fit. With the wrong side facing you, rehang the back neck stitches over 34 needles, doubling up stitches evenly as necessary. Rehang each sleeve on 4 needles at

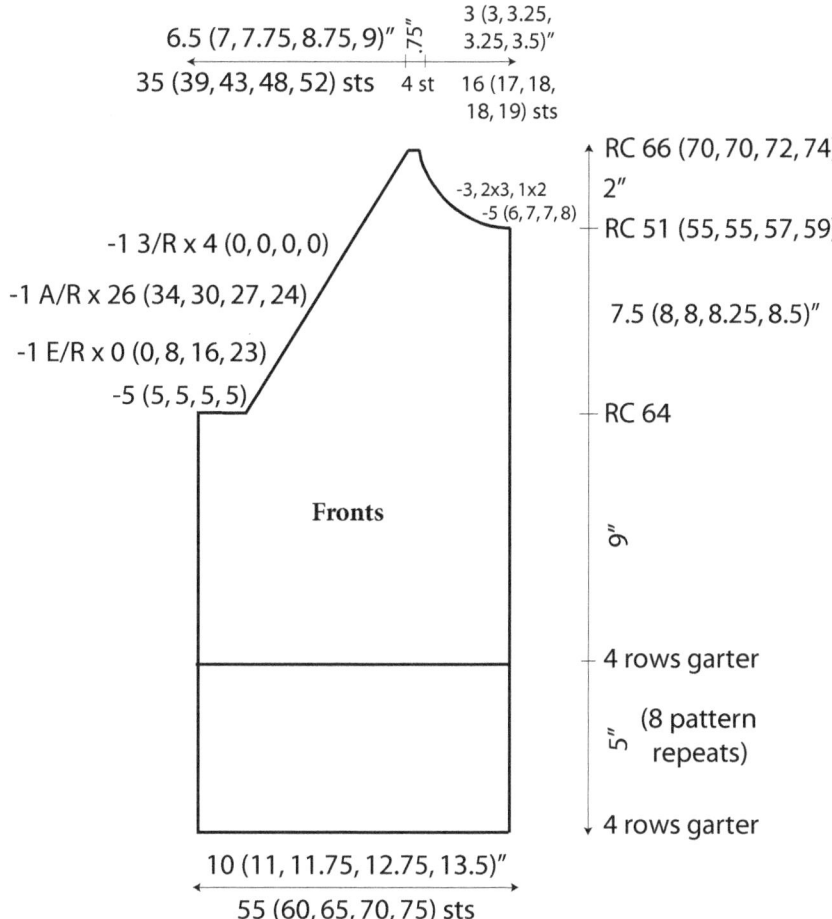

each side of the back neck, doubling the first sleeve stitch with the last back neck stitch and as necessary to reduce the sleeve to 4 needles. Rehang each front group of 4 stitches on the next 3 needles, doubling the first neck stitch with the last sleeve stitch. Lastly, rehang the 16 (17, 18, 18, 19) front neck stitches over the next 13 needles, doubling the first stitch and as necessary. 72 stitches. Knit 1 row. (Turn, knit 1 row) 8 times (4 garter ridges). Bind off loosely.

For the front bands:
Front bands are worked from the top of the lower borders to the neck edge in garter stitch.

For the left front button band:
With the wrong side facing you, pick up 80 (84, 84, 86, 86) stitches along the front edge. Knit 1 row. (Turn, knit 1 row) eight times (4 garter ridges). Bind off loosely.

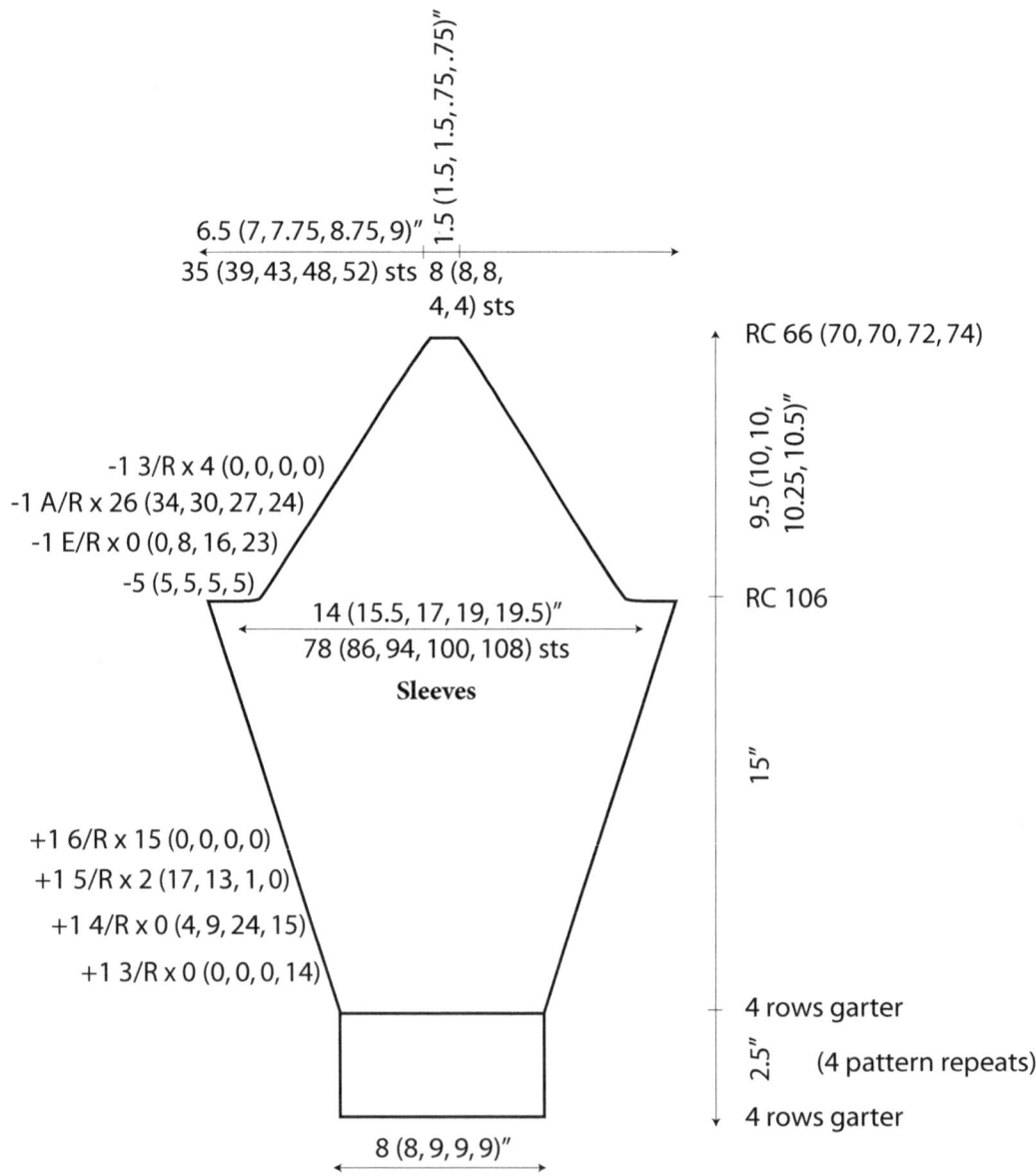

For the right front buttonhole band:
With the wrong side facing you, pick up 80 (84, 84, 86, 86) stitches. Knit 1 row. (Turn, knit 1 row) four times. The next two rows are bridged for buttonholes, spaced as shown below. With COR set to hold needles in HP, hold all needles except the first 3 (3, 3, 4, 4) on carriage side. *Knit 1 row. Bind off the next 2 stitches, put the empty needles in NWP, and return COR. Place the next 16 (17, 17, 17, 17) needles into UWP ** and repeat four times, ending with 3 (3, 3, 4, 4) stitches after the last buttonhole. Bridge the next row, e-wrapping the empty needles to complete the buttonholes. Work 4 more rows of garter stitch and then bind off loosely.

Sew buttons to left front band. Wash the finished sweater and lay it flat to dry, pinning the lower edges in place to accentuate the scalloped edge.

These cuffs were knitted with four repeats of the patterning, but cuffs can be knitted much deeper if you adjust the length and shaping of the sleeves above the cuffs.

Buttonhole Spacing

| 3 (3, 3, 4, 4) sts | 2 sts | 16 (17, 17, 17, 17) sts | 2 sts | 16 (17, 17, 17, 17) sts | 2 sts | 16 (17, 17, 17, 17) sts | 2 sts | 16 (17, 17, 17, 17) sts | 2 sts | 16 (17, 17, 17, 17) sts | 2 sts | 3 (3, 3, 4, 4) sts |

Puppet Scarf

For years, I have used a simple puppet pattern to teach the short-row knitting technique. I've adapted that same puppet pattern to create the playful ends of this textured child's scarf, while, at the same time, adding built-in hand mitts for warming frosty fingers at the bus stop. The more grown-up multicolored version, shown on page 110, features a curly fringe instead of puppet heads.

Sizes:
The puppet scarf is 22 ½ repeats long and 6"wide (the multicolored scarf is 27 ½ repeats long and 4" wide). Widths are finished widths.

Yarn:
Cascade 220 (100% wool worsted with 220 yards/200 meters per 3.5 ounce/100 gram skein), 10 ounces color #9486 (dark green), small amounts of #980 (light green), and #2410 (purple); fringed scarf color #9861 (Superwash Paint).

Notions:
4 buttons or "googly eyes," size F or H crochet hook

Stitch Size:
8 or size to obtain gauge

Gauge:
19–20 stitches/28 rows = 4"

Machine:
Models were knitted on the Studio/Silver Reed SK860, a 6.5mm midgauge machine, but these yarns are also suitable for a chunky/bulky machine.

Notes
(1) Both of these scarves were worked wider than finished width and then seamed to the back so that the texture would be framed by stockinette. You can also work this scarf to a narrower width without casting on the additional 15 (10) stitches at each side, in which case the edges roll to the back, creating a sort of boa. (2) The surface texture is created by an alternating pattern of triangular nops that are not lifted. It is easier to count repeats rather than rows. (3) The stripe pattern for the puppet scarf was knitted as follows: The single, centered nop and the row knitted immediately after the nop row were alternately knitted with two contrasting colors. Knit 2 rows of the main color before knitting the paired nops and 3 plain rows after the nop row. There will then be 6 rows of the main color alternating with just 2 rows of the stripes. (4) Reset RC 000 after each section.

Beginning Edge

With waste yarn, cast on 31 stitches (needles 15 left to 16 right) and knit some rows. Change to main yarn and knit 6 rows. RC 000. Transfer every other stitch to the adjacent needle, leaving empty needles in WP to form picots. Knit 8 rows. Fold back waste knitting to hang hem. Work to RC 28, ending COR.

First Puppet Head End

RC 000. Set carriage to hold needles in HP and thread main color. *On the side opposite carriage, bring 1 needle to HP. Knit and wrap.** Repeat * to ** until only 5 needles remain in WP and COR. Cut main yarn.

Lips:
Thread carriage with contrast color for lips. Set carriage to knit all needles and work 6 rows across all 31 stitches. Do not cut contrast yarn; instead, tuck it under the end of the bed to use later.

Mouth:
Thread carriage with contrast color for inside of mouth and set carriage to hold needles in HP. Bring all needles to HP except the center 5 needles. Knit 1 row and wrap edge needle. *On side opposite carriage, move 2 needles at center edge to UWP. Knit 1 row. Return 1 needle on carriage side to HP. ** Repeat * to ** until all needles are in WP. RC 32.

*On the side opposite carriage, bring 1 needle to HP. Knit and wrap.** Repeat * to ** until only 5 needles remain in WP and COR. RC 58. Cut the yarn.

RC 000. Rethread carriage with contrast color used for lips and repeat for second lip. Cut the yarn. RC 6.

Rethread the carriage with the main color and complete top of head as follows: Bring all needles to HP except the center 5 needles. Knit 1 row and wrap edge needle. *On side

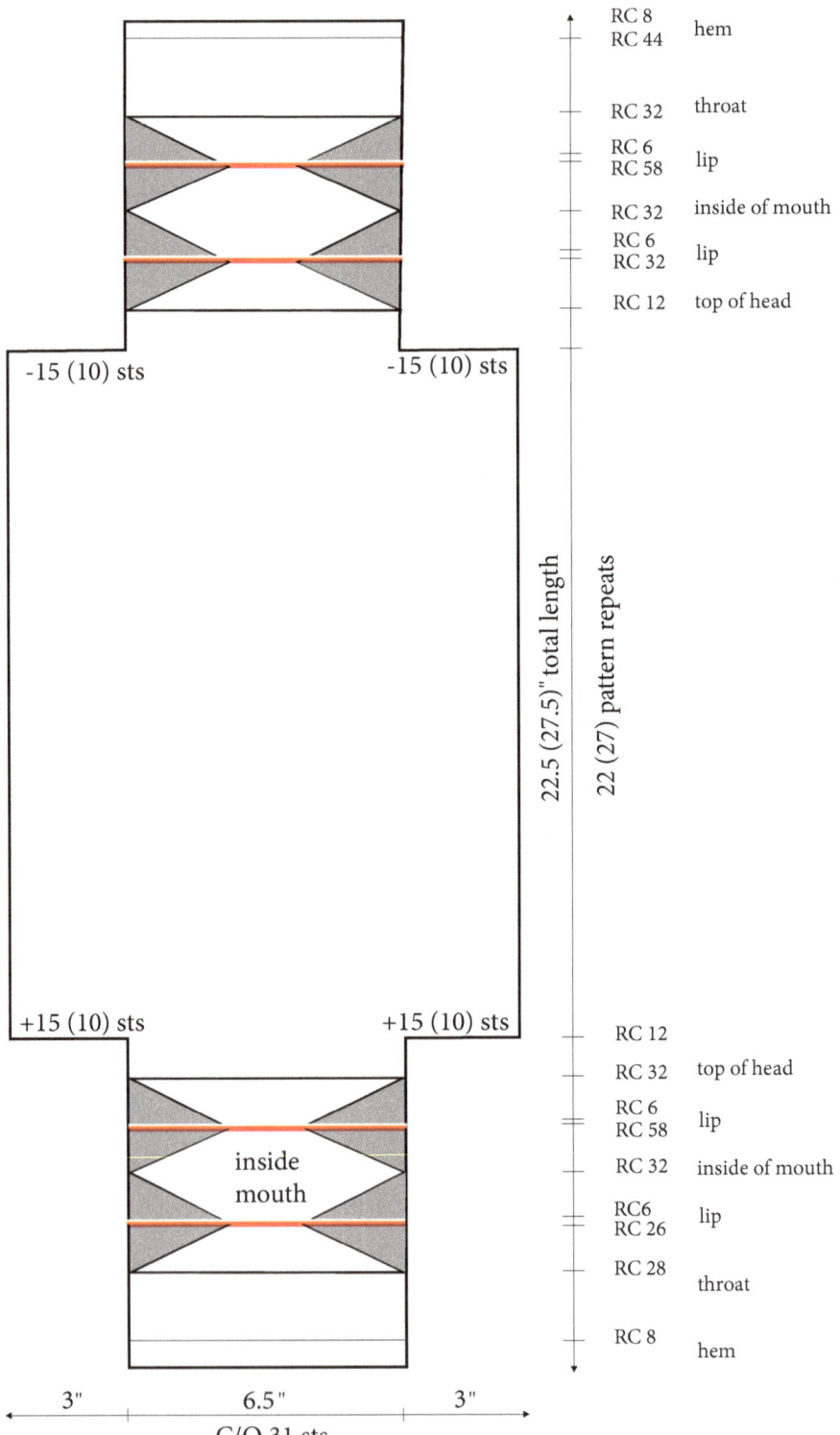

The shaded triangles along side each "mouth" section represent short row shaping. You can work rib instead of the hems at each end and the "lining" sections at each side can be eliminated if you don't mind the scarf rolling at the edges. You can also eliminate the scarf and just knit puppets!

opposite carriage, move 2 needles at center edge to UWP. Knit 1 row. Return 1 needle on carriage side to HP. ** Repeat * to ** until all needles are in WP. RC 32.

Knit 12 rows over all needles. COR. E-wrap to cast on 15 (10) stitches at right. Knit 1 row to left. E-wrap to cast on 15 (10) stitches at left. (See page 156). These additional stitches are later seamed at the back of the scarf. Knit 2 rows.

Triangular Nops

COR. Hold all needles to the left of the center 9 needles. Knit 1 row. Wrap. Hold all needles to the right of the center 9 needles. Knit 1 row and hold 1 needle on the carriage side. Continue knitting 1 row and holding 1 needle on the carriage side until only 1 needle is in WP and COL.

*Return 2 needles on the side opposite carriage to UWP, knit, and return 1 needle to HP.** Repeat * to ** until 8 needles are in WP and COR. Return all needles at left to UWP and knit 1 row. Knit 3 rows over all needles, ending COR.

Paired Nops

COR set to hold needles in HP. Hold all needles to the left of and including needle 2 (right). Knit 1 row and wrap. Hold all needles to the right of and including needle 12 (right). Knit 1 row and wrap. Knit 1 row and hold 1 needle on the carriage side. Continue holding 1 needle on the carriage side every row until 1 needle remains in WP and COL. *Return 2 needles on the side opposite carriage to UWP, knit, and return one needle to HP.** Repeat * to ** until 8 needles are in WP and COR.

Place needles 2 (right) through 10 (left) into UWP and bridge to left. Hold the bridge so that only needles 10 left to 2 left are in WP. Repeat shaping for second nop on needles 10 (left) through 2 (left). When there are 8 needles back in WP, return all needles at left to UWP and knit row. Knit 3 rows over all needles and then repeat single and paired nop pattern twenty-two (twenty-seven) times. Work 1 single nop and following 3 rows. COR.

With a curly tongue, button eyes and smacking-red lips, this creature has a winning personality coming and going. You could also give each of the heads its own personality by varying the trimmings and details.

Second Puppet Head End

Bind off 15 (10) stitches at right. Knit to left and bind off 15 (10) stitches. Knit 12 rows over all needles. Repeat shaping for top of head, lip, mouth, lip, underside of head, as for first puppet head end. Work 12 rows.

Bring all needles to HP and manually weave a strand of scrap yarn over/under all needles across the row to mark hem top. Knit 8 rows, transfer stitches for picots, knit 6 rows. Pick up the marked row to hang hem and bind off loosely.

Finishing

Work in all ends. Sew back seam with mattress stitch (see page 87). Tack the center back seam to the front of the scarf in four or five places along the length of the scarf. For puppet, sew 2 button eyes to each end. Bring underside of head to the back and use mattress stitch to sew short seams at side of head.

Make curly Q for puppet tongue or for multi-colored scarf fringe as follows: Use size H crochet hook and doubled yarn for tongue; size F hook with single yarn for fringe. Chain 25 stitches and work 1 row of single crochet back along the chain. For tongue, break yarn and pull through to secure, leaving long enough tails to tie tongue through inside of mouth. For fringe, after each curly Q, work 1 single crochet through the edge of the scarf before working next curly Q.

Ruched Cardigan

This modified drop-shoulder cardigan features a giant "seersucker" texture of ruching and stockinette that automatically creates a scalloped hemline and shaped cuffs. The sweater's lower edges are allowed to just roll, while the neckline edges are finished with stockinette sandwich bands and I-cord. Afraid of this much texture? You can actually knit fewer rows in each of the ruched sections without affecting the overall length of the garment.

Ruched Cardigan

Sizes:
Women's S (M, L, XL, XXL) with finished chest measurement 38 (42.5, 46, 49.5, 53)" and finished length 23 (23.5, 24, 25, 25)" including 2" drop from ruching (Garment sizing allows for 4–6" of ease to ensure a boxy, straight fit. Garment is shown in size L.)

Yarn:
Noro Silk Garden (45% silk, 45% kid mohair, 10% lamb's wool with 122 yards/100 meters per 1.75 ounce/50 gram skein, 19 skeins color # 252. Optional trim: 1 skein Colinette Wigwam (100% cotton tape with 42 yards/130 meters/ per 3.5 ounce/100 gram skein), color # 113 (Velvet Leaf)

Notions:
One 2" novelty button; one large sew-on snap (Dritz size 30mm)

Stitch Size:
5 or to obtain gauge

Gauge:
20 stitches/28 rows = 4" in stockinette

Machine:
Model garment was knitted on the Studio/Silver Reed SK860, a 6.5mm midgauge machine; the yarn is suitable for a chunky/bulky machine, but there will not be enough needles for the three largest sizes.

Notes
(1) Turn off RC: Each repeat accounts for 6 rows (as shown in charts on pages 115-116). Advance RC by 6 after completing each repeat. (2) Use a grease pencil to mark the bed. I marked the edges of the stockinette strips and, after a couple of repeats, was able to easily keep track of the way the ruching shifts to the left. Marking every position might be confusing unless you have grease pencils in several colors. (3) The ruching sequences differ for each size (in order to keep stockinette over the bust line) and are marked accordingly: 18 (22, 25, 28, 28) stitches. (4) Ruching is described in greater detail on page 45. (5) The last 6 rows of the fronts and back should be knitted in plain stockinette stitch for a smoother shoulder line. (6) The stockinette sleeves are knitted from the top down and end with ruched cuffs. (7) There is minimal neck shaping.

Back

With scrap yarn, cast on 94 (106, 115, 124, 132) stitches and knit some rows, ending COR. With the main yarn, e-wrap to cast on from left to right and knit 2 rows. Mark the bed for centered ruching placement and work the 6-row ruching pattern to RC 74. Note that there are 10 (10, 10, 10, 12) stockinette stitches dividing each ruched section and at both side edges.

RC 000. Continue working the ruching pattern, binding off or scrapping off 6 stitches at the beginning of the next 2 rows, to RC 54 (60, 66, 72, 72). Work plain stockinette for the next 6 rows. RC 60 (66, 72, 78, 78).

Separately scrap off 23 (29, 33, 37, 40) stitches for each shoulder and 36 (36, 37, 38, 40) stitches for the back neck.

Left Front

With scrap yarn, cast on 33 (35, 43, 47, 50) stitches as for back. Mark the bed for ruching placement, noting that there are 10 (10, 10, 10, 12) stockinette stitches at the left (side) edge, but only 5 (5, 8, 9, 10) at the right (front) edge.

Work as for back to RC 74. RC 000. Bind off 6 stitches at armhole. Then decrease 1 stitch at the right edge every row, four times. At RC 60 (66, 72, 78, 78), scrap off the remaining 23 (29, 33, 37, 40) stitches.

Right Front

With scrap yarn, cast on 62 (70, 76, 82, 86) stitches as for back. Mark the bed for ruching, noting that there are 10 (10, 10, 10, 12) stockinette stitches at the right (side) edge and between the two ruched sections, but only 6 stitches at the left (front) edge.

Work as for back to RC 60 (66, 70, 76, 76), but do not decrease at the neck edge. Separately scrap off 23 (29, 33, 37, 40) stitches for shoul-

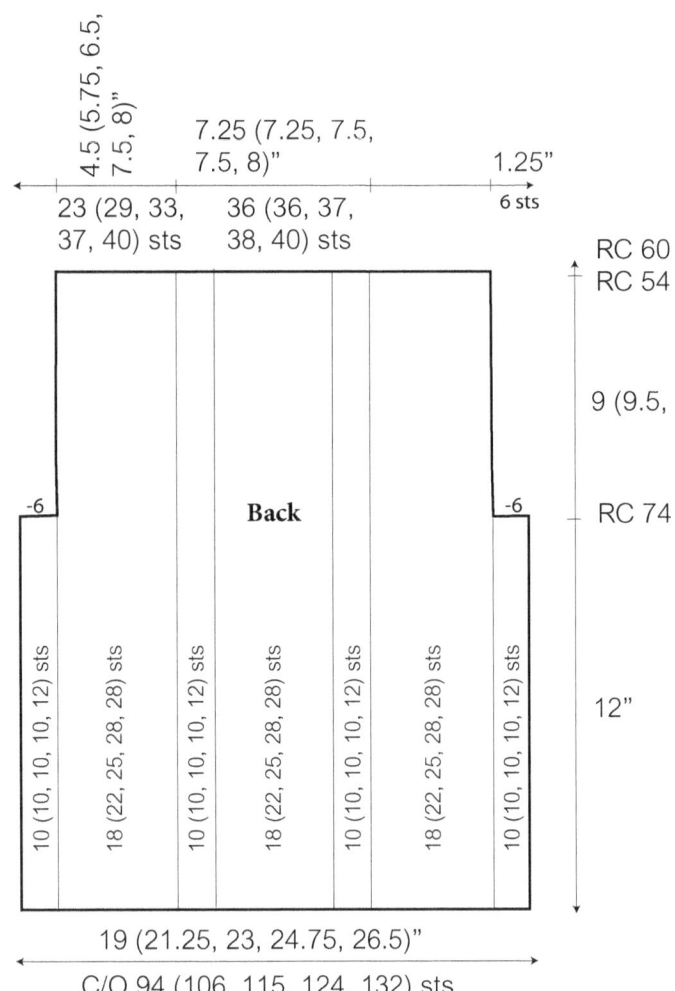

0 (0, 0, 15, 3) times, every fourth row 19 (23, 27, 16, 27) times, and every fifth row 5 (2, 0, 0, 0) times.

At RC 106 (106, 112, 112, 120), begin ruching and work 2 repeats to RC 12. Loosely bind off all 42 (46, 46, 48, 50) stitches with the backstitch method. (See page 163.)

Finishing

Join side/underarm gussets to straight section at top of each sleeve. Sew side and sleeve seams with mattress stitch. (See page 163.)

The back neck is finished with a picked-up I-cord edge. With scrap yarn, cast on 4 stitches and knit some rows. Change to the main yarn and set the carriage to knit in one direction and slip in the other for the I-cord. With stitch size 4, knit the I-cord, picking up one live stitch from the back neck below the scrap knitting every time COR. Work with the right side of the garment facing you. When all of the stitches have been picked up, bind off the I-cord by running the yarn back through the 4 stitches on the machine.

For the front bands:
Work sandwich bands on both front edges. (See page 117.) Sew the end of the left front band to the back neck.

der and 33 (35, 37, 39, 40) stitches for the front neck. (Note that this count differs from the back neck stitch count.)

Sleeves

Knit two alike. With right sides together, join both garment shoulder seams.

With the wrong side of the garment facing you, rehang the armhole edge over 90 (96, 100, 110, 110) needles. Knit 8 rows and then decrease 1 stitch at each edge every third row

When sandwich bands are complete, using the ribbon at stitch size 5 or the main yarn at stitch size 4, work a 3-stitch I-cord along the right front edge, across the back neck and down the left front edge. If you worked garter-stitch turn rows in the sandwich band, pick up the loops of the garter stitch as you work the I-cord. Alternately pick up a stitch from the front edge every time and then every other time COR—in other words, every second and fourth passes of the carriage (not RC). When working across the back neck, pick up a full stitch from the previous I-cord every time COR.

Sew a large button to the right front below the natural collar fold. Sew the snap underneath the button. Wash the finished sweater and lay flat to dry, coaxing the lower edges to form even scallops.

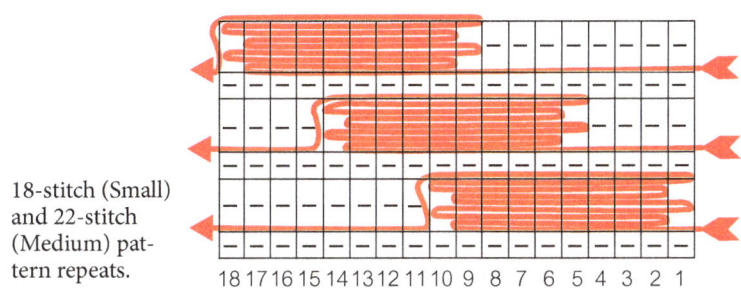

18-stitch (Small) and 22-stitch (Medium) pattern repeats.

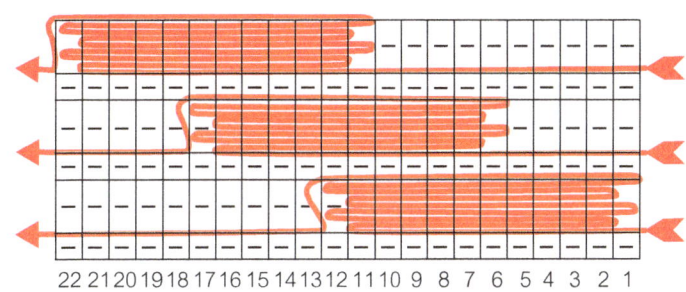

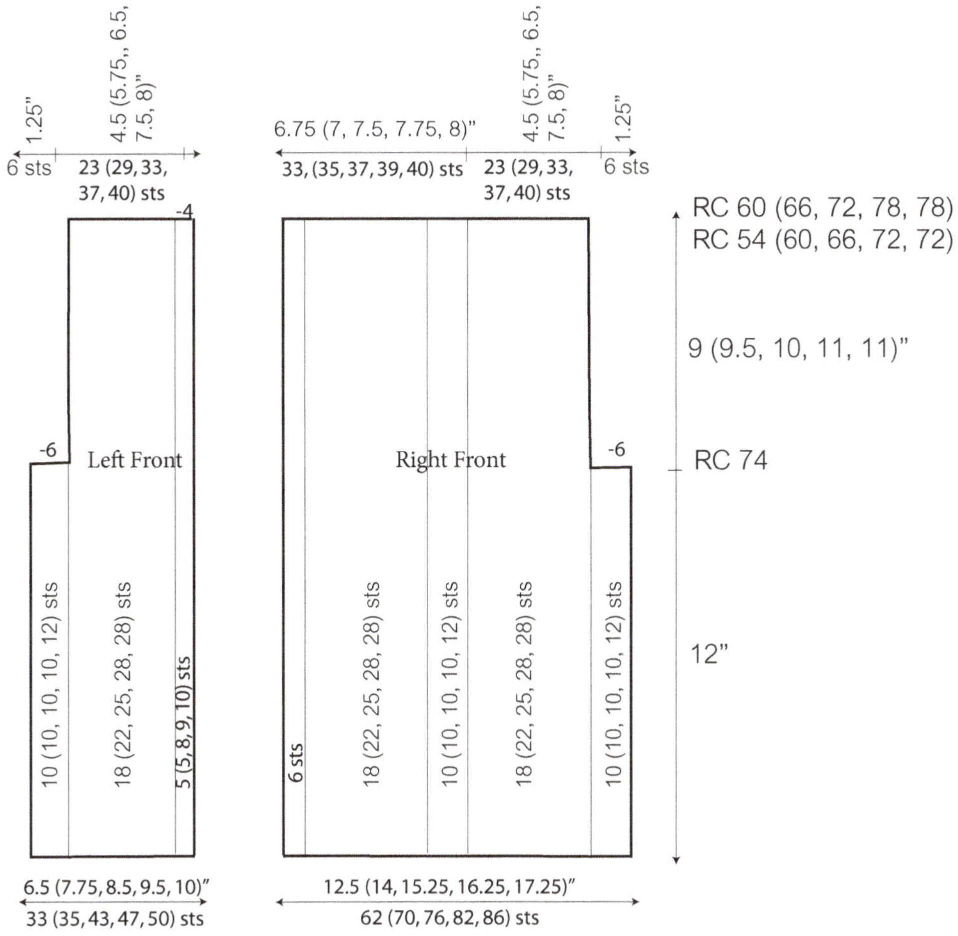

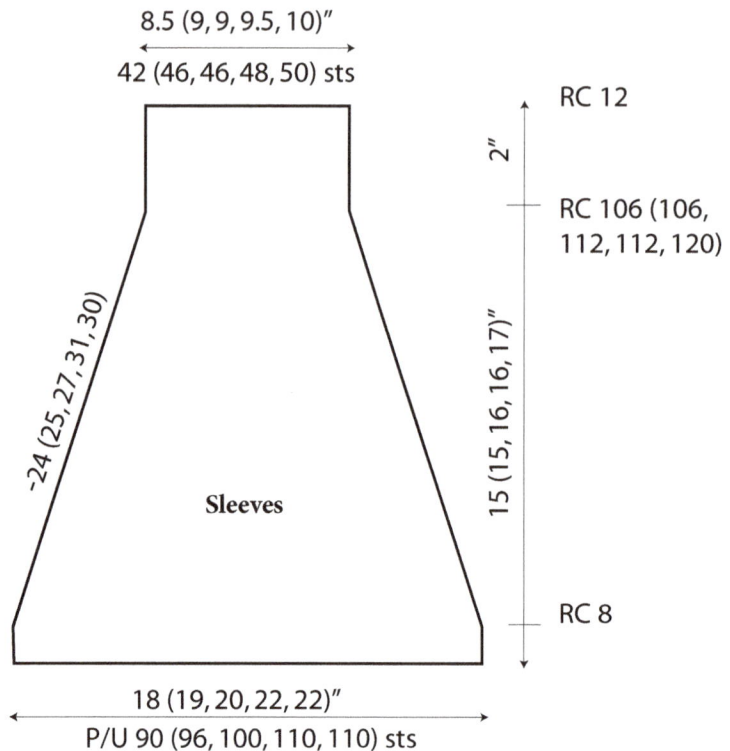

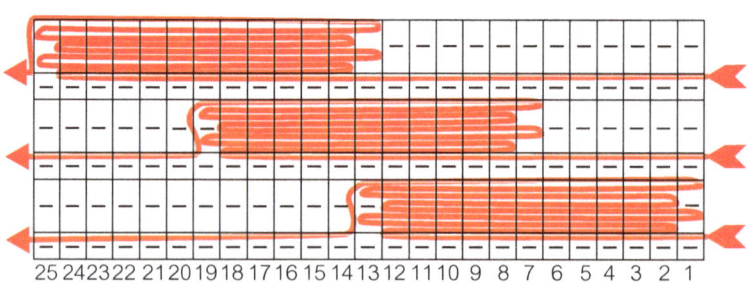

25-stitch (Large) and 28-stitch (X-Large and XX-Large) pattern repeats.

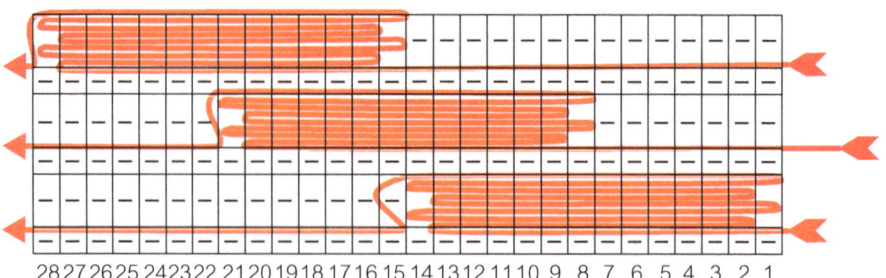

Simple Sandwich Band

This technique produces a beautiful, professional-looking band that totally encloses the edge of the fabric. On the outside, the band appears to have been hand-stitched in place, while on the inside there is a definite chain stitch. A narrower version of this band is useful for necklines. You can also work buttonholes in sandwich bands. Practice this technique on the edge of your swatch before attempting it on the garment.

With scrap yarn, cast on 106 (108, 110, 115, 115) stitches and knit some rows. Change to the main yarn and work 12 rows with stitch size 5. Turn the work with a garter bar, knit 1 row, and turn again. If you do not have a garter bar, work the row with stitch size 7–8. Work 12 more rows with stitch size 5. Do not cut the yarn.

Cover the bed with a cloth or some paper towels to avoid getting grease marks on the garment. Work with the right side of the garment facing up and with one of the front edges of the garment toward you. You will poke this edge onto the same needles that already hold the band. Working 2 full stitches from the edge, poke a few needles through at either end and at the center. Then evenly distribute the rest of the garment edge in between those needles. I bring the needles out to UWP or HP only after I have checked twice to make sure that I have poked the needles through the same column of stitches all along the edge.

The front edges of this cardigan are finished with simple sandwich bands, then further trimmed with ribbon I-cord.

Fold back the scrap knitting on the beginning edge of the band to pick and rehang the first row of band stitches in the hooks of the needles. After you've done that, each needle will hold two band stitches with the edge of the garment sandwiched between them. Bring the needles out to HP and make sure the latches are open.

The next step can be a bit clumsy, so work slowly. You'll reach back under the garment to manipulate the needle butts to manually knit each needle back to HWP. At the same time, your other hand will feed yarn into the open hook of each needle and then check that the latch is closed before you pull the needle back. To make sure that each of the stitches is the same size, I insert a ¾" strip of wood between the back rail and the needle butts. You could also cut a strip of stiff cardboard. If the unused needles are in the way, just move them forward enough to get the strip behind them and then push them back firmly against it to hold it in place.

When you've knitted all of the needles, cut the yarn and carefully lift the body of the garment off the bed and flip it forward onto your lap. The hand-formed stitches are large enough to be latched off by pulling one stitch through the next. Secure the chain by pulling the yarn end through the last loop.

Wrapped in Ruffles Scarf

Two different bridging sequences have been combined in a single chart to produce ruffles at center and along both edges of this feminine scarf. Follow the chart carefully for the first few repeats to make sure you work each of the short row sections. A soft yarn (like the yarn I used for the model) will produce a gently draped ruffle; knitted with a firmer yarn, the ruffle will stand up crisply from the surface.

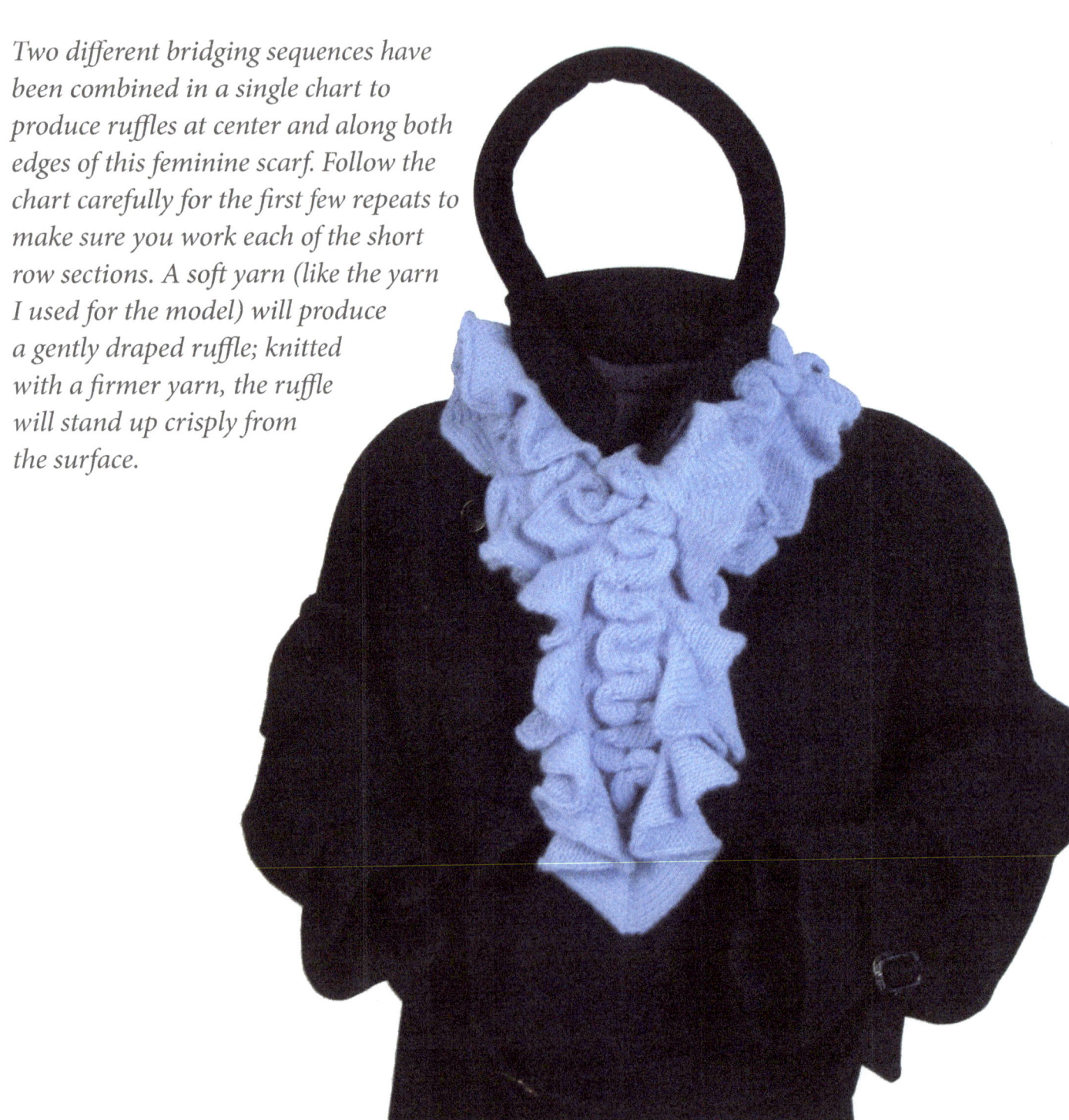

Size:
One size, 48" long x 7" wide

Yarn:
Cascade Yarn Indulgence (70% superfine alpaca, 30% angora with 123 yards/per 1.75 ounce/50 gram ball), 4 balls color #508

Stitch Size:
5 or to obtain gauge

Gauge:
22 stitches/28 rows = 4" in stockinette

Machine:
Model was knitted on the Studio/Silver Reed SK860, a 6.5mm midgauge machine, but this yarn is also suitable for a chunky/bulky machine.

Notes
(1) Work your swatch in stockinette to obtain gauge, but be aware that the swatch will not be accurate for the length of the scarf (only for the side ruffles). The open nops at center tend to elongate the fabric. The row gauge that determines the length of the scarf is closer to 4–4.25 rows per inch, so it takes only 28 repeats to reach 40–41", which is the length of the scarf prior to working the two end sections. (2) Although the chart shows only one repeat of sections A and C, the 20-row sequence for each of the edge ruffles should be worked twice. (3) The chart shows all the extra rows knitted for each of the ruffles, but accounts for only 6 knitted rows that actually contribute to the length of the scarf. Because there is extensive bridging to add extra rows, turn off the row counter and just advance it manually by 6 rows at the end of each repeat. At the same time, latch up stitches 7 and 8 at left and right. (4) The beginning point for each section (A, B, C, and D) will be easier to track if you mark the bed with a grease pencil, as indicated by the vertical red lines on the chart. (5) Make sure you keep weights under the working needles—especially when working the center of the scarf—to avoid dropping stitches.

Cast-on

Cast on 42 stitches with scrap yarn and knit some rows, ending COL. Change to the main yarn and knit 1 row to the right.

Section A *(repeat twice)*

Hold all needles except 20 and 21 right. Knit 1 row to left.

*Move needle 19 to UWP and knit 1 row to right. Move needle 18 to UWP and knit 1 row to left.

Continue moving 1 needle to UWP prior to knitting each row until 10 needles are in WP and COL.

Pass the yarn over needle 11 and under needle 10, then move needle 11 to UWP and knit 1 row.

Hold needle 12 and knit 1 row to left. Hold needle 13 and knit 1 row to right.

Continue holding 1 needle prior to knitting each row until only 1 needle is in WP and COR.**

Move needle 20 to UWP and knit the first row of the second repeat. Continue from * to **. Knit 1 row across all needles. COL.

Section B

Hold needles 5–21 right. Knit 1 row.

Hold needles 2 right–21 left. Knit 1 row.

Move needle 2 right to UWP and knit 1 row.

Move needle 1 right to UWP and knit 1 row.

Continue moving 1 needle at left to UWP prior to knitting each row until 8 needles are in WP and COL.

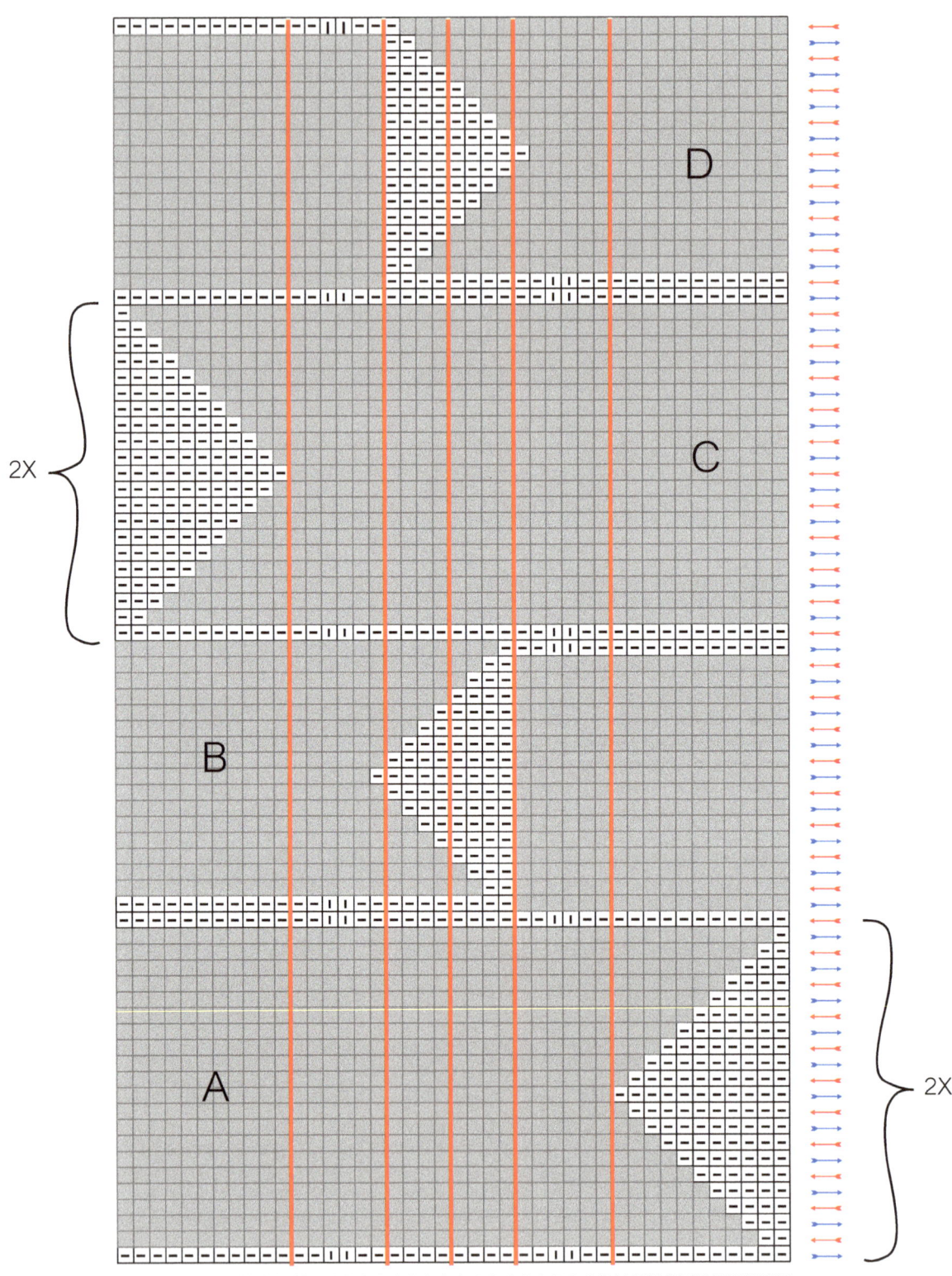

Pass the yarn over needle 5 left and under needle 6. Move needle 5 to UWP and knit 1 row. COR.

Move 1 needle at left to HP every row until 1 needle is in WP and COL. Return needles 5–21 right to UWP and knit 1 row. Knit 1 row across all needles. COL.

Section C *(repeat twice)*

Hold all needles except 20 and 21 left. Knit 1 row to right.

*Move needle 19 to UWP and knit 1 row to left. Move needle 18 to UWP and knit 1 row to right.

Continue moving 1 needle to UWP prior to knitting each row until 10 needles are in WP and COR.

Pass the yarn over needle 11 and under needle 10, then move needle 11 to UWP and knit 1 row.

Hold needle 11 and knit 1 row to right. Hold needle 12 and knit 1 row to left.

Continue holding 1 needle prior to knitting each row until only 1 needle is in WP and COL.**

Move needle 20 to UWP and knit the first row of the second repeat. Continue from * to **. Knit 1 row across all needles. COR

Section D

Hold needles 5–21 left. Knit 1 row.

Hold needles 2 left–21 right. Knit 1 row.

Move needle 2 left to UWP and knit 1 row.

Move needle 1 left to UWP and knit 1 row.

Continue moving 1 needle at right to UWP prior to knitting each row until 8 needles are in WP and COR.

Pass the yarn over needle 5 right and under needle 6. Move needle 5 to UWP and knit 1 row. COL.

Move 1 needle at right to HP every row until 1 needle is in WP and COR. Return needles 5–21 left to UWP and knit 1 row. Knit 1 row across all needles. COR.

Scarf Ends

COR, set to hold needles in HP. Hold all needles to the left of center zero. *Knit 1 row and manually wrap. Knit 1 row. COR.

Hold 1 needle at left every row until only 1 needle remains in WP and COR.**

Knit 1 row across *all* needles.

Hold all needles to right of zero and repeat from * to **. Return all needles to left of zero to UWP and knit 1 row to right. Cut the main yarn, leaving a long tail for finishing. Scrap off all 42 stitches.

Fold back the scrap knitting on the other end of the scarf and rehang the live stitches of the scarf over 41 needles and repeat the above directions. (When the work is turned upside down, there is always one fewer stitch.)

Finishing

Press *only* the scrap knitting at each end of the scarf. On one end of the scarf, fold back the scrap knitting and fold that end of the scarf in half so that the stitches are paired. Use the long tail of the main yarn to graft the live stitches together . (See page 164.) Repeat the grafting at the other end of the scarf. Work in all yarn tails. Wash the finished scarf and lay it flat to dry. Lightly steam each of the ruffles to shape.

Horizontal-Cable Pullover

This modified drop-shoulder pullover features 4x4 ribs that merge into a dramatic horizontal braided cable. The neckband is bound off with the "gourmet bind off," a hand-sewn method that matches the ribs' cast-on edges and should be part of every knitter's repertoire of finishing techniques.

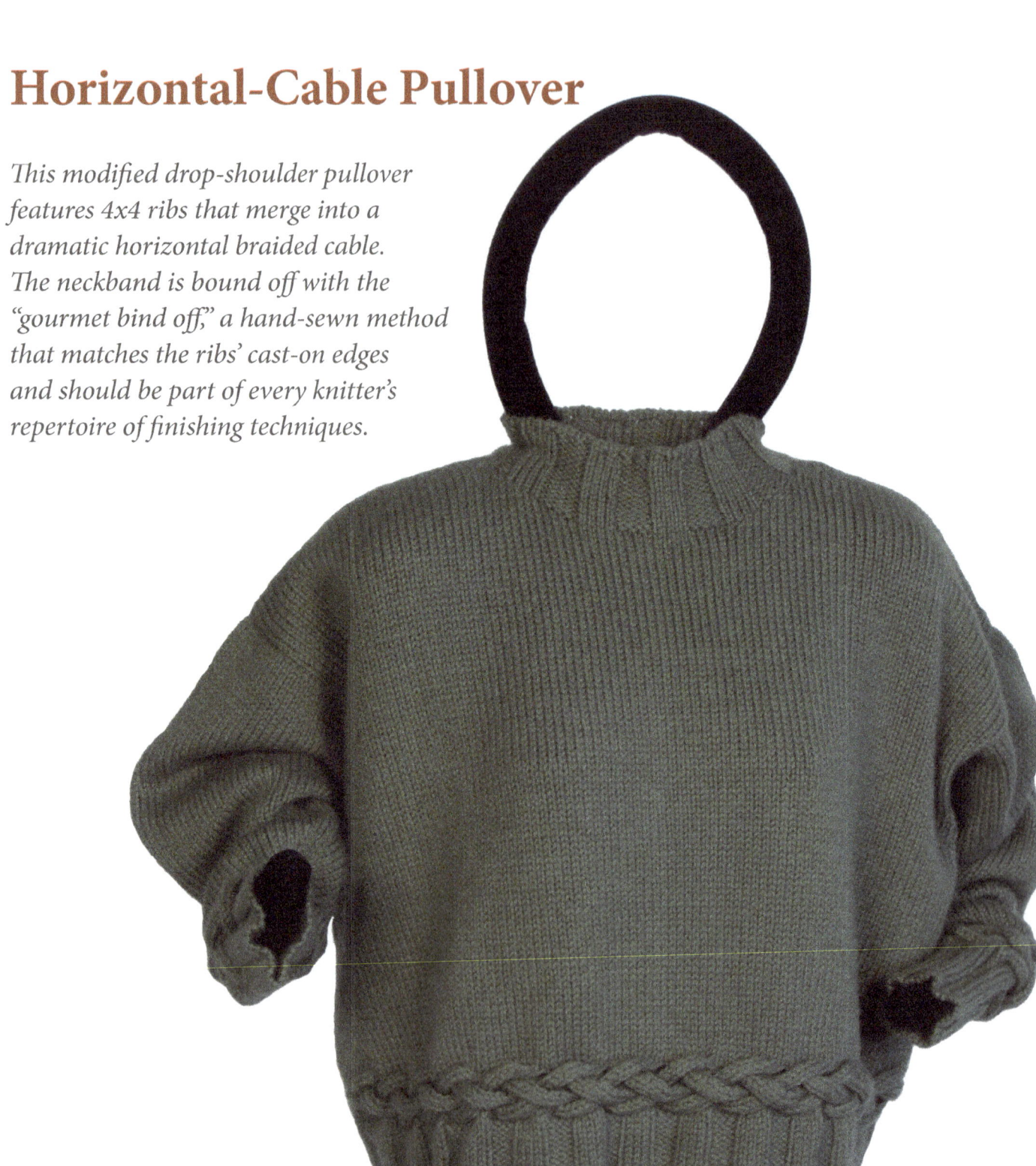

Sizes:
Women's S (M, L, XL, XXL, XXXL) with finished chest measurement 39 (42.5, 45.5, 49, 52, 55)" including 4–6" of ease to ensure a boxy, straight fit (Garment is shown in size XL.)

Yarn:
Nashua Handknits Julia (50% wool, 25% alpaca, 25% mohair) with 93 yards/85 meters per 1.75 ounce/50 gram skein), 11 (12, 12, 13, 14, 15) skeins color NHJ.0115 (Sage)

Stitch Size:
6/6 (ribs); 8 or to obtain gauge (body)

Gauge:
Ribs: 5 rows = 1"
Stockinette: 20 stitches/27 rows = 4"

Machine:
Model garment was knitted on the Studio/Silver Reed SK860, a 6.5mm midgauge machine; the yarn is suitable for a chunky/bulky machine, but there will not be enough needles for the four largest sizes. Ribber is optional. Ribs can be worked by hand or by reforming stitches with a latch tool.

Notes
(1) The 4x4x4 cables require crossing groups of 4 stitches. To do this, you will need to hold two 2-prong tools in each hand, which is much easier than it sounds. (See page 56.) (2) If knitting the ribs on the machine, cast on with scrap yarn. Hang the comb and weights and knit several rows, ending with 2 circular rows. Change to the main yarn, repeat the cast-on sequence, and then knit the rib. This method produces a better cast-on edge because the comb does not stretch out the first rows. (3) The cables require a lot of stitch transfers, and the ribber bed is apt to be in the way. I recommend removing the ribber after the stitches have been transferred to the main bed. (4) Always start the cable sections with a full skein to avoid running out of yarn midrow, where there are few places to hide the ends. (5) The specific scrapping-off directions are crucial to working the hand-sewn bind-off, even if you are hand-knitting the ribs.

Back/Front

With scrap yarn, cast on for 1x1 rib over 97 (105, 113, 121, 129, 137) needles. Hang comb and weights, knit some rows, and end with 2 circular rows. COR. Change to the main yarn and knit 1 row with stitch size R/R (the smallest size). Set both carriages for circular and stitch size 0/0 and knit 2 rows. Set both carriages to knit and knit 1 row with stitch size 1/1. Transfer stitches from one bed to the other for 4x4 rib, *beginning and ending with 3 stitches on the main bed and increasing 1 stitch at left*. This transfer ensures that the 4x4 rib meets properly at the seams, allowing 1 full stitch for seaming. 98 (106, 114, 122, 130, 138) stitches.

RC 000. Work the following rows increasing stitch size every row until stitch size is 6/6 (in other words, work 1 row each with stitch size 1/1, 2/2, 3/3, 4/4, 5/5, 6/6.) Continue with stitch size 6/6 to RC 20.

Transfer all stitches to the main bed. Remove ribber bed.

If hand-knitting the ribs:
Work 4x4 rib for 4" and then, because the wrong side of the garment will face you on the machine, transfer the stitches to the main bed so that there are 3 purl stitches at each edge.

If latching up the ribs:
Cast on 98 (106, 114, 122, 130, 138) stitches with scrap yarn. Change to main yarn and, with stitch size 4, knit approximately 20 rows. Skip the first 3 stitches at right, but then reform (latch up) every other group of 4 stitches. When the sweater is complete, the lower edge will be finished with the same bind-off method used at the neck edge.

RC 000. With stitch size 8, knit to RC 6 to begin horizontal cable. (See page 57.) When cable is complete, set RC 000 and work straight to RC 40 (40, 40, 40, 48, 54). RC 000. Bind off 3 stitches at the beginning of the next 2 rows, then 2 stitches at the beginning of the following 2 rows. Make a full-fashion

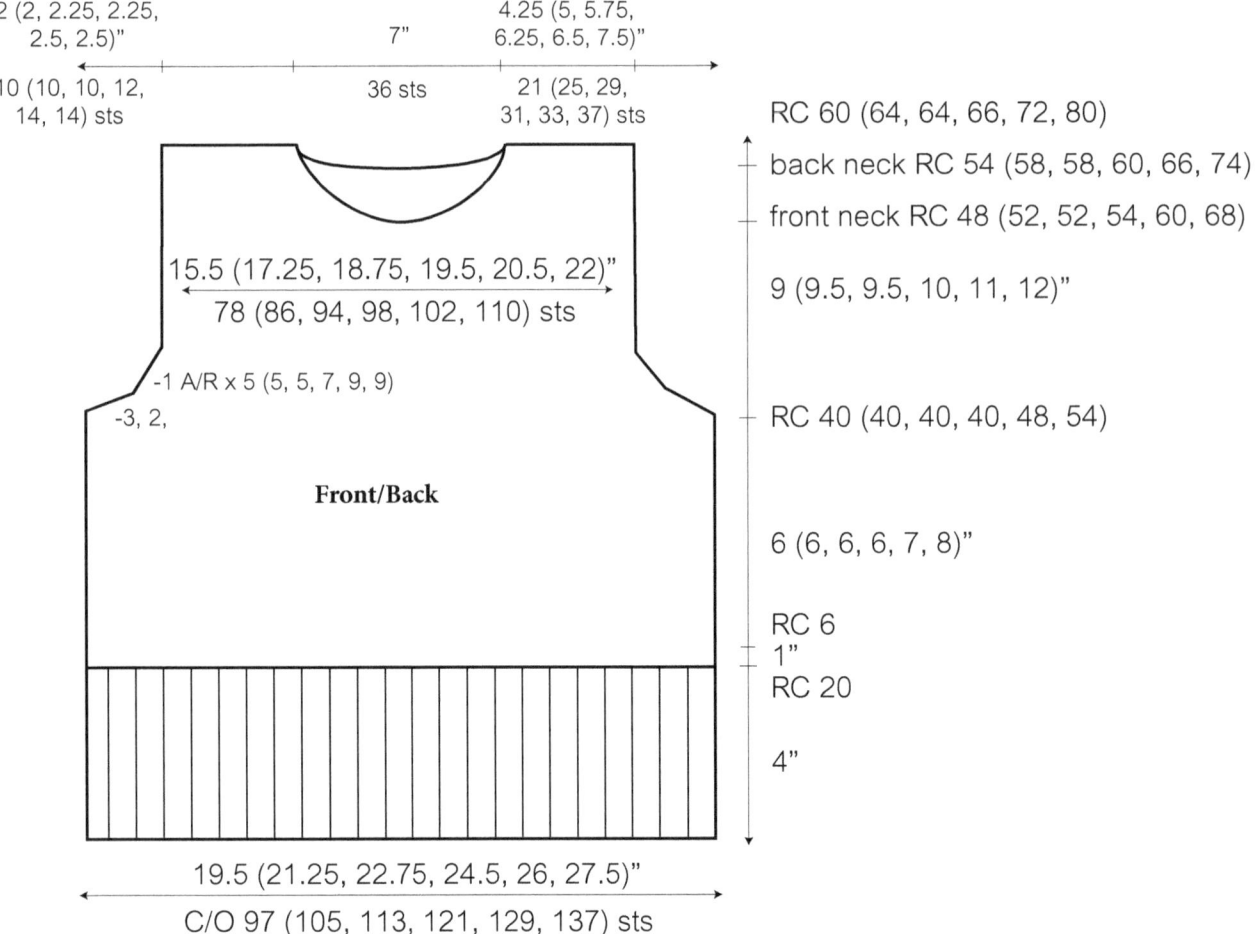

decrease at each edge, every other row 5 (5, 5, 7, 9, 9) times. 78 (86, 94, 98, 102, 110) stitches remain.

For back:
Work to RC 54 (58, 58, 60, 66, 74), ending COR, set to hold needles in HP. Hold the center 30 needles and all needles to the left of them. *KWK. Hold 1 needle at the neck edge and KWK three times. Scrap off the remaining 21 (25, 29, 31, 33, 37) shoulder stitches and place the empty needles in NWP.** Move the carriage to the left end of the bed. Move all needles to the left of 15 left into UWP and repeat * to **. With the main yarn, knit row across remaining 36 needles and then scrap off.

For front:
Work to RC 48 (52, 52, 54, 60, 68), ending COR, set to hold needles in HP. Hold the center 20 needles and all needles to the left of them. *KWK. Whenever COR, hold needles at the neck edge as follows: Hold 2 needles three times, then 1 needle twice. At RC 60 (64, 64, 66, 72, 80), scrap off the remaining 21 (25, 29, 31, 33, 37) shoulder stitches and place the empty needles in NWP.** Move the carriage to the left end of the bed. Move all needles to the left of 10 left into UWP and repeat * to **. Before scrapping off the neck stitches, pick up 1 more stitch at each neckline edge and then scrap off all 38 stitches.

Horizontal-Cable Pullover

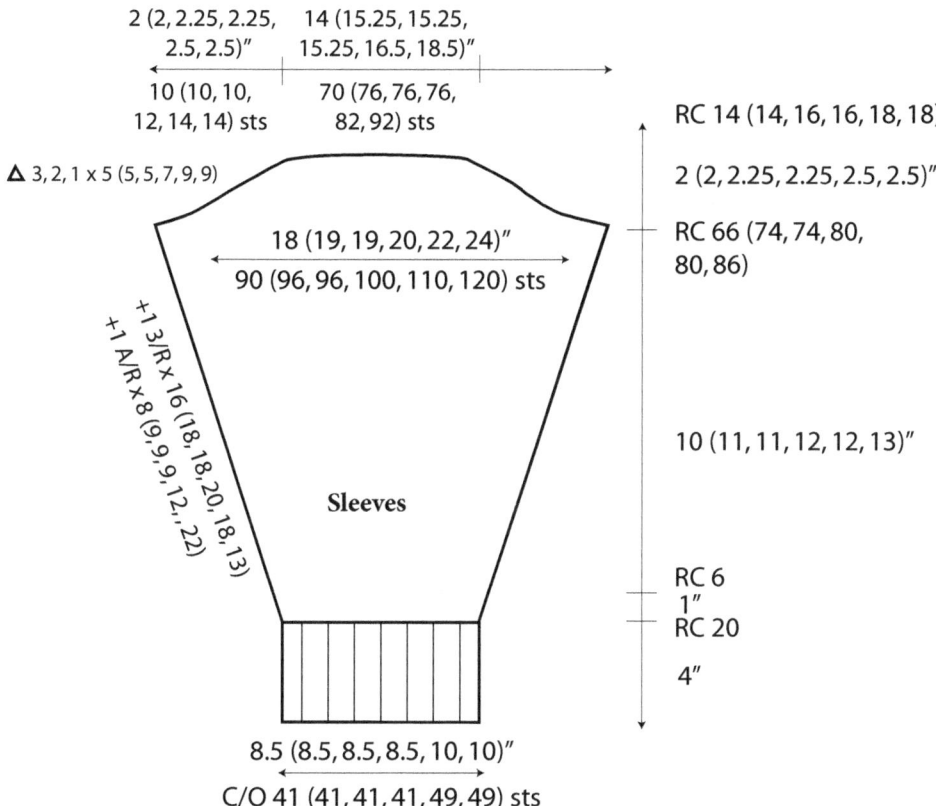

Sleeves

With scrap yarn, cast on 41 (41, 41, 41, 49, 49) stitches and work the ribbing as for the front/back, increasing 1 stitch at left for 4x4 rib. Work 6 rows following rib and then work the horizontal cable.

RC 000. Work to RC 66 (74, 74, 80, 80, 86), increasing 1 stitch at each end of every other row 8 (9, 9, 9, 12, 22) times, then at the end of every third row 16 (18, 18, 20, 18, 13) times. 90 (96, 96, 100, 110, 120) stitches.

To shape sleeve head:
RC 000. COR, set to hold needles in HP. On the side opposite the carriage, hold and then KWK at each side 3 needles once, 2 needles once, 1 needle 5 (5, 5, 7, 9, 9) times: 10 (10, 10, 12, 14, 14) stitches held at each side. COR.

Put all needles at the left end of the bed into UWP and knit 1 row. Return needles at right to UWP and knit 1 row. Tag the center of the sleeve head. Scrap off all 90 (96, 96, 100, 110, 120) stitches.

Finishing

Work in all yarn tails and block garment pieces. Ribs are bound off by hand after all other finishing.

If working ribs on the machine:
Join 1 shoulder seam and, with the wrong side facing you, rehang the neck edge over 74 needles, doubling stitches at the seam. Trans-

Triple Crossed Horizontal Cable

Visually, these 4 x 4 cables grow out of the ribs below even though there are 6 rows of stockinette between them. (Chart at right shows only 4 rows of stockinette, but the directions do call for 6.)

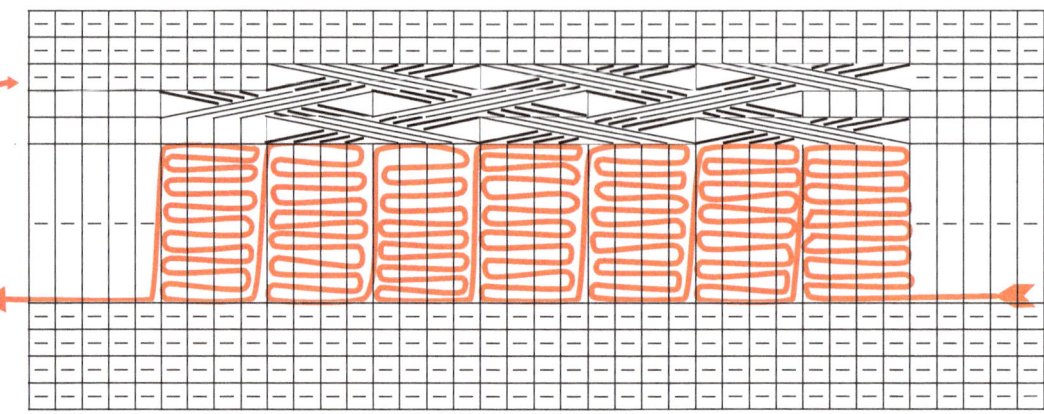

fer stitches to the ribber for 4x4 rib, beginning and ending with 3 stitches on the main bed. Work 14 rows with stitch size 6/6. Transfer stitches for 1x1 rib and work 2 rows. Transfer all stitches to the main bed, pulling needles to HP as you deposit the ribber stitches so that every other needle is in HP. Cut the main yarn, leaving a tail twice as long as the width of the knitting. Thread carriage with scrap yarn. Set the carriage to slip all needles in WP and to knit all needles in HP. Knit 1 row. Set carriage to knit all needles, work 6–8 rows, and then bind off the scrap knitting.

If latching up the ribs:
Rehang as in directions above for working ribs on the machine. Work 14 rows 4x4 rib and 2 rows 1x1 rib with stitch size 4. Bring every other needle to HP and scrap off as in directions above.

To hand-knit ribs:
Join both shoulder seams and work the neck ribbing on circular or double-pointed needles, doubling stitches at each shoulder so that the 4x4 rib is continuous. Work 3" of 4x4 rib, followed by 2 rounds of 1x1 rib. With scrap yarn, work 1 round of slip 1, knit 1. Then work 6 rounds of stockinette and bind off loosely.

Join the second shoulder seam.

To join both sleeves to the garment:
(See page 162.) With the right side of the garment facing you, and working 1 full stitch from the edge, hang one armhole over 90 (96, 96, 100, 110, 120) needles so that the shoulder seam is at the center zero. Bring the needles to HP. With the wrong side of the sleeve facing you, fold back the scrap knitting and hang the sleeve stitches into the hooks of the same needles. Carefully push the needles back to WP so that the sleeve stitches are pulled through the edge of the garment. Bind off loosely.

Use mattress stitch [see page 163] to hand-join the sleeve and side seams. Bind off ribs using the hand sewn bind off that follows.

Hand-Sewn Bind-Off

I usually work this hand-sewn, grafted bind-off after completing all the seams to produce a smooth, continuous finish that perfectly matches the circular cast-on edge. Machine knit, hand knit and latched-up bands can be bound off like this. The key to success is having scrapped off correctly (knit 1/slip 1) so that when the scrap is folded back, the stitches present themselves in two rows. The upper and lower rows of stitches alternate - just like rib does.

The first stitch of every upper or lower sequence is always worked through the same stitch the needle last exited in the previous sequence in that row. Think "in the old and out the new" as you work. The needle will always follow a down, then up path as you work the upper row of stitches (so the yarn traces a "U" shape or a smile); the "down" stitch will be through the last previously worked stitch in that row. The lower stitching path will always be up then down (tracing an upside down "U" or a frown); the "up" stitch is taken through the last previously worked stitch in that row. *Every stitch is worked twice.*

Tighten each stitch just enough to absorb any extra slack so that the bind off does not narrow the edge of the garment. Try on the sweater to be sure your head fits through the neck opening. (If it doesn't, carefully rip out the bind off and do it again – looser.) Then remove the scrap knitting.

The Hand-Sewn, "Gourmet", Bind Off

Step 1. Press the scrap knitting so that it lies flat and then fold it back to expose the main stitches (which will neatly divide into two rows because the first row of scrap was worked slip 1, knit 1.) Some of the stitches at right have already been bound off in the photograph below.

Step 2. To work the upper row, insert the needle *down* through the last stitch worked in the upper row. It is to the slight right of the stitch that the yarn is exiting in the lower row.

Step 3. Then insert the needle *up* through the next upper row stitch. This completes one upturned smile in the top row.

Step 4. Draw the yarn through to complete this "U" or smile path.

Step 5. Carry the yarn forward to work the lower row of stitches. Insert the needle *up* through the last stitch you worked on the lower row. It will be to the slight right of the stitch the needle just exited in the top row.

Step 6. Then insert the needle *down* through the next lower stitch. This completes the upside down "U".

Step 7. Draw the yarn through. Repeat steps 2 - 6 around the entire edge, always working the first stitch of each sequence through the last stitch of the previous sequence so that each stitch is worked twice. When you work the last stitch, continue to work through the first stitch to complete the edge.

Purple Posies Tote

Simple boxed construction turns this felted fabric into a sturdy tote bag. Mine is fully lined with a zippered compartment, purchased handles, and metal "feet," but you can vary the finishing details to suit your skill level and taste. Handpainted yarn adds interest to the background fabric, as does a variety of colors for the posies. You might also want to add beads to the centers of the posies as shown on page 80.

Size:
One size, approximately 10" high by 15" wide (size will vary depending on bulk of felting)

Yarn:
Brown Sheep's Lanaloft (100% wool with 160 yards/146 meters per 3.5 ounce/100 gram skein), 4 skeins #LL111W (Purple Iris Handpaint) for main color (MC) and 1 skein each #LL84W (Sailboat Blue), #LL97W (Violet Shimmer), and #LL87W (Catamaran Seas) for contrast colors (CC1, CC2, CC3). To work all of the flowers with one color, you will need 2 skeins of that color.

Notions:
Short circular hand-knitting needle or cable needle
1 yard heavyweight, sew-in interfacing or horsehair
Pair of purse handles
4 metal purse feet or large buttons
1 yard lining fabric
Craft store plastic for stiffening bottom of bag, approximately 4 x 15". Magnetic purse snaps, zippers, or other notions as required for individual finishing needs

Stitch Size:
10

Gauge:
Approximately 16 stitches and 24 rows = 4"; 20 stitches and 32 rows = 4" after felting

Machine:
Model was knitted on the Studio/Silver Reed SK860, a 6.5mm midgauge machine, but this yarn is also suitable for a 9mm chunky/bulky machine.

Notes
(1) Bridging is used to work the three-dimensional flowers, as explained on page 81. (2) If the exact size of the purse is not crucial, you don't need to knit a gauge swatch to match the given gauge (and there is always some variation after felting). I would, however, recommend working a swatch to understand the method I have used to create the single-row stripes behind each flower. (3) The schematic shows the approximate measurements after felting and gives continuous row counts for the length of the piece. You may find it easier to keep track by resetting the row counter after each flower border. The flowers take 9 rows, with 9 stitches between each flower; there are 16 rows between borders. (4) As usual, you will need to turn off the row counter for all bridged rows. It should also be off for the "dead passes" between petal rows, so it actually remains off for each flower. The dead passes enable you to knit the one-row-per-color striped background behind the flowers. (5) Use a grease pencil to mark the flower placement on the bed. (6) This fabric is easiest to knit with even weight, so I poked a ribber comb through the scrap knitting and hung weights from it. If you don't have a ribber comb, hang individual weights across the width of the fabric. (7) Thread the main color through the right side of the tension mast and the contrast colors through the left. (8) I wanted the flowers to lie flat and open against the surface of the bag so I tacked them down after felting the bag and steaming the individual petals. (9) The rows of crochet cast-on provide edges that help you fold the bag during assembly and also help to define the bag's shape.

Cast-on

With scrap yarn, cast on 77 stitches and knit some rows, ending COR. Cut the scrap yarn and set RC 000. Hang weights. Bring all of the needles to HP and, beginning at left, work a loose row of crochet cast-on over the shafts of the needles, catching the last loop on the right-end needle. Push the chain back against the bed, thread the carriage, and knit 15 rows, ending COL.

Unthread the carriage and bring all needles to HP, keeping the stitches in the hooks of the needles as much as possible. Bring the next 10 empty needles at right to HP. Work a loose row of chain cast-on behind the fabric, over the shafts of the needles, from left to right, continuing to cast on to the 10 additional needles at right. Knit 1 row from right to left. You can free-pass the empty carriage to the right and try to knit them back with the carriage, but this is pretty heavy work for any machine. Instead of straining the carriage, I hand-knitted each stitch back to WP, working from right to left. Bring 10 empty needles into WP at left and work crochet cast-on across them before rethreading the carriage.

132 Part Two

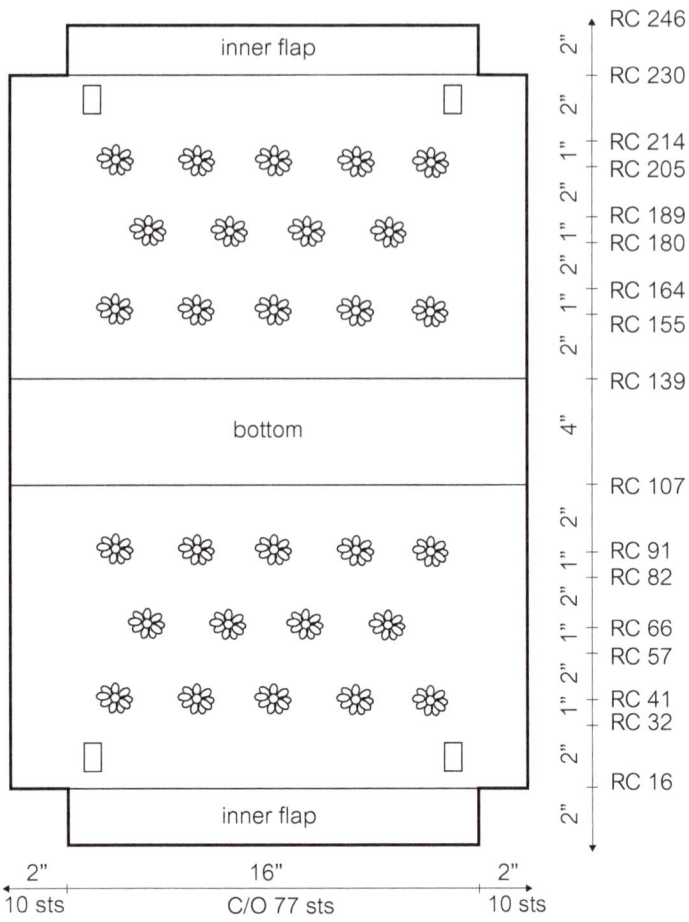

Work to RC 32, bringing the 10 needles at each end to HP, to let the carriage knit them back for the first few rows until there is enough fabric to hang weights.

At RC 32, with COR, unthread the MC, but do not cut it. Rethread the carriage with CC1 and follow the stitch chart below and the bridging directions in the charts on the next page to position the petals. Turn off the RC before bridging the first row of petals. Remember, the red and blue designations in those charts are for the right and left side placements of petals, not the actual color of the petals you are knitting.

RC 41. Knit to RC 107, *at the same time* working flower borders at RC 57 and RC 82.

At RC 107, work 1 row of crochet cast-on behind the fabric as before. Knit to RC 139 and repeat the crochet cast-on.

Knit to RC 230 *at the same time* working flower borders at RC 155, RC 180, and RC 205.

At RC 230, with latch tool, bind off the first 10 stitches on the carriage side, then work the chain cast-on behind the fabric, stopping

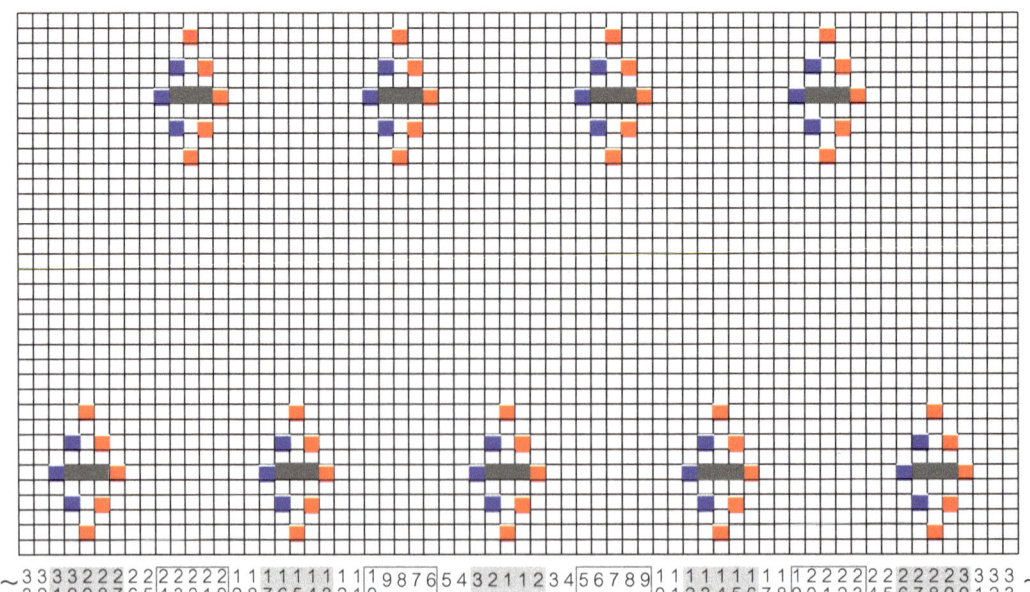

The numbers at the bottom of this chart are boxed or shaded to indicate which needles are used for each group of flowers, which alternate placement on the fabric. Use a grease pencil to mark the bed to simplify counting. The center of each flower is worked as a 3-stitch popcorn.

short of the last 10 needles. Rethread the carriage, push the last 10 needles to UWP, and knit. With latch tool, bind off the first 10 needles on the carriage side and then manually knit the remaining 77 needles back to WP.

Knit to RC 246. Bind off all stitches with latch tool.

One-Row Stripes
The chart below right and these directions describe the method used to work the one-row-per-color striped background and the flower petals at the same time.

At the end of the first bridged row, the carriage is on the left. Unthread the CC, tuck it under the left end of the bed, and free-pass the carriage to the right. Rethread the MC and knit 1 row to the left.

Unthread the MC and pass it in front of the knitting, and tuck it under the right end of the bed. Rethread the CC and bridge the next row of the chart from the left. Free-pass the carriage to the left. Unthread the CC, pass it in front of the fabric, and hook it on the left end of the bed. Rethread with the MC and work 1 row to the right.

Rethread with the CC and bridge the next row of the flower from right to left. Free-pass the carriage to the right and rethread with MC to knit the next row.

Rethread with CC to bridge the next row from left to right. Free-pass the carriage back to the left and rethread with the MC to knit the next row.

Rethread with CC and bridge the last petals from right to left. Free-pass the carriage to the right to rethread with the MC.

Turn on the row counter and advance it by 9 rows.

Bridging from left to right:

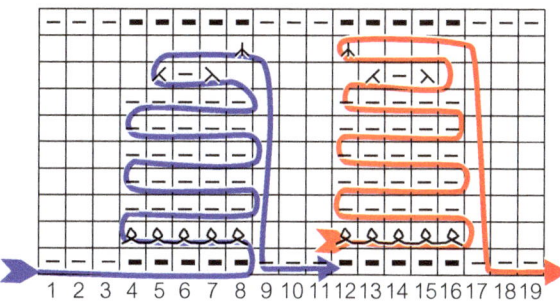

Bridging from right to left:

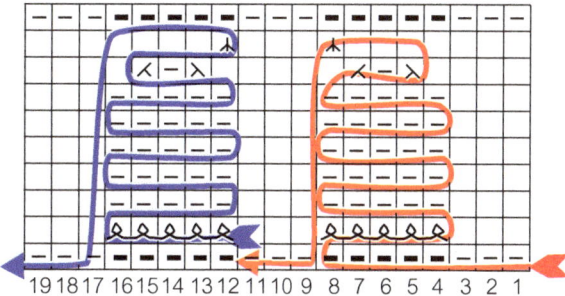

The chart on the preceding page shows the placement of the red (right) and blue (left) petals. This diagram indicates the bridging paths for each of them as worked from the left or the right.

Main color and contrast color alternation for working one-row stripes

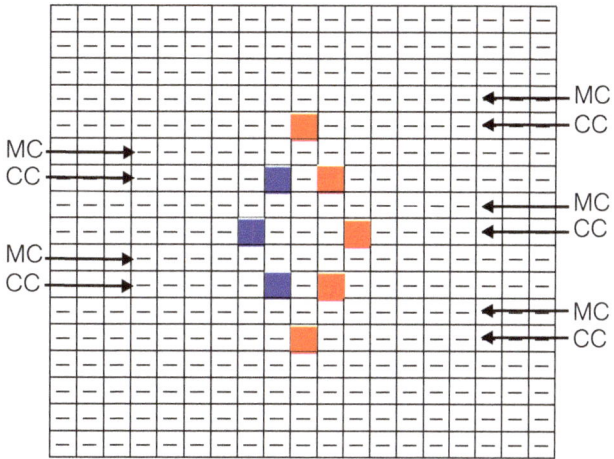

Finishing

Work in all yarn tails and remove scrap knitting.

For optional lining: Measure the felted bag flat (excluding inner flaps) and cut one piece from lining fabric adding ½" to all edges. Pockets and dividers may be added at this point. Fold in half, right sides together; stitch each side using 5/8" seam allowances. Fold under top edges 5/8" and press.

On knit bag: with mattress stitch, [see page 163] invisibly sew the two side seams, taking care to match the stripes.

Knit tabs for anchoring the straps or handles, spacing them evenly on each side of the bag. With the right side of the fabric facing you and the top of the bag facing the bed, pick up 5 stitches about 1" from the row of chaining at the top edge of bag (not from the end of the inner flap). Knit 10 rows and bind off loosely. Repeat for each tab.

Form a boxlike base for the bag by lining up the side seams and the centerline of the bottom. The inner flaps define the width of the front and back of the bag. The sides do not have flaps. Machine- or hand-stitch securely across the triangle that forms at the bottom of each side as you complete the fold, as shown in the drawing below. On the inside of the bag, tack the triangle up against the side seam. If you want to tack the flowers open, do so now.

Reinforce the strap tabs by turning them up toward the top of the bag and hand-stitching securely across each one, close to the fold. Attach the straps, turning down the tabs and sewing them securely in place. Some sewing machines may not be able to sew through such thick fabric, so you will probably have to stitch by hand.

Cut individual pieces of interfacing for all four sides of the bag ½-1" smaller than the actual sides and tack them in place, as indicated by the shaded areas in the drawing below. (This adds stiffness, but leaves the softer knit look for a stiffer box look take the interfacing all the way to each edge.) Attach the feet at the four corners of the bag bottom.

Insert a piece of heavy plastic into the bottom of the bag. For mine, I actually used a worn-out plastic kitchen cutting mat. In addition to the interfacing, I cut a piece of craft store plastic for each side panel of the bag, punched a few holes, and then sewed them in place so the bag could stand up by itself. Check your local big-box craft store for solid plastic sheets or plastic mesh.

Optional lining: Measure and stitch a triangle at each side the same width and depth as the knit bag. Insert the lining into the purse with wrong sides together, lining up side seams and top edges (before flaps). Stitch into place around the top edges.

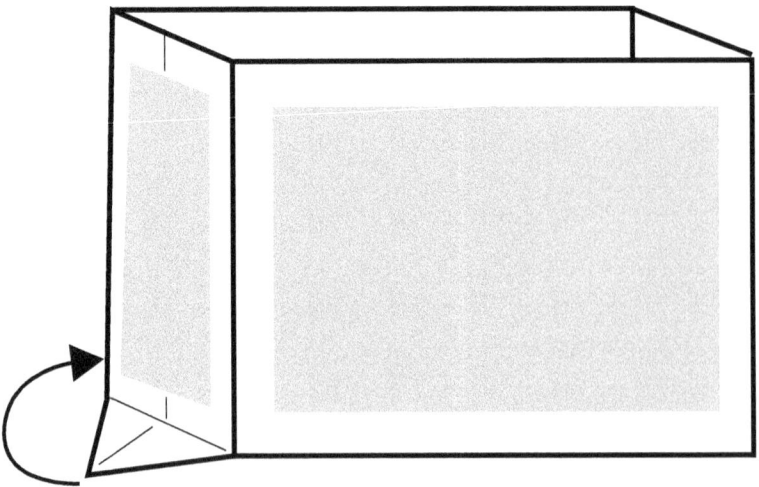

Once you have stitched the side seams of the bag (and later the lining), match the side seam to the centerline of the bottom of the bag to form a triangle as shown at left. Stitch across the base of the triangle to square off the ends of the bag and then tack the triangle to the side seam as indicated by the arrow. The shaded areas represent the placement of interfacing and/or plastic to stiffen the shape.

Felting 101
Soak the bag in a sink, in the hottest water you can—you might even want to boil some water on the stove and add it to the water in the sink. Soak the bag for 10–15 minutes and then put it into the washing machine with a couple of pairs of blue jeans (towels will leave fuzz that is impossible to remove). Run the machine through a hot wash cycle. (I allowed my bag to stay in the washer through the entire cycle because I have a front-loading washer. People with top loaders often remove their felting before the whole cycle is complete to prevent over working and possibly creasing the fabric).) If the bag has not felted enough, run it through another cycle or put it in the dryer for a while. Either way, keep a close watch on the progress, because the bag could end up felting more than you want it to. Fold a towel and insert it inside to help shape the bag as it finishes air-drying.

Assemble the lining with pockets or dividers as desired. Insert the lining into the purse with the wrong sides together. Turn the inner flaps to the inside (they fold easily along the crochet cast on ridge) and sew them in place. If you are using magnetic purse snaps, apply them to the lining before inserting the lining into the bag.

If you do not sew, it would be worth enlisting a friend who does or finding a local seamstress to construct a lining. It will help the bag hold its shape — and conceal the seams and interfacing on the inside.

Hugs and Kisses Shawl

Lots of special details give this shawl a better-than-average fit and great eye appeal. Hugs and Kisses cables encircle the shawl, while simple cables worked right on the edges create an automatic, non-roll finish. Short row darts shape a shoulder hugging fit, while a "sleeve" on the left front provides secure closure.

Sizes:
One size to fit sizes S to L, 17" wide, 70" long at neck edge, and approximately 88" long at outer edge (For extra-small or extra-large sizes, the width can easily be increased/decreased by adding/subtracting stitches between the cables and darts. Length, which affects the width across the back, can also be changed by adding/subtracting rows before, between, and after the darts. In either case, you need to renumber stitches and rows.)

Yarn:
Berroco Ultra Alpaca (50% wool, 50% Peruvian alpaca with 215 yards/198 meters per 3.5 ounce/100 gram skein), 5 skeins color #6299 (Lichen Mix)

Stitch Size:
8 or to obtain gauge

Gauge:
19 stitches/25 rows = 4" in stockinette

Machine:
Model garment was knitted on the Studio/Silver Reed SK860, a 6.5mm midgauge machine, but this yarn is also suitable for a 9mm chunky/bulky machine. Ribber is optional for the knit stitches that divide the cables and run along the right edge. (These knit stitches in the model garment were latched up to retain better visibility and easier maneuverability of cable crossings, but the shawl would be faster to knit double-bed.)

Notes
(1) Bridging is used to add 2 extra rows to each of the cable crossings. (See page 33.) The cable chart on page 139 indicates exactly which rows are bridged for the entire length of the shawl. I have also included a chart (page 140) showing the short rows *and* the bridging for the first of the 3 darts. I recommend copying this chart and adding the row counts for the following 2 darts. Numbered charts like these help keep me from incorrectly crossing cables or losing track of the short rows. (2) Use a grease pencil to mark the location of the cables at left and the reformed (latched-up) stitches at right. (3) If you are latching up the knit stitches at each border, do so every 12 rows—both to make the process easier to manage and to help you catch a mistake before you have progressed too far. (4) Before each bridged row, turn off the row counter and set the carriage to hold needles in HP. At the end of the bridged row, turn on the row counter, advance it by 1, and set the carriage to knit needles back from HP. (5) The leftmost cable is worked on needles 35–40 left, with no plain stitches at the edge, which produces a lovely, stable edging that won't roll.

Knitting Directions

Pre-knit the "sleeve" lining: With scrap yarn, cast on 80 stitches and knit some rows. Change to the main yarn, knit 36 rows, and then scrap off. Press the scrap knitting flat for easier handling.

With scrap, cast on 80 stitches and knit some rows, ending COR. Change to the main yarn, set RC 000, and knit stockinette to RC 100, following the bridged cable chart on page 139 and latching up stitches 34, 33, 20, 19, 12 and 11 at left and stitches 29, 30, 33, 34, 37 and 38 at right every 12 rows or as convenient.

With the wrong side facing you, fold back the scrap knitting on one end of the sleeve lining. Pick up the live stitches, hanging 1 on each needle. There are now 2 stitches on every needle—the front of the shawl and the lining stitches together. Bring all of the needles to HP and let the carriage knit them back to WP on the next row. (If you are using a ribber, you will need to transfer the ribber stitches to the main bed before hanging the sleeve-lining stitches and then move the doubled stitches back to the ribber before proceeding.)

Continue cable pattern and latching up stitches to RC 138. Fold back the scrap knitting on the second end of the sleeve lining and hang the live stitches on the needles as before. (See ribber note in the previous paragraph.)

Work to RC 221 to begin shaping the first dart with COL (at the same time continuing the cable pattern). Set the carriage to hold needles in HP. The chart on page 140 details the placement of the bridged rows and the short-row sequence that decreases (10 times), then increases (10 times), 5 stitches every alternate row. There are 20 steps per gore.

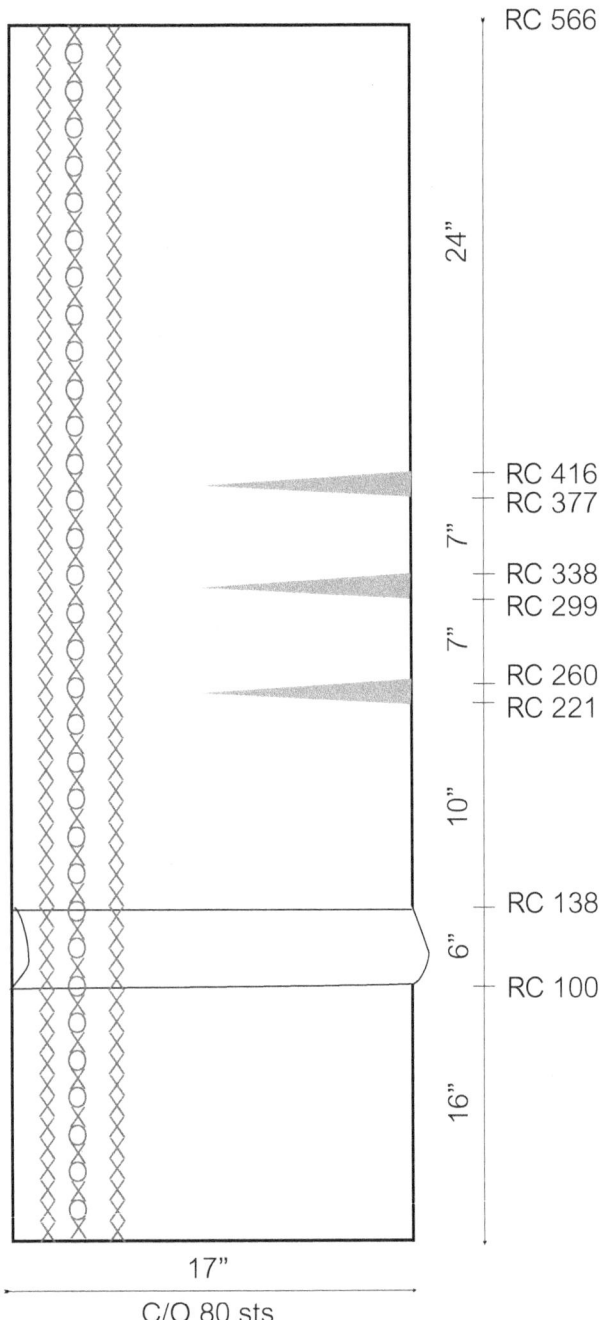

Hugs and Kisses and right cross cables run the length of the left side of the shawl. Short row darts are worked on the right to refine the fit over the shoulders.

Short Row Darts
Hold needles 36–40 right. Knit, wrap, and knit back (KWK). RC 223.
Hold needles 31–35. Knit. RC 224.
Turn off the row counter and bridge the next row, as follows:
Hold needles 16–40 left. Knit. COL.
Hold needles 12 left–30 right. Knit. COR.
Move needles 16–26 left to UWP and knit. COL.
Hold needles 23–16 left. Knit. COR.
Move needles 27–29 left to UWP and knit. COL.
Hold needles 26–16 left. Knit. COR.
Move needles 30–37 left to UWP and knit. COL.
Hold needles 27–34 left. Knit. COR.
Move needles 38–40 left to UWP and knit. COL.
Cross the cables.

Resume the short-row sequence, as follows:
Leave needles 26–40 right in HP. KWK.
Hold needles 21–25 right. KWK.
Hold needles 16–20. Knit.
Repeat the bridging sequence as before and then continue short-row shaping through RC 243, where you will begin moving needles back from HP to UWP. At RC 260, latch up stitches.

Shape the second dart at RC 299 and the third dart at RC 377. At RC 566, scrap off all 80 stitches.

Finishing

Block the shawl, allowing the darts to shape the curve. The back neck will gather easily along a blocking wire or a length of ravel cord. Press the scrap knitting at each end for easier handling. Remove the scrap from the sleeve lining, checking as you do so to be sure that all stitches have been picked up.

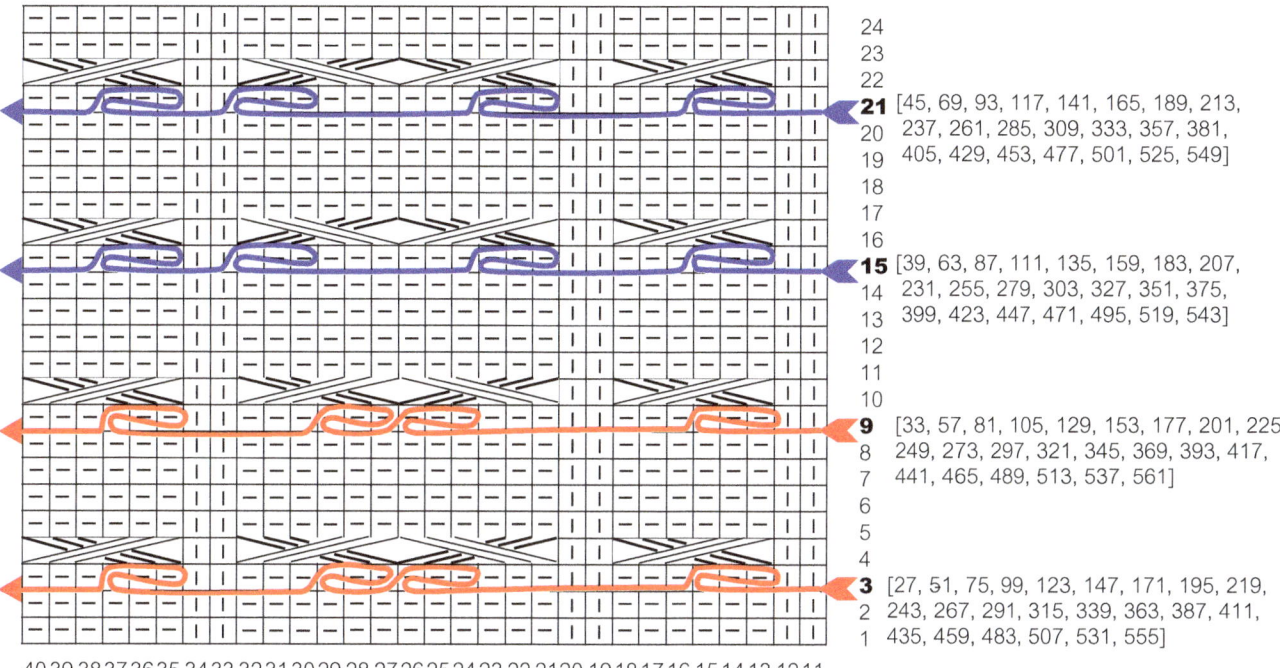

Right cross cables flank hugs and kisses cables. The red arrows indicate the bridging sequence when the center cables cross away from each other; the blue when they cross towards each other. Row numbers at right act as a guide to correct bridging and crossing for the length of the shawl.

For the lower bands:
Begin working the left front band on the right end of the bed, and the right front band on the left end.

With the wrong side of the left front facing you, pick up the 6 edge cable stitches and hang them at the right end of the bed. Begin COR. (Knit 2 rows then pick up the next live stitch from the scrap and hang on the last needle at left) twice.

Pick up 1 live stitch and hang it on the left needle. Bridge the cable: hold the 3 left needles, knit 2 rows on the remaining 3 needles, then knit 1 row across all 6 needles. Cross the cable using one 3-prong tool to move the 3 stitches at right to the next 3 empty needles at left. The tool will pass behind the bridged stitches, and the work will slowly progress across the bed to the left each time a cable is crossed. Continue picking up 1 live stitch every row and bridging every sixth row and crossing the cable until the entire edge has been worked. Reduce the stitches to 4, then 2 over the last 2 rows, and then bind off the remaining stitches.

For the neckband:
The neckband is shaped like a wide shawl collar, trimmed with the same knitted-on cable band used for the lower edges, which is turned to the outside and sewn in place. The band is not centered; it extends 24 stitches further along the left front edge to trim the upper layer of the sleeve.

With the wrong side facing you, rehang the back neck (the edge between the first and last dart) over 60 needles. Knit 1 row and then scrap off. Reduce these 60 stitches to 30 by rehanging 2 stitches on every needle. Knit 1 row, cut the main yarn, and scrap off. Turn the work over so that the right side is facing you and hang the neck stitches on needles 3 left–27 right.

140 Part Two

This chart details the short rows and the bridging for shaping the first of three darts. Copy this chart and supply the row numbers for the second and third darts. Remember, each bridged row is followed by cable crossings.

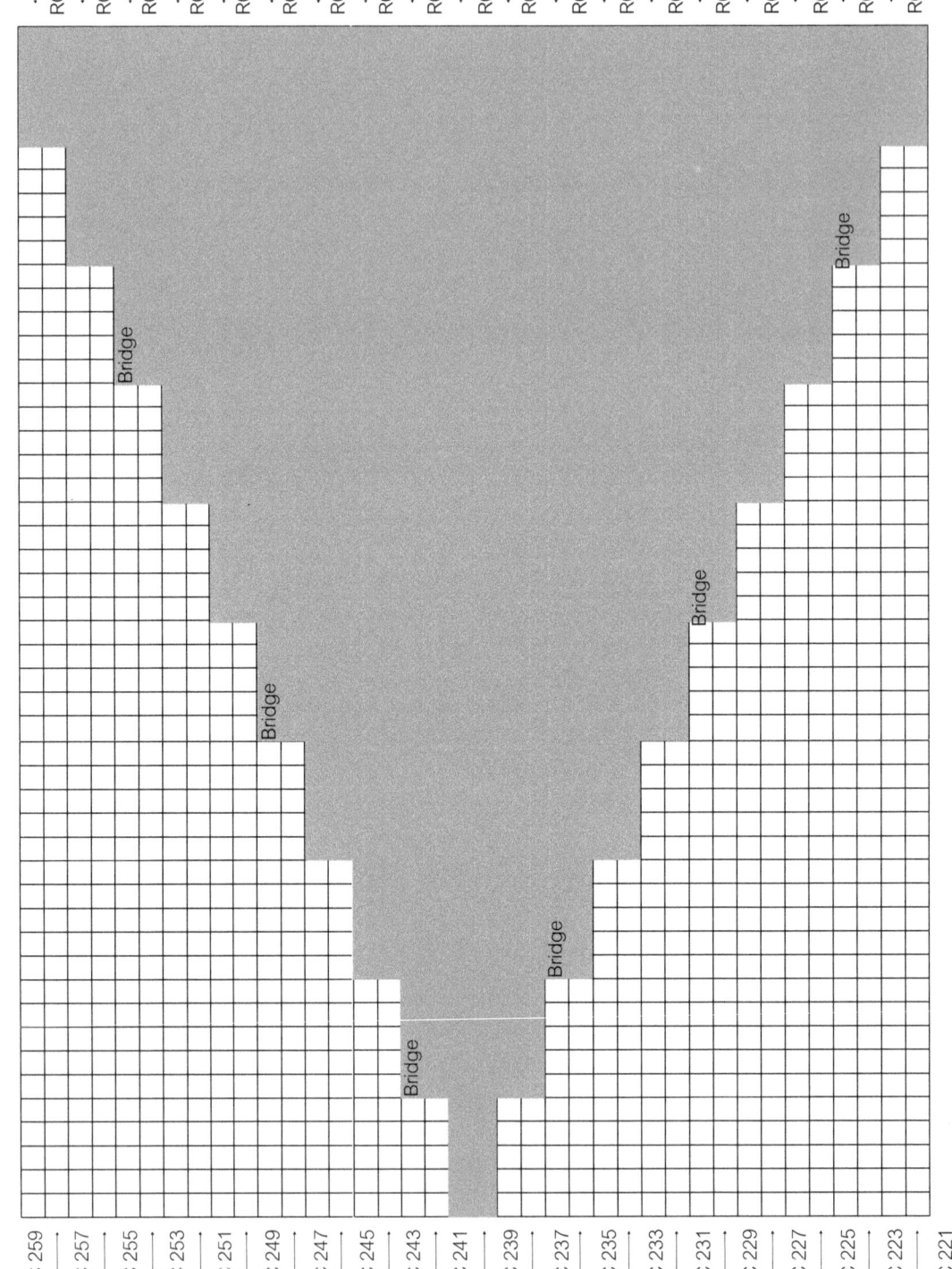

Tag the right front edge 9" below the neck (1" before sleeve). Pick up this edge and hang on the next 44 needles at right. Hang the left front between the neck and the sleeve over 44 needles and then hang the outer edge of the sleeve *only* (not the lining layer) over the next 24 needles. (142 stitches.)

COR, set to hold needles in HP. Hold 68 needles at left. Knit 1 row and wrap. Hold 44 needles at right. Knit 1 row and wrap. *Move 6 needles at left to UWP. Knit and wrap. Move 4 needles at right to UWP. Knit and wrap.** Repeat * to ** until all needles are working. The short rows are worked differently at left and right due to the off-center placement of the shawl collar. Scrap off.

Work the cabled edging as for the lower edges. Cast on 2 stitches at the left end of the bed and knit 1 row. *With the wrong side of the band facing you, pick up 1 live stitch from the scrap and, at the same time, increase 1 stitch at other edge.** Repeat * to **until there are 6 stitches working. Bridge and cross the first cable. In order to work the edging loosely enough, only pick up live stitches from the scrap the second, third, and fourth rows of each 6-row cable repeat. (Otherwise, the edging will be too tight and will prevent the band from rolling correctly to the outside.) Reduce the trim to 2 stitches over the last 4 rows. Then draw the yarn tail through the last stitches to finish off.

Carefully remove the scrap knitting from the band, checking that all the live stitches have been picked up and worked with the band. Roll the band to the outside of the garment so that the cabled edging just covers the seam line and sew the band invisibly in place. Work in all yarn tails.

Washing and Wearing Instructions
Wash the finished garment with mild soap and lay it flat to dry. Washing really brings out the beauty of this yarn and help the cables take their final shape.

When you are wearing this garment, the short-rowed darts should line up with your shoulders and center back of neck. Pass the right front through the sleeve on the left front, as shown in the photo on page 136.

Appendix 1:

Metric Schematics

Appendix 1

Tied Up In Style Cardigan

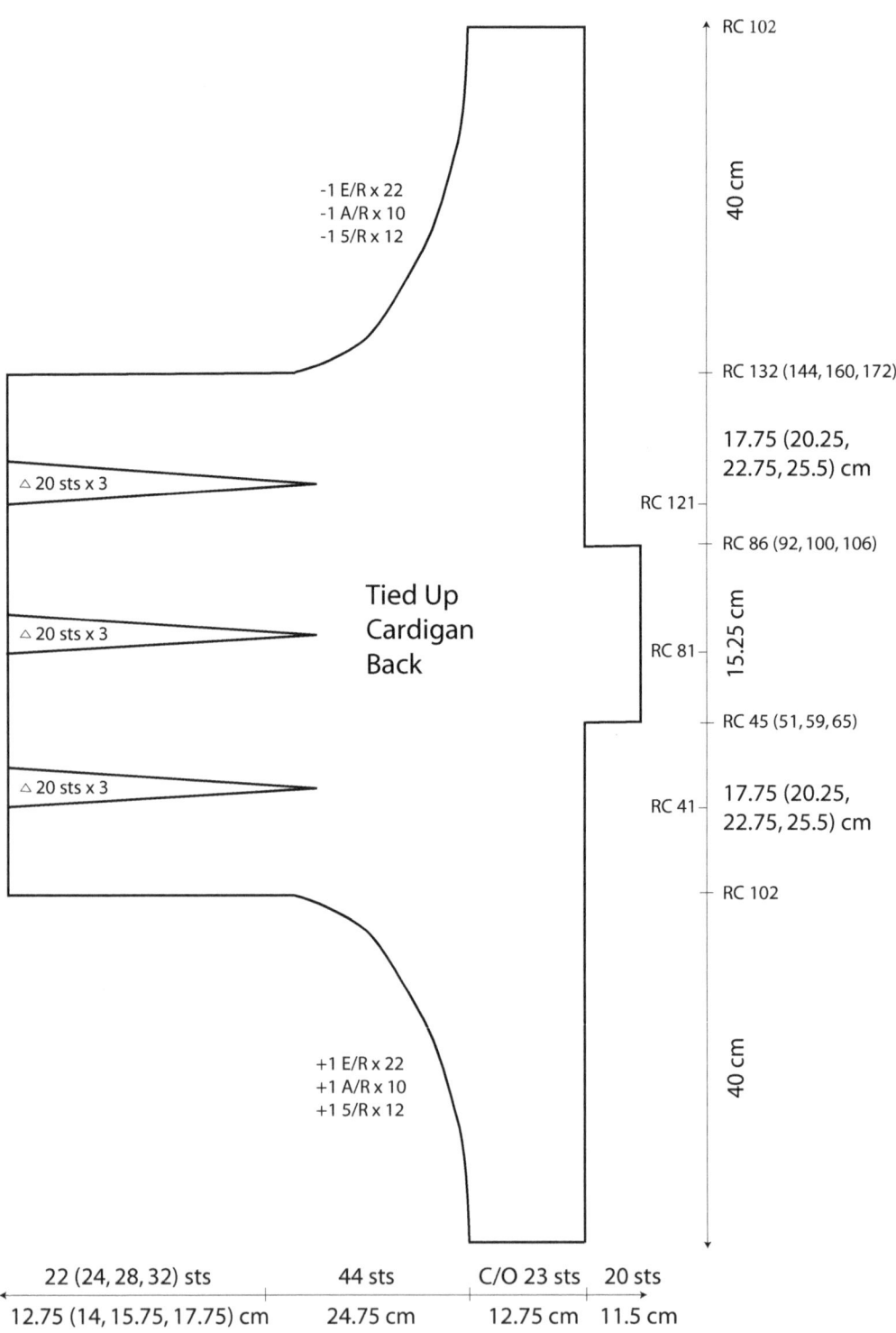

Metric Schematics 145

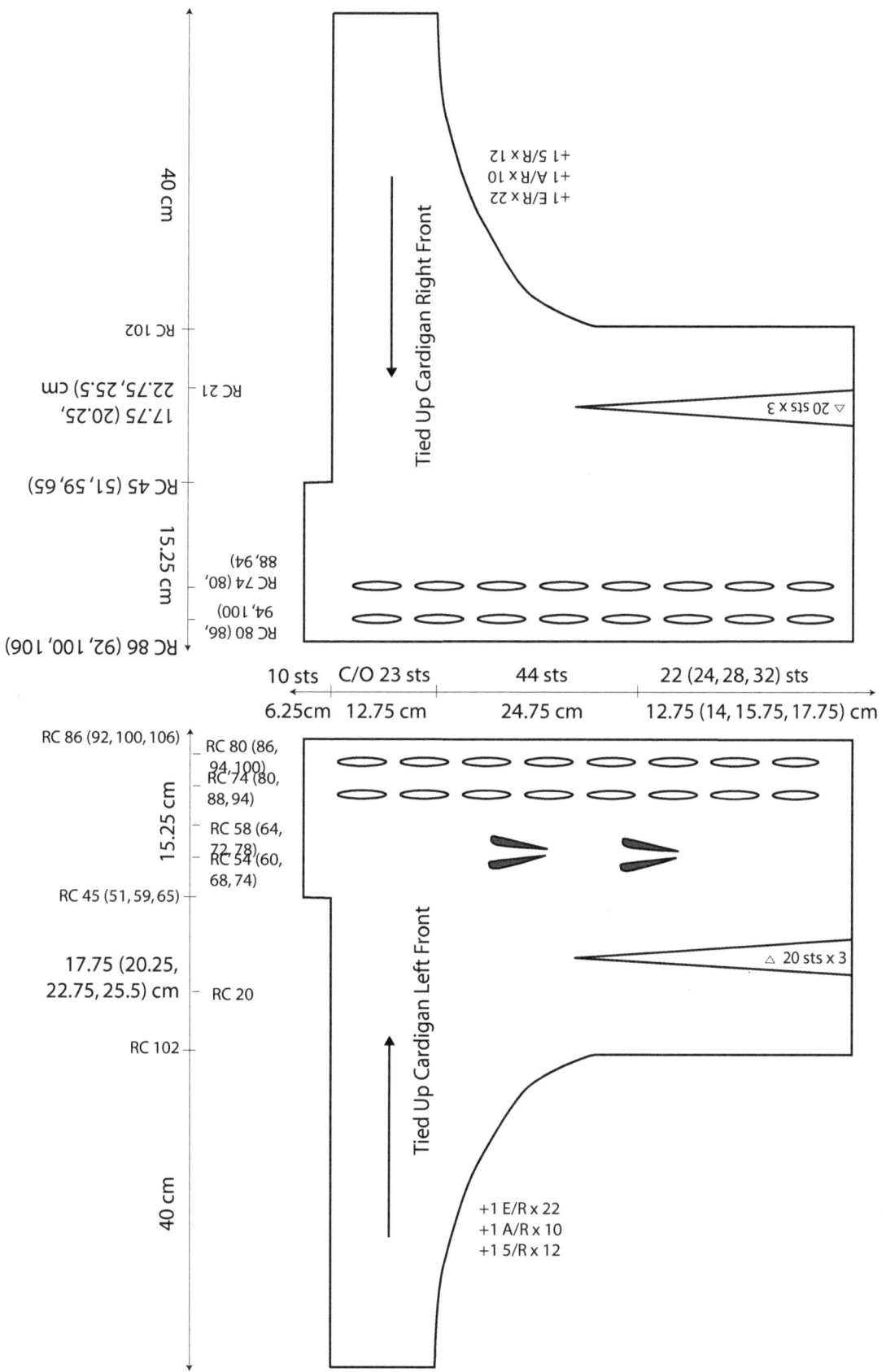

Faux Crochet Cardigan

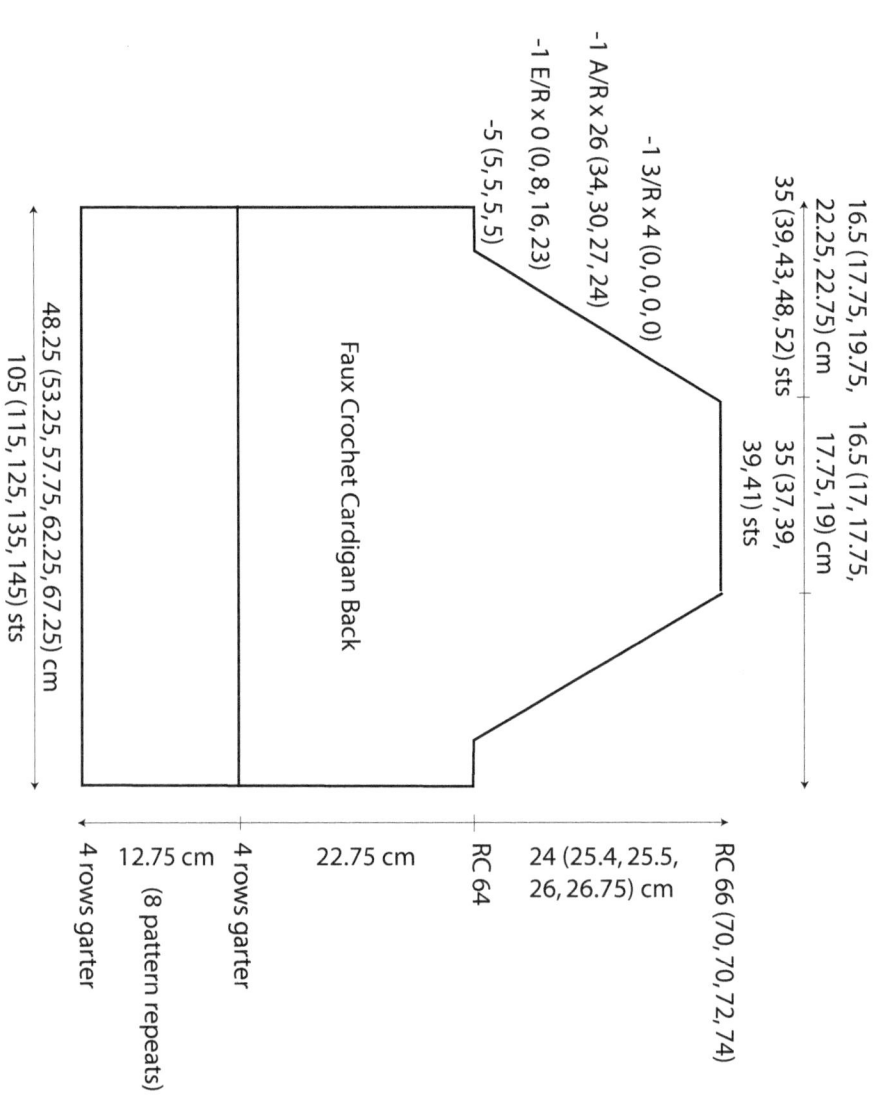

Metric Schematics 147

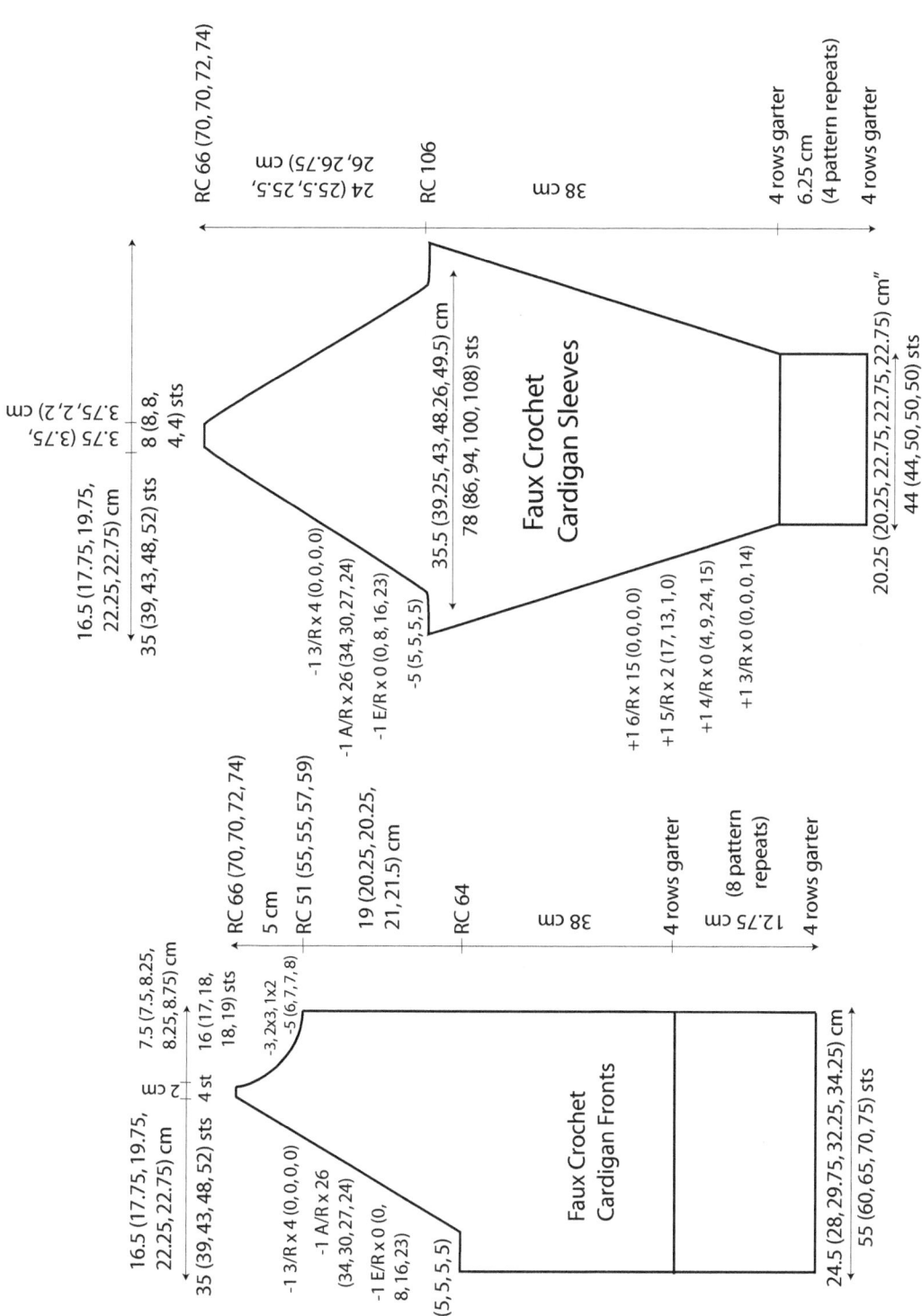

148   Appendix 1

Puppet Scarf

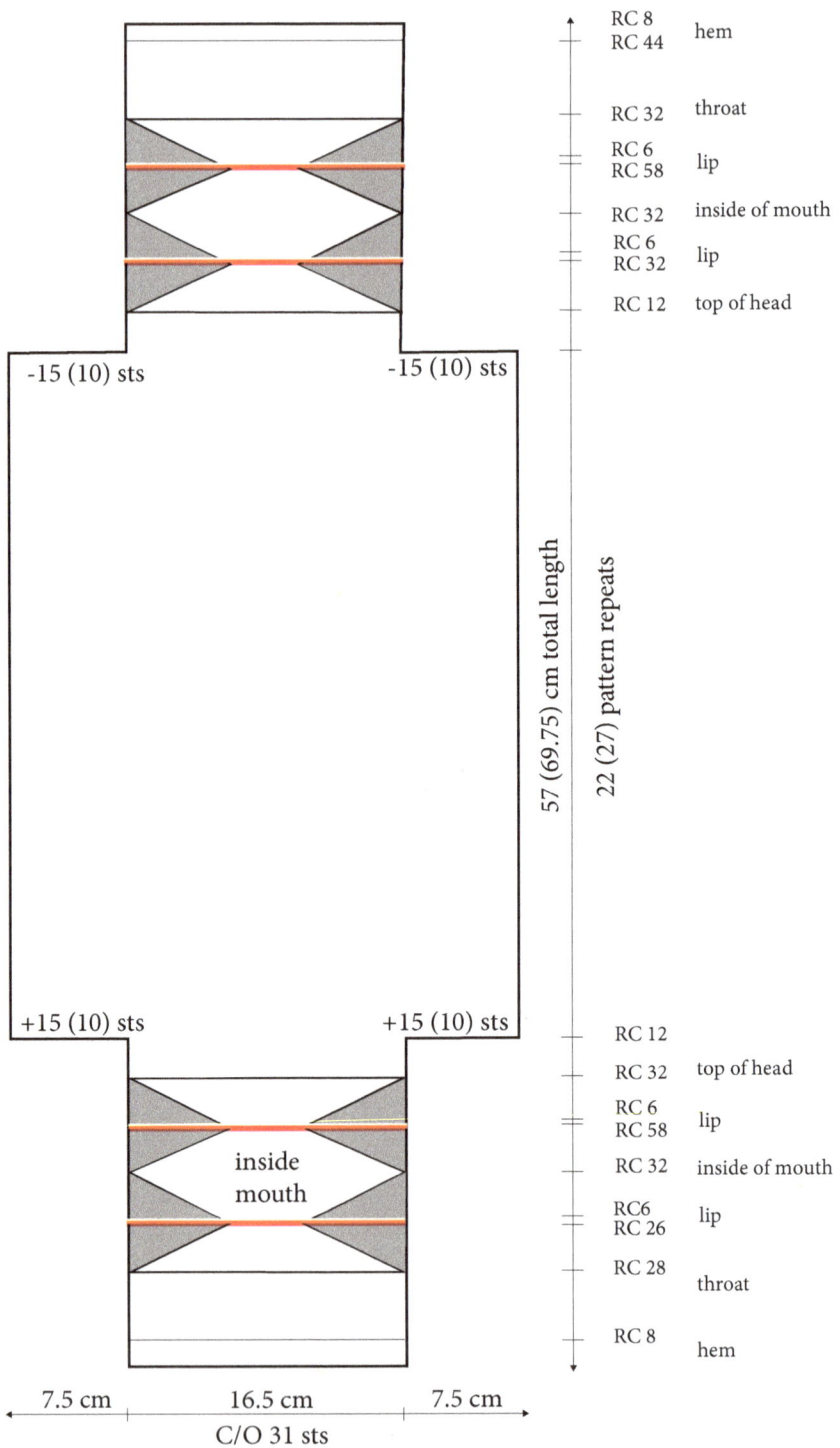

Ruched Cardigan

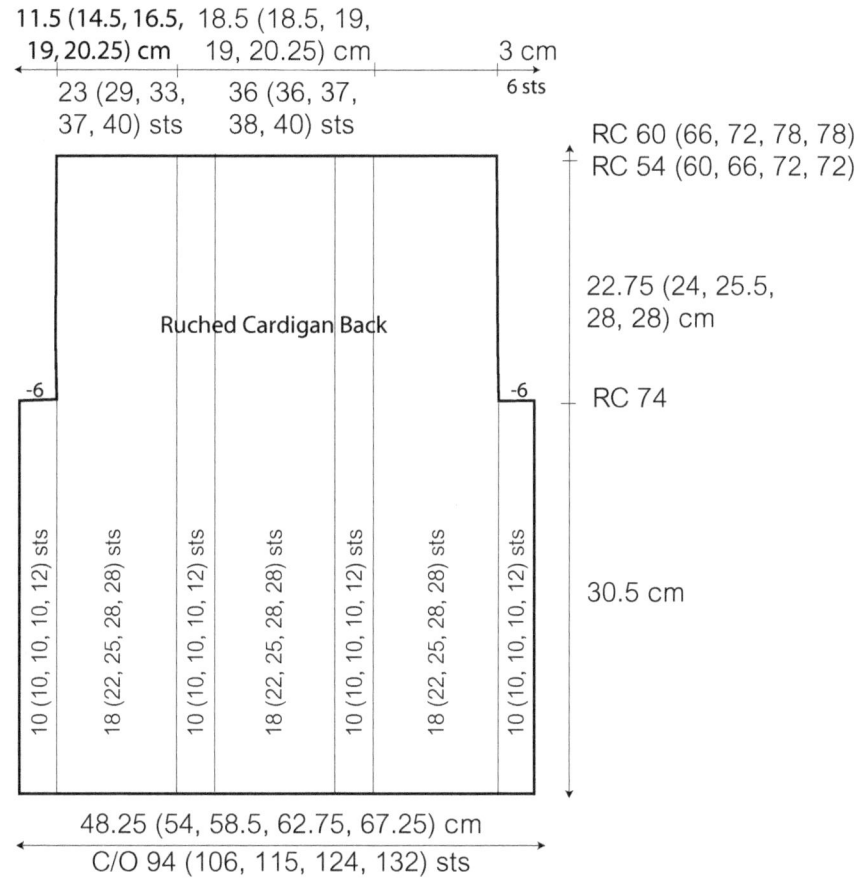

Appendix 1

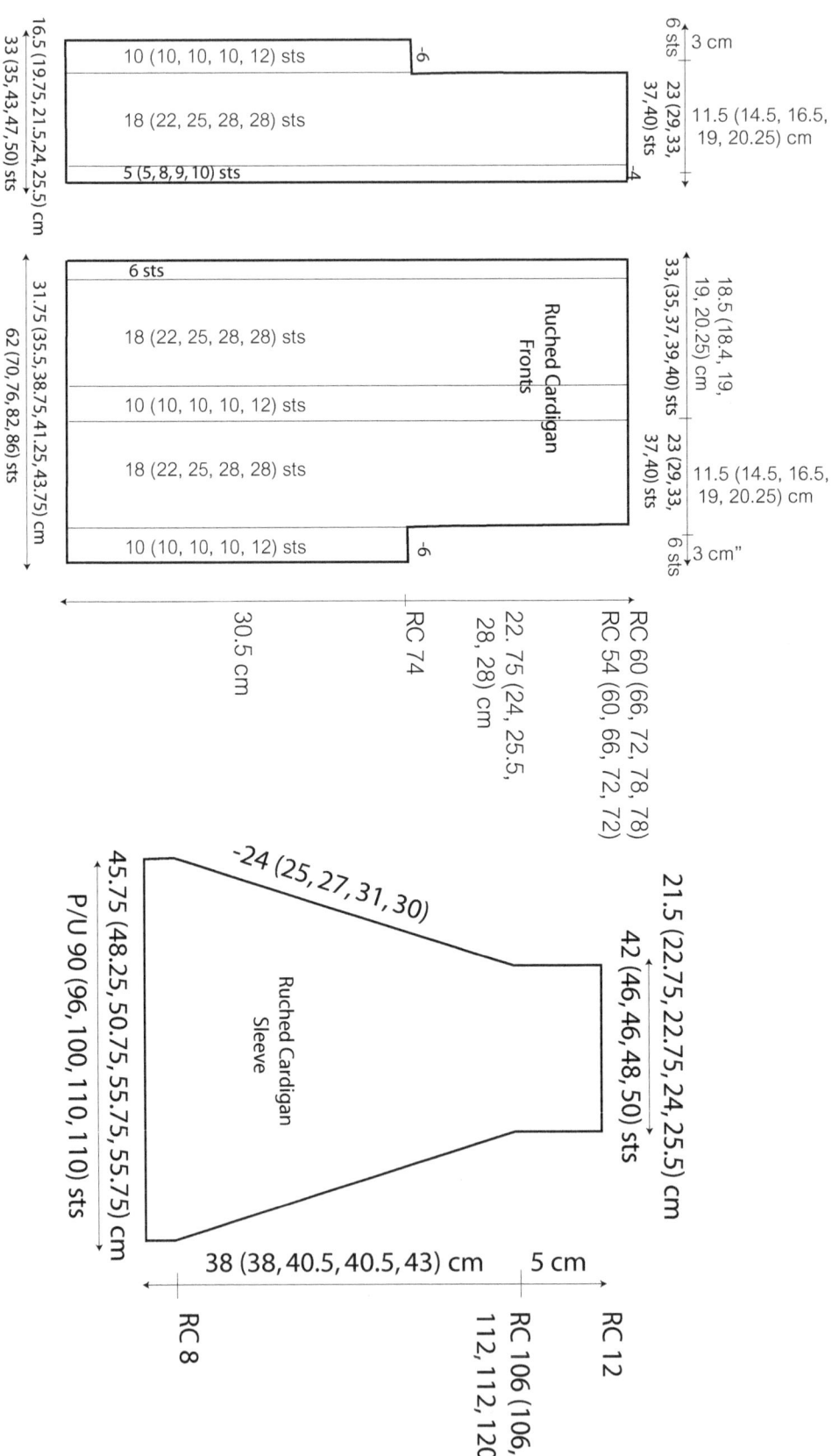

Horizontal-Cable Pullover

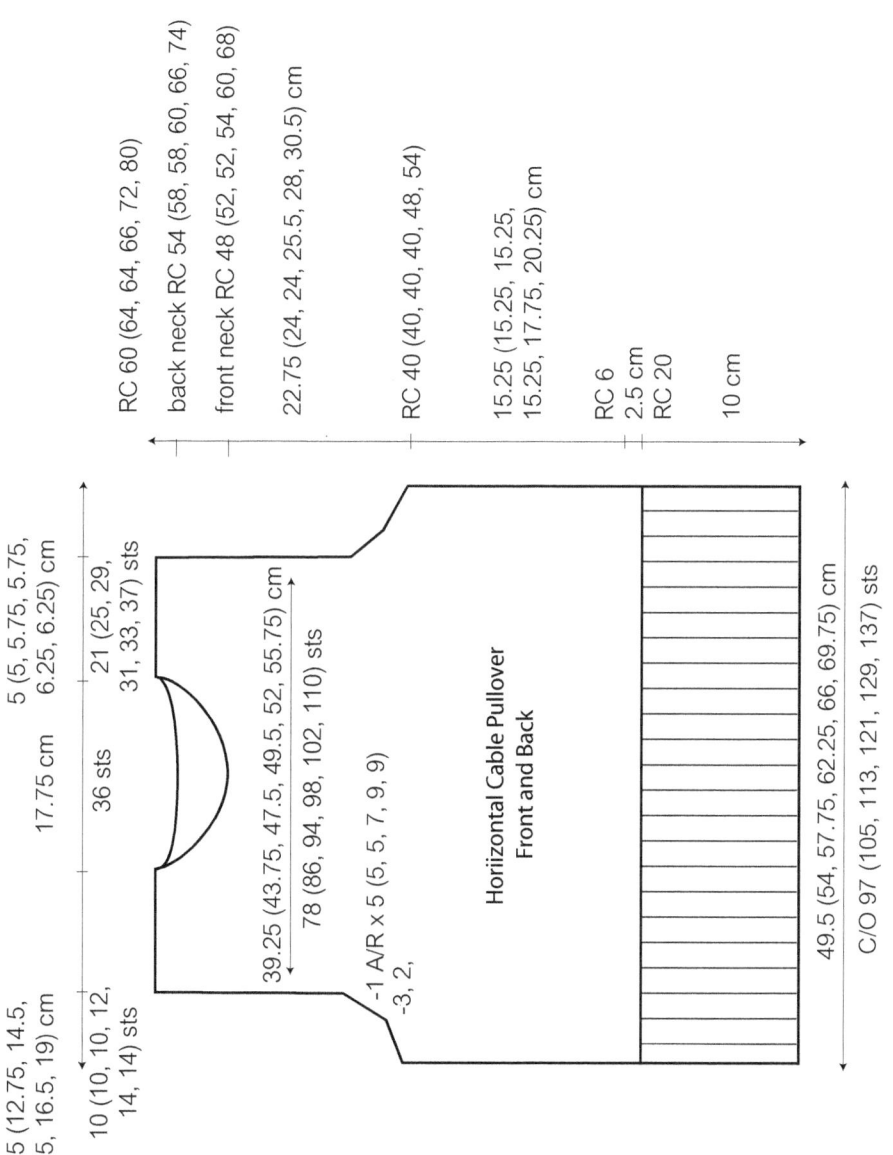

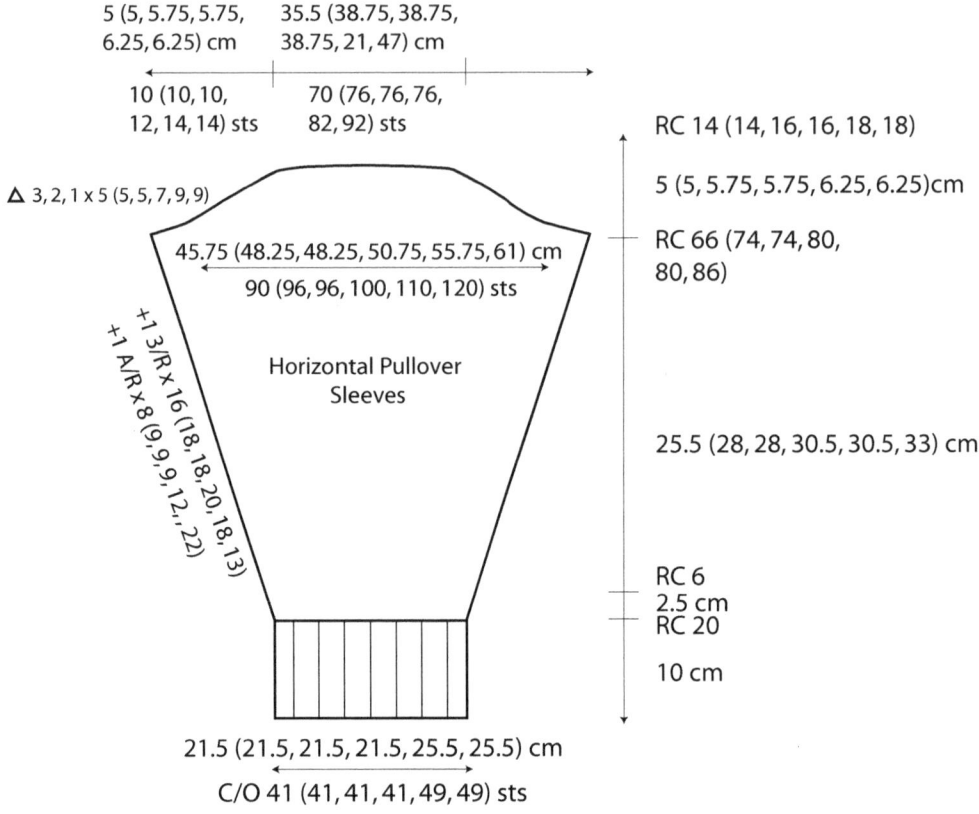

Purple Posies Tote

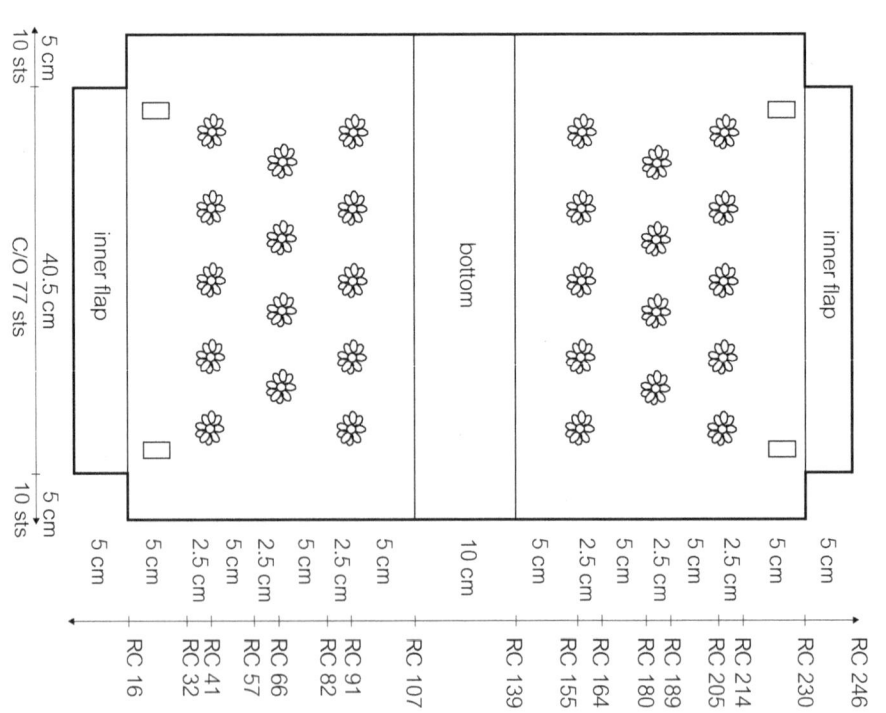

Metric Schematics 153

Hugs and Kisses Shawl

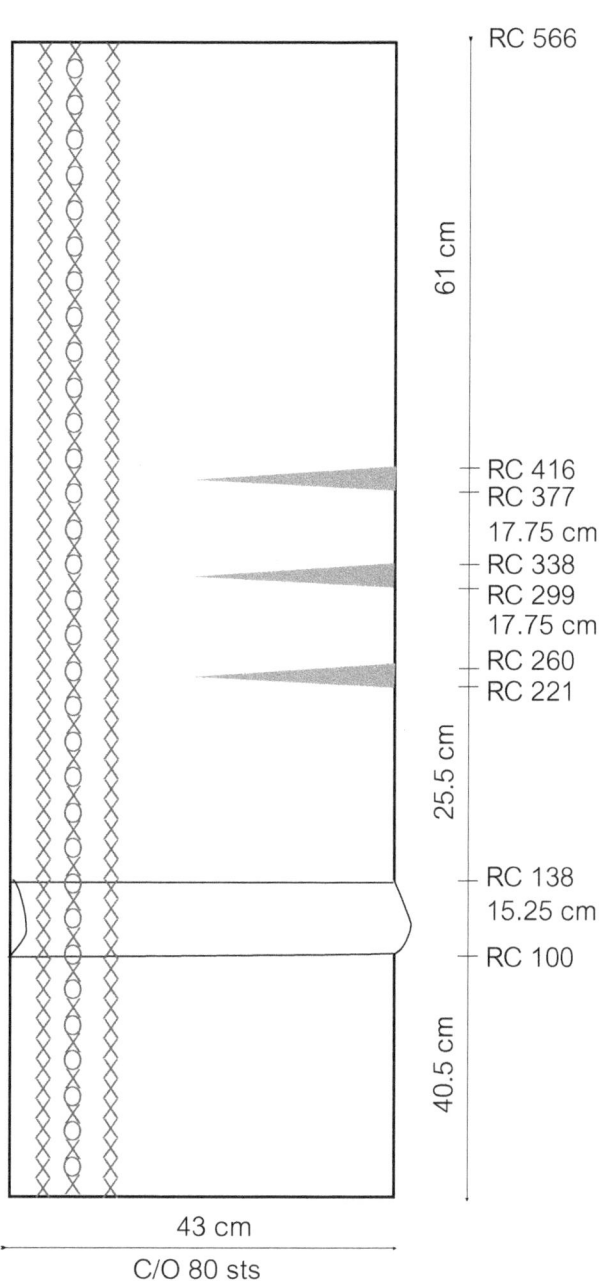

Appendix 2
The Make-Do Garter Bar

Developed by machine knitter, Colleen Smitherman, this inexpensive and very clever invention is just what you need if you do not have a garter bar for your machine (and they are no longer available for some machines). There are a number of books and web sites that offer step-by-step instruction on using a garter bar. Most instructions will refer to a raised ridge on one side of the bar, but you will not have that feature with this version. You will still be able to turn the work over, but will have to position the stitches over the needles yourself, rather than relying on ridges or grooves to help you.

Tips Before You Begin

You can combine comb sections to assemble a garter bar that is long enough for your entire machine. The combs come three to a package, but each one is a different color, so if you want the entire garter bar to be one color, you need to purchase two or more packages. (You may actually find that color changes every 20 loops or so (for example) could be helpful as you're counting.)

If you are not used to working with a hot-glue gun, practice on some scrap pieces of wood. This work can be messy if you're not careful—and dangerous if you're careless! Hot glue can burn you or melt a comb. Spread some newspaper underneath your machine to protect your work surface, too.

Let the glue gun preheat long enough for the glue sticks to melt readily. Always start each step with a full stick of glue in the gun so you do not have to add more midstep—this glue hardens quickly.

Remove any glue blobs, drips or "threads" as soon as possible so they don't harden in place. As they say, less is more, so don't use more glue than you absolutely need to hold things in place.

Materials
Scunci® "Effortless Beauty" hair combs (item #16219-A, 3 per package with 46 loops per comb)

Approximately 12" of length for each section of comb:
1.25" wide molding with .25" lip
.25" square trim
.50" wide lathing or trim strip

.25" dowel (one)

2 binder clips per section of comb

Hot glue gun and glue sticks

Discard the ends of each comb before you begin. Glue the square to the inner edge of the molding, as shown in the photographs at on page 155.

Sand off any rough edges on the wood molding before you begin. Do not cut the molding to final length until you have stretched the comb(s) across the needles and have the final measurement. Then, bind all three pieces of wood together with masking tape to cut them all to length at the same time.

The Make-Do Garter Bar   155

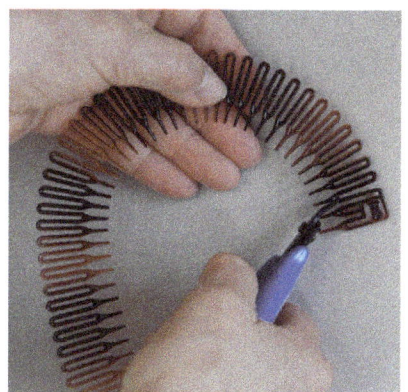

Step 1. Clip off both end pieces of each section of comb you are using.

Step 2. Glue the piece of 1/4" square trim onto the edge of the molding as shown in the photo.

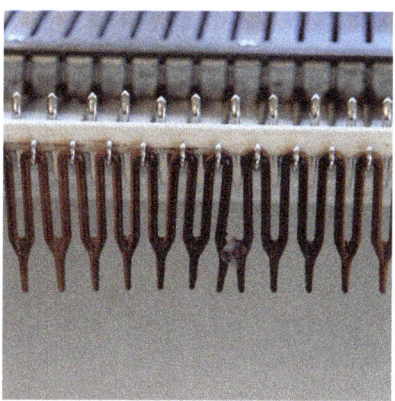

Step 3. Open all the needle latches and bring the needles to HP. Hang the comb(s) across the needles, joining sections with a dot of hot glue. Lay the dowel in the open hooks of the needles and behind the comb. Then push the needles back so that the dowel rests snugly against the front of the bed. The dowel will keep the comb even and prevent it from lifting out of the needles.

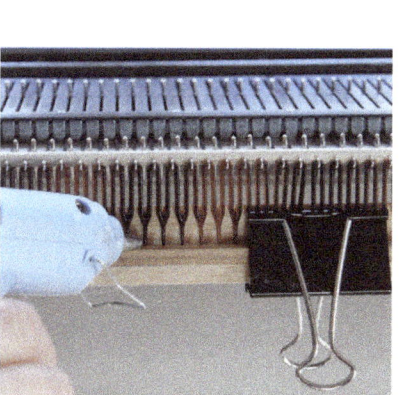

Step 4. Slip the molding behind the comb and push the comb down evenly against the edge of the molding. Use binder clips to hold the comb in place and use a few dots of glue to secure the placement.

Step 5. Double check that everything is even. Then spread a thin line of glue along the length of the comb, pressing the comb against the wood as you do so. You can work across small sections at a time.

Step 6. When the glue has set enough to hold the comb in place, carefully remove the assembled piece from the machine. Lay it flat and spread another line of glue along the comb, filling in the gaps between the teeth. Quickly place the strip of flat lathing on top of the glue, positioning it as close as possible to the comb and to the edge of the square trim. Clamp the assembly in place to finish drying. You might want to add a little more glue to the gaps at each end of the finished garter bar to secure it.

Glossary of Symbols and Abbreviations

All pattern directions rely on abbreviations in an effort to streamline the directions and reduce length. Most abbreviations are standard. In this glossary, I have listed the abbreviations I commonly use in my patterns. I have also included the symbols you'll find in the stitch charts. Take the time to familiarize yourself with these abbreviations and symbols and work through the pattern details by knitting a swatch before you begin knitting the garment.

Basic Symbols

All of these symbols represent the way the stitches look when viewed from the wrong side of the fabric—that is, the side facing you while you are working at the machine. Be aware that hand-knit charts portray the knit side of the fabric. Most of these symbols are standard international symbols, but some are my adaptations or variations, as explained below.

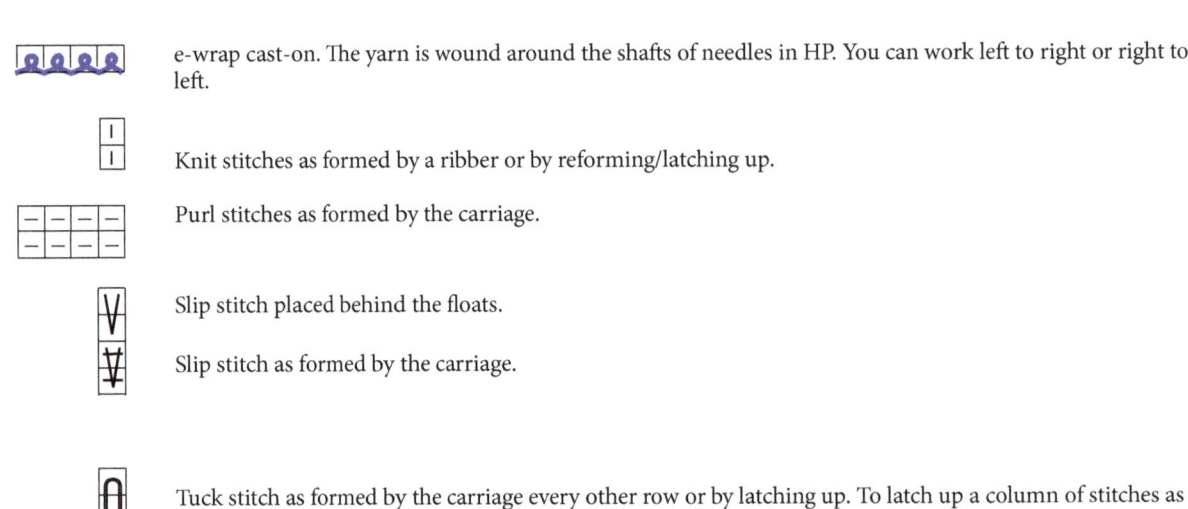

e-wrap cast-on. The yarn is wound around the shafts of needles in HP. You can work left to right or right to left.

Knit stitches as formed by a ribber or by reforming/latching up.

Purl stitches as formed by the carriage.

Slip stitch placed behind the floats.

Slip stitch as formed by the carriage.

Tuck stitch as formed by the carriage every other row or by latching up. To latch up a column of stitches as tuck stitch, drop a column of stitches to form a ladder (insert the latch tool before dropping the column of stitches to control how far they run). *Let the first stitch and one bar of the ladder slide over the latch of the tool. Then catch the next bar of the ladder in the hook and pull it through to form a (tuck) stitch.** Repeat from * to ** to reach the top of the column.

Pattern Stitch Symbols

Multiple stitches transferred to a single, central needle.
Center stitch holding a stitch transferred from left and a stitch transferred from right.
Stitch transferred to an adjacent needle at right.
Stitch transferred to an adjacent needle at left.
Stitch traveling to the right.
Stitch traveling to the left.
Closed eyelet formed by picking up the purl bar of an adjacent stitch to prevent an eyelet from forming on an empty needle.
Eyelet formed by leaving an empty needle in WP.

Glossary of Symbols and Abbreviations

Beaded stitch. The second stitch is removed from the needle with a beading needle or crochet hook, a bead is slipped over the stitch, and the stitch is returned to the needle.

Chinese knot stitch. Diagonally woven stitches individually pass in front of and behind each other. The first stitch on the right passes over the third stitch and under the fourth stitch. The second stitch from the right passes under the third stitch and over the fourth stitch.

Wrapped stitches. The second stitch from the right (left) is wrapped around the next 3 stitches and then replaced on its needle.

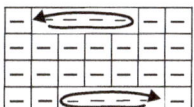

4x4 left-cross cable. This cable requires two 4-prong transfer tools or two pairs of 2-prong tools in each hand. Four stitches are removed on each tool or set of tools. The stitches on the left are returned to the needles first and show on the knit face of the fabric. The stitches on the right are returned to the needles last and are visible on the purl side of the fabric.

4x4 right-cross cable. Four stitches are removed on each tool or set of tools. The stitches on the right are returned to the needles first and show on the knit face of the fabric. The stitches on the left are returned to the needles last and are visible on the purl side of the fabric.

2x2 opposing pair of cables. The cable on the right is a left-cross cable, and the cable on the left is a right-cross cable.

Twisted stitches. Three stitches are twisted together and returned to the same needle.

Free yarn wrapping. The arrow indicates the path of the yarn as carried in the carriage and then used to wrap groups of needles or stitches.

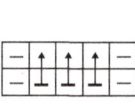

These arrows indicate stitches that are lifted to needles above them.

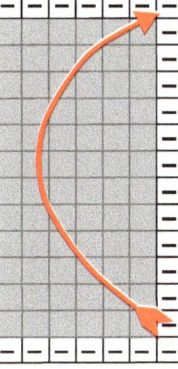

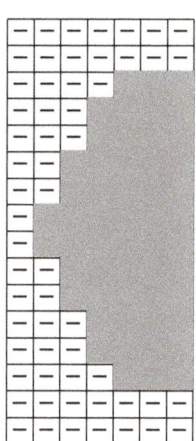

The shaded area represents needles in holding position.

Abbreviations

A/R	alternate row		R/Rs	row/rows
adj	adjacent		RC	row count or row counter
alt	alternate/alternately		S/O	scrap off
beg	begin or beginning		Δ or S/R	short row
B/O	bind off		ss	stitch size
CC	contrast color or contrast yarn		st/sts	stitch/stitches
C/O	cast on		tog	together
COL	carriage on left		UWP	upper working position
cont	continue or continued		WP	working position
COR	carriage on right		x	times
dec/s	decrease/decreases			
EN	every needle			
EON	every other needle			
E/R	every row			
fol	following			
HP	holding position			
HWP	half-working position			
inc/s	increase/increases			
k	knit			
KWK	knit, wrap, knit			
MC	main color or main yarn			
ndl/ndls	needle/needles			
NWP	nonworking position			
pat	pattern			
P/U	pick up			

* to **   Repeat the previous directions between the asterisks.

(...) Stitches between parentheses should be treated as a single unit.

Increasing and Decreasing

The following are examples of the notation that I use to indicate increases and decreases:

+1 A/R x 10 means to increase 1 stitch every alternate row, 10 times. When shown on a sleeve schematic, the process usually needs to be done at each end of a given row.

-1 4/R x 6 means that you should decrease 1 stitch every fourth row, 6 times.

Binding off around sinker posts/gate pegs or empty needles

I always bind off by catching the free yarn around a sinker post or gate peg, on machines that have them, or around an empty needle on machines that do not. This technique guarantees that each of the stitches is bound off with the same tension and spacing and also prevents the fabric edge from narrowing. This method is particularly suited for binding off large pieces as it supports the piece as you work and keeps the last few bind-off stitches from stretching.

You can use either a transfer tool or a latch tool to bind off, as shown in the following photos. Leave the work hanging from the sinker posts, gate pegs, or empty needles until all of the stitches have been bound off. Then lift the fabric from the machine to behold a perfectly straight, even edge.

When I bind off a portion of the stitches (for a straight armhole decrease, for example), I leave the bound-off stitches on the posts, pegs, or needles until I knit the next row. Then I remove them. If you leave the stitches on the machine any longer, the work will start to pile up, and the carriage will jam.

Binding off around sinker posts with a transfer tool

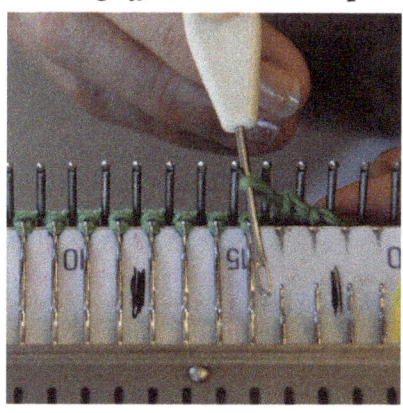

1. Stitch 17 has been removed from its needle and is deposited on needle 16 by passing the tool *behind*, rather than in front of, the sinker post between the two needles

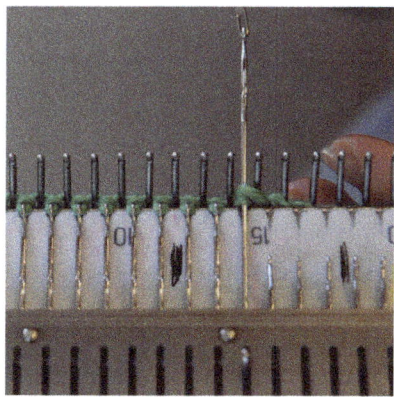

2. Bring the needle forward (I usually just pull it forward with the transfer tool while I have it on the needle) so that both stitches are behind the latch.

3. Manually knit the needle back to WP.

4. One stitch has been decreased. You can see the stitch caught behind the sinker post.

Bind Off Methods

Binding off around an empty needle with a transfer tool

1. Stitch 14 is transferred to needle 13.

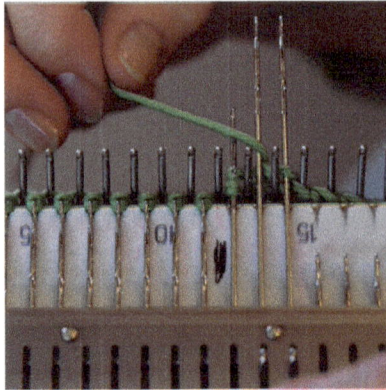

2. The empty 14th needle is brought to HP and then, passing the yarn *over* the empty needle, the two stitches on needle 13 are knitted manually.

3. The first decrease is complete.

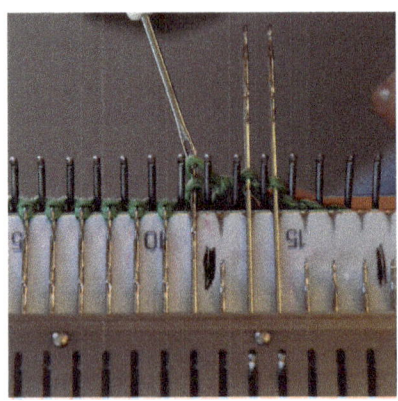

4. Stitch 13 is transferred to needle 12.

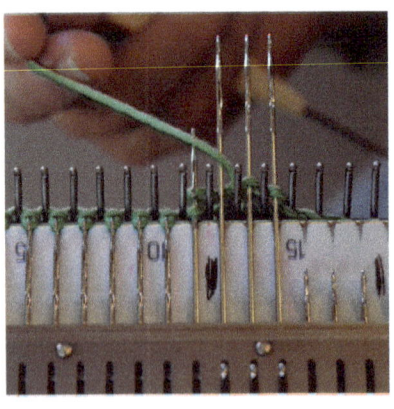

5. The empty 13th needle is brought to HP. The yarn passes over needle 13 and then the two stitches on needle 12 are manually knitted together to complete the decrease.

Binding off around a sinker post with a latch tool

1. Stitch 10 is removed from the needle...

2. ... and deposited in the hook of the 11th needle, passing the tool behind the sinker post between the two needles.

3. The yarn passes in front of the sinker post and ...

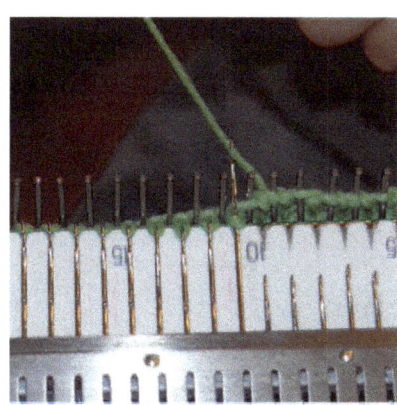

4. The two stitches are manually knitted back to complete the decrease.

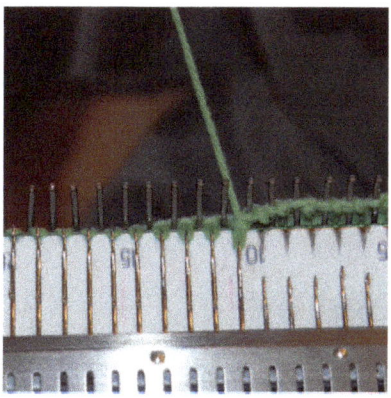

5. Then stitch 11 is moved behind the sinker post to needle 12.

6. The two stitches have been knitted together to complete the decrease.

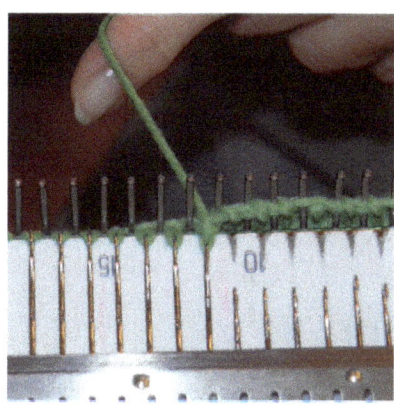

Binding off around an empty needle with a latch tool

1. Stitch 12 is deposited in needle 13 in front of the sinker post.

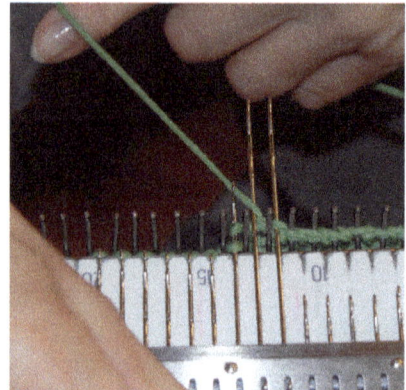

2. The empty 12th needle is placed in HP. The yarn passes over the empty needle then the two stitches are manually knitted to complete the decrease.

Joining Shoulder Seams on the Machine

Step 1.
Scrap off all shoulder stitches. It doesn't matter whether the shoulders are straight or slanted.

Step 2.
Rehang the back shoulder stitches on the machine with the right side facing you. Bring the needles to UWP or HP so that the stitches are behind the latches. Open all the latches before continuing.

Step 3.
Rehang the front shoulder stitches in the hooks of the same needles, with the wrong side facing you. The right sides of the fabric are facing each other.

Step 4.
Use a needle pusher or ruler to ease the needle butts back to WP a little at a time. The back shoulder stitches will slide over the latches and the front shoulder stitches, leaving just one set of stitches on the needles.

Step 5.
If you push the needles back too quickly, the second set of stitches might slide behind the latches and drop in the process. I usually start on the right and work my way across the bed, nudging the butts back a bit. Then I work from left to right to finish positioning the needles. This approach is a little slower but a lot safer.

Step 6.
Bind off the single set of stitches. To prevent the bind-off from tightening and shortening the seam, I always bind off around a sinker post or gate peg or, on machines without these metal dividers, I bind off around empty needles, as shown in the previous photographs.

Finishing Stitches

Mattress Stitch

Mattress stitch is worked from the right side of the fabric and, as you can see in the third photo below, produces a nearly invisible seam. Work one full stitch from the edges of the pieces you are joining, inserting the needle under two of the "bars" that separate each column of stitches. On bulky weights, you might want to work every bar or a half stitch from the edge. Each space is worked twice: the needle always re-enters the space it last exited on the opposite edge. Think "in the old and out the new" as you zig-zag back and forth from one edge to the other. Work an inch or two of the seam before drawing the yarn through to snug up the stitches and close the seam. It is easier and more even than trying to tighten each individual stitch. The edge stitches will be easiest to work if you used full fashion increases and decreases to shape your work because those methods retain the same edge stitch, placing the increases or decreases a needle or two inside the edges. As with most finishing, the pieces should be blocked prior to seaming.

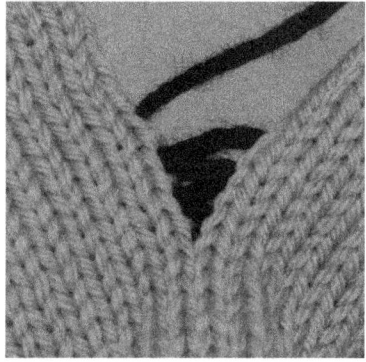

Step 1. The yarn has been worked under two bars on the edge at left. It entered the same space it exited on that edge and then exited through a new space, two bars above. "In the old and out the new."

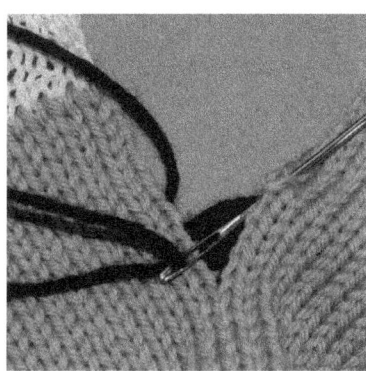

Step 2. Insert the needle into the same space it last exited on the right edge and out through the next space, two bars above.

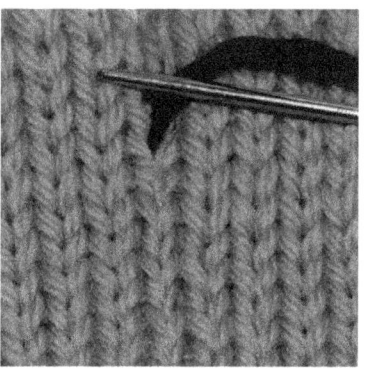

Step 3. After an inch or two, draw the yarn through the stitches to close the seam. Properly done, the seam will be invisible - even if you stitch it with a different color.

Back Stitch

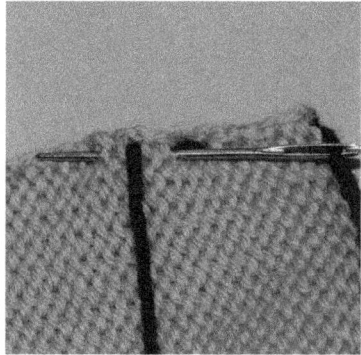

Back stitch is worked with right sides together, one stitch from the edge. The needle is inserted into the same space it last exited and comes out of the fabric a couple of spaces ahead of the last stitch, as shown in the photo at left. I think of it as "one step back and two steps forward". This produces a firm seam and can be worked along selvage or bound off edges.

Grafting

Also called Kitchener Stitch, grafting is actually a row of hand stitched knitting. The needle duplicates a row of knitting, working through live stitches held on scrap knitting. It can be worked from either the knit or purl side (I usually prefer working from the purl side as shown in the photos below), with the two pieces of fabric flat or held with right sides together. The needle travels through a new stitch on one edge and back into the last stitch worked on the opposite edge so that *each stitch is worked twice*. Follow the path traced by the scrap knitting on each side and you will hardly have to think about it as you work back and forth. Adjust your tension as you snug up each stitch so that the stitches you form with the needle will match those you knitted.

Step 1. The needle follows the (white) scrap yarn through a new stitch on the left edge and back into the old stitch on the right.

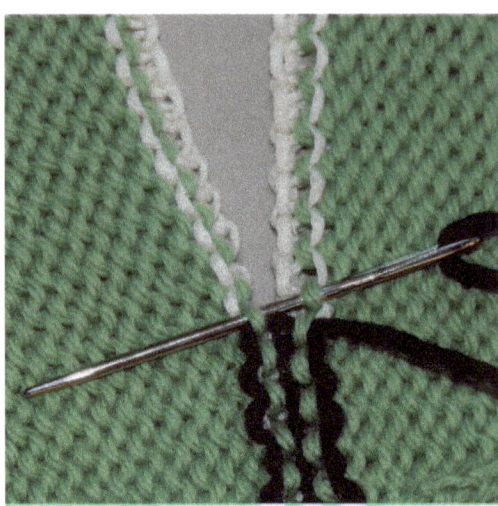

Step 2. The needle works a new stitch on the right and then the old stitch on the left.

You can hold the two pieces of fabric with right sides together to graft the live stitches.

Front and back views of grafted seam.

Sources of Supply

Yarns

Berroco
www.berroco.com

Brown Sheep Company
www.brownsheep.com

Cascade Yarns
www.cascadeyarns.com

Knit Picks
www.knitpicks.com

Nashua Yarns/Westminster Fibers
www.westminsterfibers.com

Noro/Knitting Fever
www.knittingfever.com

Trendsetter Yarns
www.trendsetteryarns.com

Materials, Services, and Periodicals

Gridded Blocking Cloths and Blocking Wires

Angelika's Yarn Store
www.yarn-store.com

Woolstock
www.woolstock.com

Knitting Machine Repair

www.needle-tek.com

Machine-Knitting Magazines

Knit Words
www.knitwords.com

Machine Knitting Monthly
www.machineknittingmonthly.com

News and Views Magazine
www.countryknittingofmaine.com

Software

DesignaKnit (DAK)
www.knitcraft.com

Cochenille Design Studio (Garment Styler and others)
www.cochenille.com

Miscellaneous

Colleen Smitherman
(patterns and original source for Make Do Garter Bar)
www.myknitpatterns.com

Scunci® (hair combs)
www.scunci.com

Index

A
Appendix 1: Metric Schematics, 142
Appendix 2: Make Do Garter Bar, 154
Abbreviations, 158

B
Back stitch, 163
Basket Weave stitch pattern, 14
Beaded cables, 22
Bind off:
    hand sewn, 127
    around sinker posts, 159, 161
    around empty needles, 160, 162
Binding-off midrow, 68
Bridging:
    defined, 2
    to add extra rows: 32
        edge ruffle, 43
        fills, 50
        giant cables, 53
        horizontal cables, 57
        popcorns, 37
        nops, 40
        oversized cables, 52
        raised cables, 33
        ruching, 44
        seashell nops, 41
        short row textures, 47
        stegosaurus cables, 48
        ties, 38
        raised triangles, 47
        wishbone cable, 35
        X and O cable 35
    to increase stitch size using the stitch dial: 8
        cables, 10
        woven stitches, 14
    to increase stitch size by manually knitting needles: 19
        beaded cables, 20
        Chinese knot stitch, 25
        openwork effect, 28
        slanted stitch pattern, 21
        wrapped stitches, 23
    with the free yarn, 60

C
Cables
    4x4, 10
    right cross, 11, 34
    left cross, 12, 34
    beaded, 20
    combination, 13, 34, 36
    giant, 52
    hugs and kisses, 35
    horizontal, 57
    raised, 33
    serpentine, 33
    stegosaurus, 48
    wishbone, 35
    X and O, 35
Cardigans
    Faux Crochet, 100
    Ruched, 112
    Tied up in Style, 90

Carriage pathways, 3
Combination methods: 72
    flowers, three-dimensional, 80
    knotted ties, 75
    lazy daisy, 73
    petal clusters, 82
    popcorn, 5-stitch, 77
    twisted eyelets, 76
Casting on midrow, 68
Chinese knot stitch, 25
Combination cables, 13, 34, 36
Corded ruffles, 42

D
Darts, short row, 138

E
Embroidery knitting, 66
Eyelets, twisted, 77

F

Faux Crochet Cardigan, 100, 146
Felting, 135
    nops, 41
Fence knitting, 66
Fills, 50
Finishing, 89
Flowers, three-dimensional, 80
Free yarn, 60
    binding off midrow, 68
    casting on midrow, 68
    fence knitting, 66
    French knots, 62
    ladders, 69
    pussy willows, 62, 64
    slits, 68
    ties,
wrapped stitches, 61
French knots, 62

G

Garter bar, make do, 154
Giant cables, 52
Glossary
    symbols, 156
    abbreviations, 158
Grafting, 164
Petal clusters, 82

H

Half-working position, 6
Hand sewn bind off, 127
Hat, Loopity Lou, 96
Holding position, 5
Horizontal cable, 57
Horizontal Cable Pullover, 122, 151
How To Photograph Series
    5-stitch popcorns, 79
    back stitch, 163
    binding off around sinker posts, 159, 161
    binding off around empty needles, 160, 162
    bridging to increase stitch size, 15
    Chinese knots, 26
    creating an open effect, 29
    crossing giant cables, 56
    crossing horizontal cables, 58
    fence knitting, 66
    forming French knots 62
    grafting, 164
    hand sewn bind off, 127
    knitting beaded cables, 22

    make do garter bar, 155
    making pussy willows, 64, 65
    mattress stitch, 163
    twisting eyelets, 77
    two tool popcorn lifting method, 39
    wrapped stitch design, 24
Hug and Kisses cable, 135
Hugs and Kisses Shawl, 136, 153

I

I-cord
    edging, 95
    2-color, 99

J

Joining shoulders on the machine, 162

L

Ladders, 69
    diamond, 71
    triangle, 71
Latching up in tuck, 22, 156
Latch tool bind off, 161, 162
Lazy daisy stitch, 73
Loopity Lou Hat, 96

M

Make Do Garter Bar, 154
Mattress stitch, 163
Mechanics of bridging, 3
Metric schematics, 143
    Faux Crochet Cardigan, 146
    Horizontal Cable Pullover, 151
    Hugs and Kisses Shawl, 153
    Puppet Scarf, 148
    Purple Posies Tote, 152
    Ruched Cardigan, 149
    Tied up in Style, 144

N

Needle positions, 5
Needle weaving (ladders), 70
Non-working position, 5
Nops, 37, 40
    felted, 41
    seashell, 41

O

One row stripes, 133
Openwork stitch pattern, 28
Over sized cables, 52

P

Patterns, 84
Popcorns, 37
    2-stitch, 38
    3-stitch, 37
    5-stitch, 77
Pullover
    Horizontal Cable, 122
Puppet Scarf, 106, 148
Purple Posies Tote, 130, 152
Pussy willows, 62

R

Raised triangles, 47
Ruched Cardigan, 112, 149
Ruching, 44
Ruffles
    edge ruffle, 43
    seashell surface ruffle, 42

S

Sandwich band, 117
Scrap knitting, 88
Scarves
    Puppet, 106
    Wrapped in Ruffles, 118
Seaming
    back stitch, 163
    grafting, 164
    mattress stitch, 163
    shoulders, 162

Seashell nops, 41
Schematics, 86
    metric, 143
Shawl, Hugs and Kisses, 136
Short rows, 89
    darts, 138
Short-row textures, 47
Slanted stitch pattern, 21
Slits, 68
Sources of Supply, 165
Stegosaurus cable, 48
Stitch charts
    3x3 serpentine cables, 33
    3-D triangles, 48
    3-D flowers, 132, 133, 81
    alternating cross cables, 55
    beaded cables, 21
    bridged fill, 52
    cast on/bind off slits, 68
    Chinese knots, 25
    circle and square ladders, 69
    closely crossed giant cables, 53
    combination cables, 13
    darts, short row, 140
    diamond and triangle ladders, 71
    enlarging all cable stitches, 10
    enlarging half of cable stitches, 11
    Faux Crochet Cardigan, 102
    fence knitting, 67
    French knots, 63
    giant left crossed cable, 54
    glossary, 156
    horizontal cable, 57, 126
    Horizontal-Cable Pullover, 126
    hugs and kisses cables, 35, 139
    Hugs and Kisses Shawl, 139
    knotted ties, 75
    lazy daisy, 73
    nops
        3-stitch, 40
        seashell nops, 42
    open effects, 28
    petal clusters, 82
    popcorns
        2-stitch, 37
        5-stitch, 78

Purple Posies Tote, 132, 133
pussy willows, 62
Ruched Cardigan, 115, 116
ruching, 44, 45, 46
ruffled edging, 43
seashell nops, 42
short row darts, 140
slanted stitches, 21
stegosaurus cables, 49
ties, 38, 75
triple crossed horizontal cable, 126
twisted eyelets, 76
wishbone cables, 35
woven stitches, 14
Wrapped in Ruffles Scarf, 118
wrapped stitches, 61, 23
X and O cables, 35
zig zag trim, 50, 51
Stripes, one row, 133
Swatching, 87
Symbols, 156

T
Tied Up in Style Cardigan, 90, 144
Ties, 38
Tote, Purple Posies, 130
Transfer tool bind off, 159
Triple crossed cables, 57
Twisted
   edging, 99
   eyelets, 76
Two tool lifting method 39

U
Upper working position, 5

W
Weaving in ends, 89
Wishbone cable, 35
Working position, 5
Woven stitch patterns
   basket weave, 14
   Chinese knot, 25
Wrapped in Ruffles Scarf, 118
Wrapped stitches, 61, 23

X
X and O cables, 35

Z
Zigzag trim, 50